RETURN ON STRATEGY

RETURN ON STRATEGY

How to Achieve It!

*Michael Moesgaard Andersen,
Morten Froholdt and
Flemming Poulfelt*

Routledge
Taylor & Francis Group

NEW YORK AND LONDON

Simultaneously published in the UK
by Routledge
2 Park Square, Milton Park, Abingdon, Oxon OX14 4RN

First published 2010
by Routledge
270 Madison Ave, New York, NY 10016

Routledge is an imprint of the Taylor & Francis Group, an informa business

© 2010 Taylor and Francis

Typeset in Baskerville by Wearset Ltd, Boldon, Tyne and Wear
Printed and bound in the United States of America on acid-free paper by
Sheridan Books, Inc.

Library of Congress Cataloging-in-Publication Data
Andersen, Michael Moesgaard.
Return on strategy : how to achieve it! / Michael Moesgaard Andersen, Morton
Froholdt, Flemming Poulfelt.
p. cm.
Includes bibliographical references.
1. Strategic planning. 2. Organizational effectiveness. I. Froholdt, Morton.
II. Poulfelt, Flemming. III. Title.
HD30.28.A515 2009
658.4'012–dc22   2009015688

ISBN10: 0-415-80509-0 (hbk)

ISBN13: 978-0-415-80509-4 (hbk)

CONTENTS

FOREWORD

The rationale behind a strategy is to set the future direction of a company. To do this many companies invest heavily in developing a strategy plan with the main focus of capitalizing on the strategy, and thereby achieving the best Return on Strategy as possible.

But how do companies embark on the strategy and how do companies develop their strategic behaviour?

Our studies throughout the last 25 years of how companies develop over time show not surprisingly that there are very few, if any, easy picks. To develop a successful strategy is mostly hard work combined with diligent and often unconventional thinking. In addition there needs to be a passion for execution to ensure that the strategy is being well implemented all the way through the organization.

Therefore, it is interesting to see the outcome of many of those companies who had opted for following the conventional recipes of hallmark literature within the areas of "excellence", "great companies" and "best practice" or some of the "easy-to-go" recommendations like "It's all about leadership", "Only people count", "Execution is the only thing that matters". Even for companies used as models for exercise, the outcome turns out badly. In fact a good deal of these end up in a fatal crisis in the traditional sense of the term and fall apart.

Crisis is often used as a term for a drama that will unavoidably lead to not less than the sudden death of a company or a major reconstruction.

On the other hand, our initial analyses showed that Skype, Hotmail, Ryanair, Saxo Bank, Honda, Samsung Electronics and many others diligently managed to use a crisis or special situation as a trigger event. More detailed studies even showed that such companies deliberately started their journey with a crisis as take-off, heading towards an attractive destination characterized by something hugely different from the conventional recipes.

Crisis originates from Greek and means turning point, which is precisely the way we found that smart business managers and boards leapfrog the recipe universe into a radically different universe which we choose to label the X-factor universe.

Notwithstanding the fact that we believe that this may be an evergreen issue, we also believe that the 2009 escalating financial crisis may be yet another interesting ticket to admission to the X-factor universe. During times when the business climate is cash-strapped, when state intervention supersedes the invisible hand, and when peers struggle, some companies help themselves achieve a disproportionately high Return on Strategy. Instead of solely viewing the economic downturn as a threat, many companies would gain by viewing it as a simultaneous threat and opportunity and therefore act more offensively.

Whether a crisis or not, we have been puzzling with a fundamental question for some years, namely how companies can achieve a high Return on Strategy knowing that no single or easy formula exists. To further explore this question we embarked on an extensive research journey. This has included a search in literature, journals and newspapers, informed interviews with many executives from various parts of the world, analyses of specific companies and intense discussions with peers.

In this book we report our findings including an answer to the question: What characterizes the road map to achieve Return on Strategy?

The book is neither a handbook on strategy nor a book on strategy recipes. Instead it's a book on how some companies have developed a substantial Return on Strategy. It's also a book illustrating examples on elements and issues companies should work with in order to develop a high Return on Strategy. And like a road map various options on how to get to a destination exist. However, some routes are more fruitful and beneficial than others. In the corporate world companies can choose various ways to achieve their strategy, but only one provides the company with the optimal Return on Strategy.

Our own map shows how some companies have successfully developed their road map. It also illustrates how some companies have failed to develop an appropriate map, including reflections on what went wrong. But foremost the book provides the reader with insights and inspiration on how to work with various strategy components in order to achieve a better Return on Strategy.

In writing a book it is important to have supporters. Therefore special thanks goes to the publisher John Szilagyi at Routledge, an imprint of the Taylor & Francis Group. We appreciate very much his constructive support of the idea of our research project and for transforming it into a book.

We also want to thank the many executives we have interviewed as part of our research project and colleagues with whom we have had many stimulating dialogues on strategy. Special thanks goes to our families. Although they sometimes wondered what type of universe we had embarked on when the project was launched, they fully believed in our efforts to write a book on a topic for which we all have a passion. Therefore, thanks for all your support and encouragement.

Finally, we sincerely hope that readers working with strategy in practice will strive to significantly improve their Return on Strategy based on the experience, ideas, frameworks and tools as presented in this book and at www.returnonstrategy.org.

Michael Moesgaard Andersen
Morten Froholdt
Flemming Poulfelt
Copenhagen June 30, 2009

ARE WE ABLE TO PRODUCE GOLD?

During medieval times alchemists tried to find the right formula for producing gold. According to the legend, Dr Faustus was one such alchemist, but Faust also appears in many other contexts, such as poetry and the natural sciences. Later on Faust became a legend and was utilized in many contexts related to art and science, notably by Goethe.

Today's literature on strategy and management also strives to find the right formula for success in the sense that success equals outstanding financial results, namely "gold". So essentially, Faust is still operating. However, notwithstanding the fact that many recipes have been tabled and are still being tabled, an equal amount of failures and fallacies have been reported.

In essence, all recipes seem very much alike as they often comprise a listing of a few variables which trigger success. The listing of such five to eight variables may change in wording. However, there is a considerable common body operating as the same substantial strategic behaviour may be labelled differently and used to justify different recipes. Moreover, the output also seems to represent a common body as "success" in practically speaking all recipes is measured by way of financial performance, notably by way of stock performance.

The recipes have developed over time in different phases. In the first phase, a considerable number of the recipes originated from management consulting practices. This was the case with the so-called first-generation recipes, for example when two McKinsey consultants wrote "In Search of Excellence" with the conclusion that companies adhering to eight variables had determined the success of the 43 companies included in their sample. Second-generation recipes have emerged during the last 20 years on the basis of much more refined analysis, in particular with many more companies included in the samples and with a gradually emerging focus on not only measuring companies according to a static here-and-now picture but also taking companies' development over time into consideration.

So far so good. Does this mean that the recipe for gold has at last been discovered in the literature on management and strategy?

Unfortunately not, as at least one very serious problem occurred. A good deal of the companies included in the samples meant to illustrate and justify the recipes, actually later underperformed, ceased to exist or went bankrupt! In other words, they had no or a very low Return on their Strategy. Invariably, a number of companies that were never included in the samples of successful companies turned out to achieve a disproportionately high Return on Strategy.

Consequently, this book is the opposite of working with recipes and cook books. Rather, it takes the viewpoint that there is no such thing as a "one size fits all" recipe for success and that success has to be viewed in the context of what this book terms the X-factor universe.

What does the X-factor universe comprise and implicate? How is the X-factor defined? What does it take for a company to stay tuned in this universe and achieve a high Return on Strategy?

This book intends to provide the answer to such questions in the light of the fact that far too many companies are in strategic error and that their Return on Strategy is consequently far too low. The book provides insight into how companies in the X-factor universe outperform. Simultaneously, the book also provides insight into how and why some companies may stop outperforming.

The book is based on research comprising companies covering several industries as well as several continents, notably North America, Asia and Europe. The companies involved are listed in Appendix II.

The purpose of the book is to provide the readers, whether active business executives, board members, management consultants or students of strategy, with food for thoughts and reflections when it comes to how companies can develop their strategic position and edge and by this achieve a higher Return on Strategy than their peers.

The book also presents toolkits as to how companies may facilitate the journey into the X-factor universe, whereby they can increase their Return on Strategy. First of all, a Return on Strategy framework is presented (see Figure 4.5), encompassing events that triggers strategy, key success drives and Return on Strategy as the outcome of this framework. But also parameters for "out-of-the-box-thinking", a number of road maps utilizing key success drivers (see Figures 12.2–12.6) and a number of revenue-cost related tools (see Chapter 8 and Appendix I) are there to help increase the Return on Strategy. However, the toolkits presented are by no means a holy grail that exhaustively determines ultimate and sustained success. They merely help companies achieve a higher Return on Strategy.

1

THE X-FACTOR UNIVERSE IS OVERLOOKED IN STRATEGY!

Hatched in a Swan's Egg?

Fifteen years have passed since Kim Fournais and Lars Seier Christensen met for a drink to discuss an idea that would lead to a billion-dollar business within the financial services industry. As founders of Saxo Bank, a top 25 foreign exchange (FX) provider and the recipient of multiple awards for contributions to the industry, they have managed to successfully navigate the competitive seas of the financial services industry. Since 1998 the compounded annual growth rate (CAGR) of the company's profits before tax computes to more than 60%. For the financial year 2007 the profits before tax increased by 78% on the previous year leading to Saxo Bank receiving the "Euromoney" award for the fastest growing FX bank of the year.

Aside from their performances and their doings within the financial services industry they are one of the sponsors behind the cycle team that won the Tour de France of 2008. Saxo Bank therefore also displays an ability to pick winners outside their business that can increase the brand of their company.

How did Saxo Bank achieve this? Which business book recipe did they follow? And what type of strategy did they pursue?

Saxo Bank is widely recognized among its peers in the industry as an innovative and pioneering company and has received numerous awards for its trading platform, the SaxoTrader. In 2008 they received the award for the best retail platform for the fourth consecutive year at the e-FX awards, sponsored by

"FX Week" magazine. Since 2003 the awards presented to Saxo Bank, by "FX Week" magazine, World Finance magazine, "Euromoney" and "Profit & Loss" magazine, have grown at a steady pace cementing their place in the industry as a leading edge player.

Is the successful company hatched in a swan's egg right from the outset? And what does it take – what is the recipe if one exists at all – for eventually turning an ugly duckling into a beautiful swan?

Initially, the bank started off with performing mediocre brokerage activity attracting a somewhat negative publicity. However, the company changed business model and went on the route of leading players of IT and financial services with online trading as the foremost tactical weapon. When the company achieved its banking licence in 2001 it changed its name to Saxo Bank.

Banking business is often considered a conventional industry where success is dependent on a long track record, history, strong local presence and a service delivery apparatus comprising friendly front-line officers.

However, the entrepreneurs behind Saxo Bank did not adhere to any of these industry rules of the game. Neither do they stick to prevailing CEO norms, as Lars Seier Christensen and Kim Fournais jointly share the CEO responsibilities, which is also an unprecedented construction not only in the management literature but also in managerial practice.

Can Entrepreneurs Have Their Cake and Eat It Too?

When asked about the strategy they had followed over 15 years, the founders of Saxo Bank did not just refer to an existing well-known strategy or management book. As Kim Fournais puts it:

We did not follow a specific strategy described in a business book. We may even be unable to describe or fully explicate what we have done in terms of strategy. What matters to us was the passion to create our platform and that we have been inspired by the execution power of others, such as Jack Welch.

Even more importantly, it seems difficult, if not impossible, to efficiently correlate the success elements of Saxo Bank with the strategies and recipes outlined in the current literature.

Imagine that Saxo Bank adheres to both a differentiator and a cost leader strategy. Imagine that they run the company with two CEOs with equal responsibility. Imagine that they deliver their core IT platform on a wholesale basis to some of their competitors, whilst at the same time generating channel conflict by addressing banking customers directly.

How come that Saxo Bank can have its cake and eat it too? How come that Saxo Bank can combine various generic strategies, such as differentiation, cost leadership and niche excellence? Why do they pursue blue and red ocean strategies simultaneously? How come that you can be successful when breaking many of the rules from strategy theories as they do?

The path to success has not been an entirely rosy one, but the thorns encountered along the way have, to a large degree, been instrumental in the strategic direction of Saxo Bank and thus its remarkable top line growth. The top line has grown by more than 50% annually each year and with a continued strong underlying trend. Saxo Bank has not been focused on identifying the holy grail of strategy by devising the one and only generic recipe for success. In fact, they did not use any recipe at all. As true entrepreneurs they did it their own way.

Building Unprecedented Bridges, Breaking Conventions?

Invariably, part of the Saxo Bank road map resembles well-known aspects, although often mixed in a creative way. Saxo Bank succeeds because the company is keen to execute either something which is not described in the standard recipes or something which is the complete opposite of the prescribed behaviour.

In order to fully understand the achievements of Saxo Bank it is necessary to look into two widely different universes. One universe is characterized by companies adopting textbook strategies or companies, which incidentally fit an easy-to-understand recipe. As foremost examples of recognized typical cost leaders, IKEA, Dell, Wal-Mart, Anheuser-Busch, Samsung Electronics and Hyundai Electronics are often mentioned and admired cases. Virgin, Harley Davidson, JetBlue, Toyota, Glaxo Wellcome and IBM are often quoted as examples of successful differentiators. Ferrari, Gucci and Louis Vuitton are all examples of a focus strategy, while Costco and Lidl go for discount strategies. Finally, we have Cirque du Soleil and Starbucks as prime examples of blue ocean strategy. As these examples are primarily based on conventional strategy frameworks. This space is labelled the *recipe universe.*

Another universe is defined by companies which do not fit the conventional recipes and are tainted very much by out-of-the-box-thinking. Many of these companies display highly profitable growth which is often correlated with unconventional thinking, as is the case with Saxo Bank. Other examples to be addressed later include Google, Skype, Facebook, Huawei, Yahoo, Hotmail, eBay, Ryanair, PayPal, Naturhouse and Wahaha. This universe is characterized by companies that do not fit the recipes but rather deliberately work in contrast to the recipes and make use of what is called the X-factor. Therefore, this space is labelled the *X-factor universe.*

How come that we are so keen on recipes in the management literature? How come that case stories like Saxo Bank moving out of the recipe universe and successfully into the X-factor universe are untold? How come that no alarm bells ring at conventional companies, when newcomers are building strategic bridges that they should not be able to build according to traditional theory? And how come that some companies are deliberately and successfully breaking industry conventions?

It is somewhat unfortunate that the dominant strategy literature has expended so much energy on establishing rules and recipes, leaving top-level management and boards almost on autopilot once a business book on strategy was adopted. The out-of-the-box initiatives are therefore largely uncharted today and no room is left for what could be labelled the X-factor in strategy.

At the same time there has been a competition in the theoretical landscape between different approaches to strategy. Various perspectives and schools have been introduced, often leaving executives uncertain on which approach to apply as the theoretical prescriptions often emphasize the importance of not mixing perspectives.

Inevitably, easy procrastination of companies' tendencies to adopt certain strategies has been the consequence of conventional thinking. However, more and more companies are making their stewardship in the out-of-the-box strategic landscape moving into the X-factor universe. As this trend evolves, there is a growing need to effectively manage the risk of business books on strategy being successfully conquered by disruptive strategies from the X-factor universe.

Optimizing the Exploitation of Trigger Events

How did Saxo Bank manage to transform itself from a brokerage company deploying a full service model to a global online success, and what are the reasons behind their innovative strength and ability to continuously develop their award winning trading platform?

Back in the 1990s, the company was in a crisis as negative press coverage for the industry as a whole emerged, leading to some major clients leaving the company and potential clients hard to convince. True entrepreneurs do not give up just because of temporary head wind. In this case, the SaxoTrader platform was developed during the subsequent years. Saxo Bank relied heavily on this IT platform in conjunction with their increased focus on the Internet. Maybe this platform would never have been built if the entrepreneurs had not met with temporary opposition in the market?

A parallel example is the case of Hotmail. When trying to develop a web-based personal database company, the entrepreneurs were frustrated because their employer's firewall prevented them from accessing their personal email accounts. Subsequently, they developed the idea of email accounts that could be accessed anonymously through a web browser leading to Hotmail as we know it.

A crisis, head wind or temporary opposition may be an important stepping stone to bankruptcy for some companies and a golden opportunity for others.

In addition to a crisis, important events that lead to golden opportunities may be largely down to luck or initial failures. While developing an online facebook for his local university in response to the traditional paper-based versions, Mark Zuckerberg stumbled upon a worldwide demand for a social networking web site that has since led to the growth of Facebook. When the Spanish dietary company Naturhouse opened their first retail shop in the early 1990s it failed miserably, calling for a revised strategy that has since proven highly successful.

The X-factor Narrowed Down

Performing a Google search on the term "X-factor" will yield just over 70 million hits within 0.25 seconds. Many of these hits will lead to information about the talent show of the same name broadcast in more than 20 countries across the world. However, this is not the X-factor of interest in this publication. The X-factor of interest is what the Shorter Oxford English Dictionary defines as:

> A critical but indefinable element. Also a noteworthy special talent or quality.

In other words, the X-factor comprises an element of surprise or something which goes far beyond what could be found in a standard business book recipe. It comprises features that make a company superior in a special way while not necessarily following the typical management recipes.

To avoid paging through the many hits that the "X-factor" search returns, the above definition can also be found by performing a search on the word combination of X-factor and dictionary. What such a search, however, does not return is the

X-factor of the company Google itself – a company which has been very successful by not following business book strategies. Neither will a search performed on the X-factor of Saxo Bank, Huawei, Facebook or some of the numerous companies that have had success without relying on business book recipes yield any results.

This book sets out to explore the X-factor universe and what companies belonging to this universe have done in order to break the rules of the conventional game or otherwise thought "out-of-the-box" whereby they outperform, i.e. achieve a disproportionately high Return on Strategy.

This book also sets out to illuminate: how major parts of the existing literature have derailed or even extinguished the X-factor, being part of the recipe universe. How Saxo Bank and other companies have found inroads to diligent exploitation of the X-factor. How Google and similar business cases have worked with, for example, reverse pricing mechanisms and other unprecedented strategic elements in the X-factor universe. How the X-factor needs to be rethought and redefined over time. How difficult, yet very relevant, the X-factor as an "indefinable element" is to catch, describe and evaluate thereby making it irrelevant to create a new recipe. How the use of the X-factor often disrupts the establishment and conventional thinking.

The book will depart in Chapter 2 with an analysis of existing managerial recipes on how to achieve success. The survey is based on some of the most successful business books during the last 25 years. It shows that the recipes for success seem quite short termed as well as ambiguous when it comes to the specific conclusions which can be made. As such the recipe game for business success formulated in some bullet points seems to be a mirage for several reasons.

One main reason is that a considerable number of the companies on which basis the recipe for success was crafted in the first place, turned out to be unsuccessful. Another main reason is that the recipes are crafted, formulated and marketed under an assumption of full validity without any room for other or additional explanations. The mirage is then already evident when just these two reasons are combined, because how can you trust a recipe, if a recipe pretends to be exhaustive, but ends up with companies that are not successful because they go bankrupt or otherwise cease to exist?

This recipe game is taken over in Chapter 3 by a guided tour in the strategy landscape with the purpose of demonstrating the scope and variety of strategy perspectives. The strategy "jungle" is narrowed down to four different perspectives, namely strategy as positioning, resource-based strategy, blue ocean strategy and disruptive strategy.

These four perspectives lead directly forward to a combination of the four different perspectives in what is labelled "The Strategy System" and a focus on how to achieve Return on Strategy (RoS), which are presented in Chapter 4. Arguably, companies in the X-factor universe diligently achieve a high Return on Strategy, in fact they outperform not only their peers, if such exist, they outperform their own strategic goals and subsequently often reach a degree of effectiveness over and above 100% (when companies outperform their own goals).

Generically, a number of strategy modes are identified and discussed in Chapter 5. Within the X-factor universe, strategy often occurs out of a crisis, on the back of failures, by luck or – rarely – as fully planned. Surprisingly, many companies in the X-factor universe have struggled strategically in their infancy. Having then developed and executed their strategy, they have found a direction which was not foreseen, which was unprecedented or which took the market by surprise and even made it impossible for (potential) competitors to adequately respond or strike back.

The following chapters intend to depict the combination of salient X-factor issues and empirical data with ample evidence of companies exercising "out-of-the-box"-thinking. Chapter 6 deals with the customer attitude as well as the attitude of customers. Practically all companies in the X-factor universe have the pro-sumer approach to customers, i.e. to regard customers as consumers and producers alike. Companies may have either a transactional or relational view on customers, however, both companies and their customers often regard customers as the social capital of the company.

Where Chapter 6 deals with the demand side of the company, Chapter 7 is more focused on the supply side. A lean product line with stickiness of the core product is here the starting point, but also considerations about life-cycle, pull tactics, products as part of an ecosystem and the view of a product as a business model fit into the equation.

The financial circuit addressed in Chapter 8 seems to be an overlooked aspect of strategic success as this aspect does not occur in the business book recipes. However, it takes a prominent place in this book. It turns out that many of the recent successes in the X-factor universe come out of unprecedented pricing and/or working with the cost base far beyond usual cost cutting exercises and even lean programmes. Some of the findings are explicated further mathematically in appendix I.

The organizational design which is the focus in Chapter 9 also attracts attention in the X-factor universe. Creation of a "wolf-culture", establishment of a dual-CEO structure, strongest possible dissociation from peer groups or complacent monopolies are examples of how organizational aspects operate in the X-factor universe.

Chapter 10 comprises an outline of the technology chain. Technology is often listed as a "more-is-better" factor in companies. However, in many cases the technological exuberance is operating to the effect that companies are overinvesting in technology, leading to failure when resources are poured into deep water. Rather, the use of proven, simple and scalable technology and – from time to time – groundbreaking technology attracts attention in the X-factor universe.

The leadership genes are the core of Chapter 11. This is a relevant and interesting theme as it seems to be a matter of fact that many successful companies are top-managed by charismatic personalities. However, such successes are often instant and not sustainable. In the X-factor universe, quite a number of leaders seem to have an entrepreneurial background without necessarily being overly narcissistic. A main challenge in this universe is to keep up the entrepreneurial spirit over time.

The concluding Chapter 12 further elaborates on the overall characteristics of companies operating in the X-factor universe and addresses what it takes to enter, stay and remain in this universe and thereby achieve a high Return on Strategy. Specifically, Chapter 12 provides inroads and road maps as to how companies may achieve a disproportionately high Return on Strategy.

2

THE RECIPE GAME

Managerial recipes are beliefs and approaches that based on experiences have been developed over time until they have become institutionalized. When a business formula has worked once, it is often convenient to believe that it will do so again.

Since the 1980s, much of the management literature has been characterized by its attempts to identify and describe the recipe for success. Success is often defined as something equal to top performance or outperformance, and typically by growth in stock prices and actual profitability numbers. Despite providing valuable insight, none of the recipes offered over the past three decades have stood the test of time in the changing world of business.

Excellence Is in the Eye of the Beholder

In 1977, the two McKinsey consultants, Tom Peters and Robert H. Waterman, were put in charge of a project concerning organizational effectiveness. This project led to the publication of, what is, arguably, the first bestselling book on management and how to become successful. First published in 1982 the book entitled "In Search of Excellence: Lessons from America's Best-Run Companies" became an instant success with business leaders in America who were desperately seeking answers on how to combat the growing competition from Asian companies, in particular, and the economic downturn of the 1980s.

The findings of the book were based on a sample group of 62 American companies of which 43 were labelled as excellent. Entry into the club of excellence was given on the back by three quantitative measures for growth, three quantitative measures for return on capital and finally a qualitative measure for innovativeness.[1]

Having identified the 43 excellent and innovative companies, the authors continued to search for common attributes that could then be argued to constitute the building blocks of excellence. In doing so they identified the eight attributes of corporate excellence that are listed in Table 2.1.

Selling more than three million copies in the first four years alone, the book became a long-lasting success not only in the

Table 2.1 **The eight attributes of excellence from "In Search of Excellence"**

Attributes	*Description*
A bias for action	Getting on with it exemplified by a standard operating procedure described as "do it, fix it, try it"
Close to the customer	Learn from the people they serve and provide unparalleled quality, service and reliability thus succeeding in differentiating their offering
Autonomy and entrepreneurship	Encourage practical risk taking, and support good tries.
Productivity through people	Treat the rank and file as the root source of quality and productivity gain
Hands-on, value driven	Explicit attention to company values and the ability of the leaders to create exciting environments through personal attention, persistence and direct intervention
Stick to the knitting	Stay within the businesses you know
Simple form, lean staff	Simple underlying organizational structures and lean top level staff
Simultaneous loose–tight properties	Centralized and de-centralized at the same time pushing autonomy down to the shop floor while being centralists around the core values

US but also globally. The success of the book itself did, however, not characterize all of the 43 companies it identified as being excellent performers.

In 1984, only two years after its publication date, an article in "Business Week" entitled "Oops. Who's excellent now"[2] found that one-third of the 43 companies were experiencing financial difficulties. Among those less fortunate companies listed as excellent performers in Peters and Waterman's bestseller one can find the likes of Atari, Digital Equipment Corporation (DEC) and Wang Laboratories of which none exist today.

In contrast to these, companies such as Exxon, General Electric, Ingersoll-Rand and United Technologies that did not gain entry to the club of excellence are still in existence today.

In the case of Atari, the fall from excellence is believed to result from their failure to develop and market products to succeed the hugely popular Atari 2600 video game console and the emergence of the home computer. What is known as the North American video game crash of 1983 also piled additional problems onto a troubled Atari and the share price of Warner, the owner of Atari, tumbled from US$60 to 20.[3] In 1984 Warner sold off the home computing and games console division to Jack Tremiel for US$240 million under who's leadership they continued to develop state of the art consoles but failed to market these with any significant success thus losing market share to Nintendo's Game Boy. The failure to market products and the desire of the Tremiel family to exit the business eventually led to the demise of Atari.

The tumble of Digital Equipment Corporation is indeed remarkable considering that they were among the largest computer companies in the world by the late 1980s and by many considered to be the company that created the minicomputer and arguably the first computers for personal use. At their peak the company employed in the region of 100,000 people and held subsidiaries across the globe, but a desire to branch out into other complementary industries, such as software, and strong aversions to traditional marketing as well as the rise of

RISC-based architecture ultimately led to the demise of the company.

Wang Labs was founded by Dr An Wang and Dr G.Y. Chu in 1951 and manufactured calculators, word processors and personal computers. At the height of their business in the 1980s it had annual revenues in the region of US$3 billion and employed approximately 40,000 people. It is a common belief that the company's subsequent failure stemmed from a narrow focus on computers designed specifically for word processing and a lack of industrial foresight as general computers would take the place of computers designed for a single purpose only.

Did these three companies stray from the recipe as laid out by Peters and Waterman? The answer to this question is primarily "No". Atari failed to develop and bring to market new competitive products, Digital Equipment Corporation strayed from their original "knitting" (core business) by branching out into a host of other markets and Wang Labs perhaps stayed too close to their knitting failing to see where the industry was heading.

Interestingly, the company Ingersoll-Rand that did not make it into the category of excellence is still in business today due to the very fact that they decided to go beyond their core products of heavy machinery and pursue commercial products. Ingersoll-Rand reported revenues of US$8.7 billion for the year 2007 growing from US$6 billion in 2003.[4] What this seems to suggest is that the recipe for excellence is not as excellent as its bestselling success may imply.

One reason for this is that the formula for excellence rests on eight factors and only those eight, leaving neither room for other variables that may have been instrumental to the success of a particular company, nor room for any residuum to be addressed. The mere fact that the eight factors identified can be attributed to those 43 companies that were deemed excellent in the late 1970s does not mean that these were the exact factors paving the way for their success. Invariably, the X-factor had operated considerably in many cases without being identified by the authors; the proof of the pudding being that companies excluded were actually successful and many companies included failed within a very short time frame.

The authors' underlying assumption – that the correlation between the presence of these eight factors and a company's success perfectly exists – is made despite it being commonly known within statistics that correlation does not equal causality. So the success of these 43 companies could just as well be attributed to different or additional variables, which may be heterogeneous in the sense that each company follows its own specific recipe to achieve success and gain a competitive advantage.

Other critics were phrased as follows:

Critics suggested that excellence was oversimplified and trendy but managers saw little to criticize in the prescription for success and rushed to be excellent. When the popular business press began to point out the less-than-excellent performance of some of the excellent companies, even managerial proponents had to acknowledge that perhaps the emperor was naked. One West Coast bumper sticker proclaimed "I'd rather be Dead than Excellent".[5]

As can be seen there were obvious shortcomings in the findings of "In Search of Excellence". Although presented as a recipe for success, it did not stand the acid test. Also the road was paved for finding more formulas for success.

Built to Last but not Necessarily to Stay Ahead

If "In Search of Excellence" was the management book of the 1980s, then "Built to Last: Successful Habits of Visionary Companies" written by two Stanford professors Jim Collins and Jerry Porras was definitely the management book of the 1990s with sales topping 3.5 million copies to this date.

Collins and Porras compiled a list of visionary companies by asking a representative sample of 700 CEOs to name up to five companies that were perceived to be highly visionary. The CEOs were chosen among the four indices, namely Fortune 500 industrial companies, Fortune 500 service companies, Inc. 500

private companies and Inc. 100 companies. The responses were subsequently used to create a list of 18 companies that were most frequently mentioned by the CEOs as visionary companies and had outperformed the general market in terms of stock returns.

Published in 1994, the book paired the 18 visionary companies that had performed extremely well over a long period of time with another company that was founded in the same period that carried similar products and acted in similar markets that fewer CEOs had listed in their responses and finally had shown a good but not excellent performance. By performing this paired comparison, an overarching concept for what it takes to build a visionary company was identified as well as the managerial principles for doing so.

The concept in all its simplicity was that visionary companies were able to preserve the core ideology of the company whilst simultaneously stimulating and constantly driving progress. The methods for achieving this that distinguished the visionary companies from their comparisons fell into the five categories described in Table 2.2

Contrary to the list of companies presented in Peters and Waterman's "In Search of Excellence", all of those companies identified by Collins and Porras still exist to this very day making it hard to argue with the fact that they were, or are, indeed built to last.

Their ability to outperform the market, however, was not a lasting feature for all of these as companies such as Ford, Merck, Motorola, Sony and Walt Disney have since experienced some difficulties and performed below the S&P 500 index when measured from 1994 until 2008.[6]

Of the above the worst case scenario is Ford Motor Company that ended the fiscal year of 2007 with net losses of US$2.7 billion, down from an astounding loss of US$12.7 billion in 2006, dropping from the position of second to third ranked automaker for the first time in the previous 56 years. This development is attributed to, among other things, the increasing

Table 2.2 **Five methods of visionary companies**

Method	Description
Big Hairy Audacious Goals	Commitment to challenging, audacious – and often risky – goals and projects towards which a visionary company channels its efforts. Argued to stimulate progress
Cult-like Cultures	Great places to work ONLY for those who buy in to the core ideology; those who do not fit with the ideology are ejected like a virus. Argued to preserve the core
Try a Lot of Stuff and Keep What Works	High levels of action and experimentation – often unplanned and undirected – that produce new and unexpected paths of progress and enables visionary companies to mimic the biological evolution of species. Argued to stimulate progress
Home-grown Management	Promotion from within, bringing to senior levels only those who've spent significant time steeped in the core ideology of the company. Argued to preserve the core
Good Enough Never Is	A continual process of relentless self-improvement with the aim of doing better and better, forever into the future. Argued to stimulate progress

Source: "Built to Last."

demand for higher fuel efficiency and failure to globalize the model line. Following hot on the heels of Ford one can find Motorola, which posted losses of US$49 million for the fiscal year 2007 due to their failing handset division which recorded losses of US$1.2 billion for the fourth quarter of 2007 alone. One of the reasons given for this development is Motorola's lack of innovative products which stands in major contrast to the label of a visionary company.

The remaining three companies, Merck, Sony and Walt Disney, all posted healthy profits for the fiscal year 2007 and may be regarded as sound companies albeit no longer outperforming the average in terms of stock returns as was the case when "Built to Last" was published in 1994.

Again, the notion that a clearly defined set of factors and only these are the cause for success is argued to explain why some of those companies, labelled as visionary, subsequently encountered problems. Correlation does not equal causality and as such the factors presented may well be attributable to a visionary company but not necessarily its success.

The generic recipe for success resting on a defined number of variables is as achievable as the alchemist's transmutation of common metals into gold. An argument that is supported by the fact that many of the same companies have been used as role model companies in both "In Search of Excellence" and "Built to Last".

One Plus One Equals None

When comparing the companies included in the two publications, "In Search of Excellence" and "Built to Last", one will find that 16 companies feature in both of these as shown in Table 2.3. As can be seen from this table, only two of these 16 companies (General Electric and Texas Instruments as shown

Table 2.3 **Companies common to "In Search of Excellence" and "Built to Last"**

Common companies	In Search of Excellence	Built to Last
3M	Excellent	Visionary
Boeing	Excellent	Visionary
Bristol-Myers	Non-Excellent	Non-Visionary
Burroughs	Non-Excellent	Non-Visionary
Walt Disney	Excellent	Visionary
General Electric	*Non-Excellent*	*Visionary*
General Motors	Non-Excellent	Non-Visionary
Hewlett-Packard	Excellent	Visionary
IBM	Excellent	Visionary
Johnson & Johnson	Excellent	Visionary
Marriot	Excellent	Visionary
Merck	Excellent	Visionary
Procter & Gamble	Excellent	Visionary
Texas Instruments	*Excellent*	*Non-Visionary*
Wal-Mart	Excellent	Visionary
Westinghouse	Non-Excellent	Non-Visionary

in italics) receive a different label from one publication to the other in terms of their performance, indicating that the remainder fits both recipes. How come that 14 out of 16 companies achieve success by following markedly different recipes?

Yet again, there is no room left for any X-factor operating. "Built to Last" therefore runs into the same fallacy as "In Search of Excellence", namely that following the recipe is assumed to equate causality with regard to company success.

One might wonder which recipe these companies actually subscribe to, if any, or if they added the findings of the two publications to come up with the master plan. Perhaps they devised entirely their own recipe for success. What can be stated with a reasonable degree of certainty, however, is that one generic recipe leaves little room for another so the mere presence of two must add up to a total close to none.

As if two generic recipes for how to excel within business and outlast the competition were not enough, the new millennium brought about an additional two publications which have also received substantial success.

From Good to Great to Evergreen

Perhaps inspired by the two building blocks "Big Hairy Audacious Goals" and "Good Enough Never Is", one of the authors of "Built to Last", Jim Collins, decided that a recipe for how to become a visionary company was not quite good enough. As such he embarked on a project that aimed at identifying the factors that catapult a company from being good to becoming great.

Published in 2001, the book "Good to Great" examines what it takes for companies to make the leap from good to great and is based on the study of the 1,435 companies that had been among the Fortune 500 companies during the period from 1965 to 1995. Of the 1,435 only 11 companies displayed the desired pattern of being average performers for 15 years followed by 15 years of exceptional performance, even beating the usual stars among high performing companies such as 3M, Boeing, General Electric, Hewlett-Packard and Procter & Gamble.

A comparator company for each of the 11 great companies that operated within the same industry and argued to hold the same resources and opportunities was subsequently identified in order to determine how they differed. By performing this analysis with paired comparisons as the instrument the six characteristics described in Table 2.4 were identified as those instrumental in elevating companies from good to great.

In addition to these six characteristics, the concept of the fly wheel and the doom loop was also introduced as an illustration of how the companies made the leap from good to great. It is argued that none of the companies that made the leap did so through a single defining action or grand scheme for turn-around, but instead reached greatness through a constant

Table 2.4 **Six characteristics of how to go from good to great**

Characteristics	Description
"Level 5 Leadership"	The fifth and ultimate level of leadership characterized by a leader's desire to build sustainable and remarkable results through a combination of intense professional determination and profound personal humility
"First Who, Then What"	First get the right people on board before deciding what to do
"Confront the Brutal Facts"	Face the facts of the company's current situation regardless of how brutal they may be in order to determine what is really going on
"The Hedgehog Concept"	Focus on what you can be the best in the world at, what drives your economic engine and what you are deeply passionate about
"Culture of Discipline"	Develop a culture of discipline in terms of disciplined people deploying disciplined thinking and taking disciplined action
"Technology Accelerators"	Develop and implement technologies that are fundamentally compatible with strengths and objectives

Source: "Good to Great".

movement, which was initiated long before the breakthrough was reached. This development is compared to that of a fly wheel slowly beginning to spin and constantly gaining speed in order to eventually take off.

The doom loop is the opposite process of multiple quick fixes designed at creating a breakthrough that, however, never materializes and instead leads to doom as the course is frequently changed, creating an atmosphere of uncertainty within the company.

Few can argue with the identified six characteristics given their highly generic nature, which allows for endless interpretation. As such many business leaders may look at these six characteristics and feel that this is common sense or at least the fundament for sound business decision making. Few business leaders will thus feel that they have the wrong people onboard and are not facing the brutal facts of market movements or pursuing activities which they do not think they are particularly good at and passionate about. Given this, the characteristics may also apply to companies that never make the leap from good to great or even companies performing below average.

When viewing the set of identified great companies only one company, Philip Morris, can be found in the lists of both visionary companies presented in "Built to Last" and great companies identified in "Good to Great".

How can this be? Does this imply that the recipe for how to become a visionary, lasting and high performing company is different from the recipe that will catapult you to greatness? The short answer provided by the author, Jim Collins, is a "yes".

Despite "Good to Great" being the latest publication to emerge from the realms of Jim Collins, the author argues that this precedes "Built to Last" in terms of when the two recipes are applied. First the ideas of "Good to Great" are applied in order to transform a company from the obscurity of being an average performer, after which the ideas of "Built to Last" are applied in order to sustain this achieved greatness. This approach is illustrated in Figure 2.1.

Good to Great ⟹ Great results ✛ Built to Last ⟹ Sustainable
concepts   concepts   great results

Figure 2.1 **The relationship between "Good to Great" and "Built to Last".**

What this suggests is that the recipe for success changes depending on the situation a given company finds itself in. Different measures must be used for different circumstances underlining that no generic recipe for success exists. If the combined ideas presented in "Good to Great" and "Built to Last" are thought to represent such a recipe would it not then be logical to assume that the ideas presented in other publications such as "In Search of Excellence" could be added in order to distil an even better mixture for success? If so, then the concepts and ideas presented in all of the literature on strategy and management that seeks to identify the formula for success are merely lists of ingredients that the individual company can mix and match as they see fit.

However, even such a pick-and-choose list seems problematic. Should we pick all cherries or only a few cherries? How do we assess whether some "cherries" are better than others? And how does the X-factor come into the equation?

Does It Work?

The last example within the management literature that shall be drawn into the light as yet another attempt to identify the one and only recipe for success is the result of what was called the Evergreen Project. Published in 2003, the book "What Really Works: The 4+2 Formula for Sustained Business Success" was a result of this Evergreen Project. The three Harvard professors William Joyce, Nitin Nohria and Bruce Robertson spearheaded the project undertaking a study of 160 companies and their performance during two different periods of time with the first lasting from 1986 to 1991 and the second from 1991 to 1996. The 160 companies were selected on the basis of total return to shareholders, a market cap between US$100 million and six billion and represented 40 narrowly defined industries each holding four companies for analysis.

Table 2.5 **The company categories**

Performance 1986 to 1991	Performance 1991 to 1996	Category
High	High	Winners
Low	High	Climbers
High	Low	Tumblers
Low	Low	Losers

Source: "What Really Works".

Using total return to shareholders as the measure, the 160 companies were divided into four categories based on their performance over the two periods as shown in Table 2.5.

Following this categorization more than 200 management practices of both broad and specific nature that were thought to influence business success were analysed with the purpose of identifying which of these could be correlated with the winning companies.

This analysis identified two sets of management practices a company must adhere to in order to ensure a high return for its shareholders. The first being a set of primary management practices that a company must excel at in order to achieve success supplemented with a second set consisting of secondary management practices of which the company must excel in at least two out of four characteristics. The 4+2 formula for sustained business success became a reality covering the management practices shown in Table 2.6.

Unfortunately, the 160 companies are not revealed, which makes it impossible to determine whether the formula did indeed work for these companies. Nor are the more than 200 management practices that went into the analysis communicated, and as such it cannot be determined whether those chosen were in fact the basis for success or if there were others among the 200 that could have been argued to present a better cause for success. This and the highly generic nature of the identified practices make it practically impossible to disagree with the findings of "What Really Works", whereas the missing data are a cause for concern.

Table 2.6 **The practice of "What Really Works"**

Primary Practices	Secondary Practices
Strategy: Develop a strategy that is sharply defined, clearly communicated, and well understood by employees, customers, partners and investors	*Talent:* Hire, retain and develop talented employees
Execution: Develop and maintain flawless operational execution	*Innovation:* Develop innovative products and services and anticipate disruptive events rather than reacting to them
Culture: Develop a culture of high expectations concerning performance	*Leadership:* Choose the great chief executives
Structure: Develop a structure that reduces bureaucracy	*Mergers and partnerships:* Although internal growth is essential, mastering mergers and partnerships can lead to high performance

Source: "What Really Works".

What can be argued to constitute a point of disagreement, however, is the notion that this formula, or rather recipe, presents a generic road map for all companies wishing to achieve sustained success. The recipe states that a company must excel at all four primary practices and at least two of the secondary ones. Again, the correlation between the recipe and success is presented as being perfect. The implication is that no X-factor is operating, although some flexibility is granted at the secondary level where two out of the four parameters are "optional".

The Mix of Excellence, How to Last, Great Leaps and Things that Work

Having discussed four different recipes for success that have appeared in the management literature over the past three decades it is argued here that no such thing as a one-and-only best recipe for successful strategic stewardship of a company exists.

This is not to say that the management books presented and discussed in the previous sections do not provide the reader with useful insights and good pointers on how to develop the business and potentially achieve success, but rather to stress the point that recipes do not guarantee success.

When comparing the ideas presented in each recipe, whether these be known as attributes, methods, characteristics or practices (emphasized in Tables 2.1, 2.2, 2.4 and 2.6), as shown in Table 2.7, it is argued that these do not represent recipes for

Table 2.7 **The four recipes compared**

In Search of Excellence	Built to Last	Good to Great	What Really Works
A bias for action	Big Hairy Audacious Goals	Level 5 Leadership	Clear strategy
Close to the customer	Cult-like Cultures	First Who, Then What	Focus on execution
Autonomy and entrepreneurship	Try a Lot of Stuff and Keep What Works	Confront the Brutal Facts	Culture of high performance
Productivity through people	Home-grown Management	The Hedgehog Concept	Structured to reduce bureaucracy
Hands-on, value driven	Good Enough Never Is	Culture of Discipline	Talent must be hired, developed and retained
Stick to the knitting		Technology Accelerators	Innovative products and services anticipating disruptive events
Simple form, lean staff			Leadership through great chief executives
Simultaneous loose–tight properties			Mergers and partnerships as a vehicle for high performance

success but rather an à la carte menu from which the business leaders can be inspired to mix and match in order to progress.

The argument that the above presents a list of ingredients rather than four individual recipes for success is underlined by the fact that the same companies to a large extent are used as case examples across the publications. No less than ten out of 18 companies touted as visionary in "Built to Last", can be found on the list of excellent companies in "In Search of Excellence" suggesting that these companies can be made to fit any of the formulas if so desired. The company Philip Morris features in both "Built to Last" and "Good to Great" again allowing for a fit of two generic recipes. Given that a list of companies used in the research leading to the 4+2 formula for "What Really Works" has never been published, it cannot be determined whether companies used in the other publications appear in this as well. It would, however, be of little surprise if this was, in fact, not the case.

Troubled Waters

As earlier addressed there is some resemblance between the alchemist's hunt for finding the recipe to produce gold and the recipe game in the literature on management and strategy in order to identify the five to eight criteria of ultimate success.

This hunt has so far proved unsuccessful due to a number of reasons, not least the following:

1   As discussed, an unacceptably high number of the companies listed in the recipe books eventually fail. This is very critical because the performance of the companies was utilized to identify the underlying recipe of companies like Digital Equipment Corporation, Wang, Atari, Fannie Mae and many others having been demonstrably unsuccessful.

2   Some of the same companies are used as models for exercise to justify different recipes as is visualized in Table 2.3. This was the case for companies like 3M, Boeing, Walt

Disney, HP, IBM, Johnson & Johnson, Marriot, Merck, Procter & Gamble and Wal-Mart in some of the older comparisons. However, just think of how many times Starbucks, Southwest Airlines, Virgin, IKEA and others have recently been utilized over and over again in many business books to justify (different) recipes.

3 The recipes leave no room for residual factors or something unexplained. Eventually this implies that a considerable number of the companies in the X-factor universe may not qualify for being successful in the recipe game. Hotmail, Google, Huawei and Ryanair would probably not qualify for being a member of the recipe universe, yet they are highly successful in the X-factor universe.

4 The recipes pretend to see perfect correlation between the recipe and success. However, in reality they expose no perfect correlation. In an increasingly complex world it is inexplicable how all things to be aware of could be reduced to one or typically five to eight parameters.

5 No proof has been issued to justify the assumed cause–effect relation between the recipes and success. Many other factors may influence the success of companies than those assumed in the recipes and in some instances it may even be that it is the intermediary success of a company that allows for the creation of a stronger culture, more resources expended on recruitment or stay-close-to-the-customer programmes.

6 Hidden and even unhidden problems in many of the success companies are often not addressed. So when company leaders are asked to explain their success they often overemphasize the good stories and disregard failures.

7 A pervasive delusion namely a so-called Halo Effect takes over, meaning that company leaders and reader alike are blinded by positive performance,[7] see below and Figure 2.2.

8 Best practice is difficult, from time to time impossible, to transform from one company to another. *Quod licet jovi non licet bovi*.[8]

Consequently, success in the corporate world of today cannot be reached by following a generic recipe for success. Far too much of the literature on strategy and management has failed in its attempt to engineer a generic recipe for success.

The extensive use of the same companies within the strategic literature and the fact that they somehow can be made to fit nearly any strategic approach is perhaps what prompted Phil Rosenzweig to introduce the notion of "the Halo Effect" (2007). He offers a sharp critique of the current strategic thinking arguing that it is pervaded by the tendency to offer specific evaluations based on general impressions, the Halo Effect. It lists nine delusions (see Figure 2.2) currently present in the literature as Rosenzweig sees them and suggests that business managers should adopt a clear-eyed, critical and thoughtful approach to strategy rather than seeking the recipe for success as the majority of these are flawed.

This book explores some of the yet unknown or even ignored elements of success, including the important X-factor and how companies can utilize this to position themselves within the

---

The Halo Effect – The tendency to just look at a company's overall performance and correlate this with certain attributions

The Delusion of Correlation and Causality – Do we always know which thing causes which?

The Delusion of Single Explanation – There seldom exists one particular factor which can explain everything

The Delusion of Connecting the Winning Dots – It's impossible to isolate the reasons for being successful as most studies don't compare them with less successful companies

The Delusion of Rigorous Research – Sometimes the data haven't the right quality

The Delusion of Lasting Success – Sustainable formulas for success don't exist

The Delusion of Absolute Performance – Company performance is always relative

The Delusion of the Wrong End of the Stick – It may be true that successful companies pursue a focused strategy but this doesn't mean that a focused strategy always leads to success

The Delusion of Organizational Physics – Company performance hasn't the sense of an immutable law of nature. Therefore it cannot be predicted with the accuracy of the natural sciences

---

Figure 2.2 **The nine delusions related to the Halo Effect.**

X-factor universe and thereby achieve a high Return on Strategy.

When strategizing, it is fully recognized that companies – instead of following just one generic strategy – may diligently craft a strategy puzzle based on a mix of all jigsaw pieces from all recipes (see Table 2.7) and also other jigsaw pieces.

However, even though a number of jigsaw pieces may be the same, the strategy puzzle will often differ widely from company to company, between contingencies and across time, geographies and managerial cultures. When crafting and executing a strategy it may prove disastrous to ignore the X-factor.

3

THE STRATEGY LANDSCAPE

Yes, they said, we considered ourselves lost and waited for the end. And one of us found a map in his pocket. That calmed us down. We pitched camp, lasted out the snowstorm, and through the map we discovered our bearing. And here we are. The lieutenant borrowed this remarkable map and had a good look at it. He discovered to his astonishment that it was not a map of the Alps, but a map of the Pyrenees.[1]

(Karl E. Weick, 1995)

Over the past five decades the field of business strategy has grown to become a complex landscape within which the business leaders and academics of today must navigate. The development of strategy has led to various schools of thought and perspectives on what business strategy is and how it should be applied to achieve success.

In this chapter the more specific philosophies and the groundings of these perspectives will be presented and discussed with the purpose of illustrating the complexity and heterogeneity of the field. Also the chapter will be used to illustrate some of the underpinnings later used in the development of the X-factor universe mode of strategy thinking.

Strategic Management in Brief

Since the concept of strategic management was developed in the 1960s, the contributions to the field have been many,

drawing on a number of different disciplines. The main con-
tributors and the concept or underlying discipline as well as the
corresponding period in time are summarized in Table 3.1,
illustrating that strategy has developed substantially in scope
and scale and that strategy has been drawing on a wide variety
of disciplines.

As can be seen from Table 3.1, the strategy discipline is quite
multidisciplinary. Therefore the table should be seen as an
indication of those areas which have shaped strategic thinking
and led to the current state of affairs within the strategic
landscape.

The Dawn of Strategic Management

The concept of strategic management grew out of the research
and writings of, in particular, Alfred Chandler, Igor Ansoff and
Kenneth Andrews in the 1960s. Other non-academic contribu-
tors included Alfred Sloan, the former president of General

Table 3.1 **History of strategy**

Decade	Concept/discipline	Contributors
1960s	Corporate Strategy/Strategic management	Chandler, Ansoff, Andrews
1970s	Transaction Costs Economics	Williamson
	Business policy & Strategic management	Schendel, Hofer
1980s	Industrial organization economics	Porter, Rumelt
	Resource-based theory	Penrose, Wernerfell
	Evolutionary theories of economics	Nelson & Winter
	Strategy processes and change	Pettigrew
1990s	Core competence	Prahalad, Hamel, Grant, Barney
	Critical strategic management	Mintzberg
	Knowledge based theory of the firm	Nonaka
2000s	Simple rules	Eisenhardt
	Blue Ocean	Kim & Mauborgne
	Disruptive strategy	Christensen, Moesgaard Andersen & Poulfelt

Motors, and the consulting companies McKinsey & Co. and Boston Consulting Group (BCG) were very early in entering the strategy stage.

The book "Strategy and Structure: Chapters in the History of the Industrial Enterprise" (Chandler, 1962) was a landmark in strategy as it describes a historical account of the evolution of strategy and organization in large American companies. The four central case companies were: The Du Pont Company, Standard Oil, General Motors and Sears, Roebuck & Co.

Based on the analysis of these four companies, Chandler developed a definition of strategy that emphasizes the long-term goals and objectives of an enterprise. According to Chandler, strategy is:

> *the determination of the basic, long-term goals and objectives of an enterprise, and the adoption of courses of action and the allocation of resources necessary for those goals.*[2]

Chandler further argues that managerial organization develops in response to the company's business strategy, underlining the importance of managers to organize and manage large-scale corporations.

One of the main arguments in Chandler's strategy thinking was the notion that "structure follows strategy". Corporate strategy is the long-term goal of the organization as well as the courses of action and associated allocation of resources necessary to achieve the goals. Changes in the strategy would lead to organizational revisions. New organizational forms therefore become primarily a derivative of strategy according to Chandler. Since the thesis was explicated many have discussed the correlation between strategy and structure as some will argue that structure in many cases is a determinant for strategy.

Inspired by the work of Chandler, Andrews divided strategy into the four components of (1) market opportunity, (2) corporate competence, (3) personal aspirations and (4) social responsibility.[3] Strategy thus became an issue of external and internal factors. The decision to balance these to gain an optimal fit led to the development of the SWOT analysis, which seeks to analyse the strengths, weaknesses, opportunities and threats of a given company.

Alfred Sloan also recognized the need for a long-term strategy, albeit calling this policy, which was kept separate from the day-to-day business of operations. The positioning of the company in those markets where maximum profit could be obtained was at the centre of his strategic definition. In his autobiography "My Years with General Motors" published in 1963, Alfred Sloan outlines the goal of strategy as:

> *The strategic aim of a business is to earn a return on capital, and if in any particular case the return in the long run is not satisfactory, the deficiency should be corrected or the activity abandoned.*[4]

Ansoff, being inspired by the management approach and work of Alfred Sloan, built on the work of Chandler by adding detail to the area of strategy focusing on the planning efforts of the same and the generically designed strategy.

In 1965, Ansoff published the first textbook on corporate strategy to focus entirely on corporate strategy and the process of how to make it ("Corporate Strategy", 1965).

Chandler, Andrews and Ansoff are by many viewed as the founding fathers of the concept of strategic management and corporate strategy. Their approach to strategy focuses around the readiness and capacity of managers to adopt strategies of profit maximization through rational long-term planning. Given this focus on rationality, a number of tools have been developed by these founding fathers of which the best known are: SWOT analysis, Ansoff's Product-Market Growth Matrix and Gap Analysis.

With such a strong focus on rational factors and the task of analysing the external and internal environment to determine the best fit, it is no surprise that the indefinable element of strategy – the X-factor – was never in contention.

Through the 1970s, a number of tools were developed by the consultancies and major corporations which also focused on rationality in long-term planning. The Boston Consulting Group introduced the experience curve and developed the BCG growth matrix of Cash Cows, Stars, Question Marks and Dogs, whereas McKinsey developed the GE Matrix (Market Attractiveness–Business Strength) in cooperation with General Electric. In addition various scenario analyses were introduced as well as the PIMS (Profit Impact of Market Strategy) database. PIMS was a large-scale study designed to measure the relationship between business actions and business results. It contained market, competitive profiles and business results for approximately 3,000 businesses providing valuable data to study, *inter alia*, the importance of market leadership.

The main other contribution to the field of strategy that was introduced in the 1970s was the concept of transaction costs economics championed by Oliver E. Williamson. According to Williamson, a transaction cost is a cost incurred in making an economic exchange. The determinants of transaction costs are (1) frequency, (2) specificity, (3) uncertainty, (4) limited rationality and (5) opportunistic behaviour. Put in a strategy perspective, it can be used in evaluating potential actions of future behaviour, such as outsourcing possibilities.

Various Modes of Strategy Thinking

In the 1980s, major contributions were made to the field of strategy that had widely differing approaches to how strategy should be formulated and developed. The unit of analysis is argued to be the differentiating factor for the contributions of Michael E. Porter, Edith Penrose, Birger Wernerfelt, Jay Barney, Richard R. Nelson, Sydney G. Winter and Andrew Pettigrew.

Drawing on industrial organization economics, Porter argued that it was the structure of a given industry that determined the extent of competition and thus the amount of profit potential available. In the book "Competitive Strategy: Techniques for Analyzing Industries and Competitors" (1980) he presents his framework for analysing the competitors ("five forces model"), the use of strategic groups and the three generic strategies. Initially criticized for focusing too much on the external factors of a company, Porter published another book a few year later introducing the concept of the value chain and thus provided an extensive toolbox for business managers around the world covering both internal and external analysis (Porter, 1985).

The approach of Porter has later become known as the "outside-in" framework given his focus on how a company can best position itself in a given industry in order to gain a competitive advantage.

Contrary to this approach are the views of the resource-based approach championed by Wernerfelt, Penrose and Barney. Barney introduced a framework for applying the resource-based view. Here the focus is not on matching the internal resources to the external competitive situation, but rather to identify what resources a company holds that can be termed specific to that particular company and use these to develop a competitive advantage.

The framework was initially named the VRIN framework as a sustained competitive advantage could be achieved if the resources of a company were Valuable, Rare, Imperfectly imitable and Non-substitutable and offered business managers with a new tool that allowed for an "inside-out" approach to strategy.

Other prominent strategic contributions of the 1980s were made in response to the focus on rationality and were offered by Nelson and Winter who took on an evolutionary perspective on strategy. This approach radically downgrades the importance of rational analysis, and instead argues that strategy is an emerging and constantly changing process.[5]

Strategy as a process was also the focus of Pettigrew whose contributions covered the identification of strategy development and organizational learning.[6] Pettigrew considers human, political and social aspects of organizations and their strategies in contrast to the purely economic view where the main unit of analysis is the firm or the industry.

Given these contributions, strategy evolved in the 1980s to cover the outside-in approach characterized by rational thinking, the inside-out approach focusing on the resources of the company and the heterogeneous nature of these as well as the evolutionary and emerging nature of strategy. Despite the varying nature of these approaches, they all share the common theme of arguing to be the only viable approach to strategy. Although they do not all provide ready-made recipes for success, they still leave very little room for any residual factors operating, notably such factors which play an important role in the X-factor universe.

Competence and Critical Management

The 1990s are marked by the contributions of C.K. Prahalad, Gary Hamel, Henry Mintzberg and Kathleen M. Eisenhardt, where core competencies, critical strategic management and knowledge-based theory of the firm gained centre stage.

The notion of core competencies are built upon the resource-based view of strategy in which the company holds specific resources that are unique in the marketplace. An argument put forward by Prahalad and Hamel is the importance of a company's core competence, which is argued to present opportunities to gain a competitive advantage and even holds the key to unlock new and future opportunities.

A core competence is defined as a bundle of skills and technologies rather than a single discrete skill or technology.[7] This means a bundle of skills which could be deployed across different industries allowing for diversification or the creation of new markets.

Some of the company examples included in the publication by Prahalad and Hamel are: the Sony Corporation, whose core competency includes miniaturization and their ability to produce pocket size radios; Honda, who leveraged the core competency of building engines into the production of cars, lawn mowers, garden tractors and generators; and Canon, whose skills in fibre optics, precision mechanics and electronics have taken the company far beyond their core camera business.

Mintzberg outlines the traditional views of strategy in which planning holds a central place (1994). He argues that strategic planning is mainly concerned with strategies that already exist, thus leaving little room for strategic manoeuvrings or flexibility. With statements such as "Sometimes strategies must be left as broad visions, not precisely articulated, to adapt to a changing environment",[8] he advocates for a more informal approach to strategy making in which the planning is concerned about the process around strategy making as opposed to being central to it. Minzberg later summarized his strategy map in ten school: (1) Design, (2) Planning, (3) Positioning, (4) Entrepreneurial, (5) Cognitive, (6) Learning, (7) Power, (8) Cultural, (9) Environmental and (10) Configuration. Of these 1–3 belong to a prescriptive category while the remaining seven, i.e. 4–10, are more descriptive in nature. The ten schools provide a nice picture although they, at the same time, seem to lose the strategic face value owing to their scope.

Another contribution, which argues that traditional views of strategy are no longer the answer to all questions, is made by Kathleen M. Eisenhardt and Donald N. Sull. They argue that strategy is a matter of pursuing opportunities by focusing on key processes and establishing simple rules rather than establishing a position in the market or leverage resources.[9] In doing so they summarize the framework in five simple rules: (1) How-to rules that spell out how a process is executed; (2) Boundary rules that focus on which opportunities can be pursued; (3) Priority rules that assist in ranking opportunities; (4) Timing rules that synchronize managers with the pace of emerging opportunities and other parts of the company; and finally (5) Exit rules that govern when to pull out of yesterday's opportunities. This can be illustrated by Cisco. When Cisco started on their acquisition mode in the 1990s, it followed the "75 people, 75% engineers" rule. This was introduced to ensure a match with Cisco's entrepreneurial culture and left the company with lots of space to manoeuvre meaning that candidates should have at least 75 employees of which 75% should be engineers. As the company developed

Cisco recognized the need for adding some more rules. These were: (1) A target must share Cisco's vision of where the industry is headed; (2) It must have potential for short-term wins with current products; (3) It must have potential for long-term wins with the follow-on product generation; (4) It must have geographic proximity to Cisco, and (5) Its culture must be compatible with Cisco's. These were used to screen the candidates. If a potential acquisition met all five criteria, it got a green light. If it met four criteria, it got a yellow light with further consideration required. A candidate that met fewer than four got a red light, and was excluded from the list.

By the end of the millennium, strategic management had developed from its founding fathers and their focus on rational planning to approaches drawing on industrial organizational economics, transaction cost economics, organizational theory and evolutionary theory to name a few. Tools had been developed for outside-in and inside-out approaches as well as a fit of the external and internal environment and the notion of strategy as a formal process had been questioned. The field of strategic management had grown in complexity and yet the majority of contributions were still adamant that a particular approach was the only one or the best. Mixing and matching of strategies was unheard of and the X-factor continued to shine through its absence.

Strategy as an Ocean

After the turn of the millennium, the concept of no competition was introduced by W. Chan Kim and Renée Mauborgne in their notion of Blue Ocean Strategy and the book of the same name (2005).

Their basic view on strategy is "to create uncontested market space and make competition irrelevant", equivalent to the basics of monopolies. In the short term this might be attainable, but in the long run it might be a complacent attitude.

The cornerstone of a Blue Ocean Strategy is "Value Innovation" which is achieved when a company creates value for both the buyer and the company by simultaneously pursuing a strategy of differentiation and low cost.

A strategy which was rendered doomed to failure by Porter as he labels such a strategy as being "stuck in the middle". Porter however is assuming that the structural conditions of an industry are given, whereas a Blue Ocean Strategy assumes that market boundaries and industry structure can be reconstructed, offering the opportunity to create new market spaces.

To support their audacious idea of a strategy that will render the competition irrelevant, Kim and Mauborgne offer a number of analytical tools to be used when crafting a Blue Ocean strategy. These include the Strategy Canvas, which is used to identify the range of factors a given industry is competing on and whether a company scores high or low on each of these factors, and The Four Actions Framework, which is used to determine which factors should be eliminated, reduced, raised and created in order to break the existing value curve.[10]

The case companies used to back up the idea of Blue Ocean Strategy are, among others, Southwest Airlines, Yellow Tail, Cirque du Soleil and Starbucks, of which the latter has experienced recent difficulties.

Another publication from 2005 that also has the idea of no competition as a central theme is the book "Monopoly Rules" by M. Milind Lele.[11] The main message is that companies could achieve a favourable strategic position by adopting the much disliked monopoly rules in order to win or rather extinguish the competition game. Starbucks is highlighted as a foremost case of a company that has adopted this type of strategy. Another prominent example that is used throughout the publication is Southwest Airlines which, as is the case with Starbucks, is also extensively used in Kim and Mauborgne's "Blue Ocean Strategy".

The ideas presented in "Blue Ocean Strategy" and "Monopoly Rules" are very similar in nature, as illustrated in Table 3.2. At the centre of both these strategies lies the notion of a non-competitive market position which can either be obtained

Table 3.2 **High-level comparison of two "non-competitive" strategies**

	Blue Ocean Strategy	*Monopoly Rules*
Main aspiration	"How to create uncontested Market Space and Make the Competition Irrelevant"	"How to Find, Capture, and Control the Most Lucrative Markets in Any Business"
Means of measurement	Blue Ocean Idea Index (BOI) and the Strategy Canvas	The Monopoly Quotient
Terminology around the ideal positioning	Uncontested market space	Situational monopoly
The role of competition	Competition to be made irrelevant	Capture and control as a monopolist

through a situational monopoly or by unlocking uncontested market space.

Value Creation versus Disruption

In contrast to the notion of rendering the competition irrelevant by creating uncontested market space, Michael Moesgaard Andersen and Flemming Poulfelt introduced a strategy perspective on disruptive business strategy (2006), somewhat similar to the notion of "red ocean" mentioned but not elaborated by Kim and Maubourge in their book on blue oceans. They focus solely on companies in hypercompetitive markets, as characterized by Richard D'Aveni,[12] and where blue ocean is closely tied to the creation of value in an uncontested market space, Andersen and Poulfelt deals with the possibility of value destruction in hypercompetitive contingencies.[13]

Rather than value innovation, discount strategy thus focuses on creating value for oneself, while destroying value for the remaining competitors, notably by aggressive pricing even to the extent of offering a product or service for free as is the case with some Skype telephony. Other cases used in the book are the Scandinavian mobile telephone operator CBB Mobil that attacked the establishment leading to an overall decline in prices,

Ryanair which attacked the flag carriers by aggressive pricing, and finally the German discount store Lidl that by merely announcing entry into a new market caused price reductions.

When comparing Blue Ocean Strategy with Discount Business Strategy it is worth noting that the former uses Southwest Airlines as a case example to illustrate the substitution of road transportation by flight, whereas the latter uses Ryanair to illustrate how existing monopolies in the form of old flag carriers may be attacked by way of better core services, a lower cost base, cheaper prices and strong price elasticity. Apparently, two widely different strategic approaches were applied by seemingly similar types of companies.

Other contributions to the field of strategy are made by Constantinos C. Markides. The central theme of Markides is how to craft breakthrough strategies by innovating the "who, what and how" combination of the business model.[14] Who pertains to the customers, with what being the products or services these customers should be offered and, finally, how as the way a company can best deliver these.

The Ongoing Development of the Toolbox of Strategy

The positioning school and the resource-based view are arguably the main pillars of today's strategy thinking and will therefore be described in terms of their contributions to identifying the holy grail of strategy. In addition to these two strategic perspectives, the perspective of a non-competitive strategy, as argued for in "Blue Ocean Strategy" and "Monopoly Rules", and the hypercompetitive and disruptive strategy presented in "Discount Business Strategy" have impacted on the way to think about and act on strategy in practice. As such the perspectives Positioning, Resource-based, Blue Ocean and Discount/disruption form the four main pillars of strategy thinking.

Strategy as a Position – a Porter Toolbox

The positioning school, championed by Porter, is perhaps the best known strategic view over time. By developing a toolbox consisting of Porter's Five Forces, the Three Generic Strategies and the value chain, Porter has cemented his place as one of the most read strategists since the 1980s. Of these the three generic strategies, as shown in Figure 3.1, have been widely used since they were devised more than three decades ago.

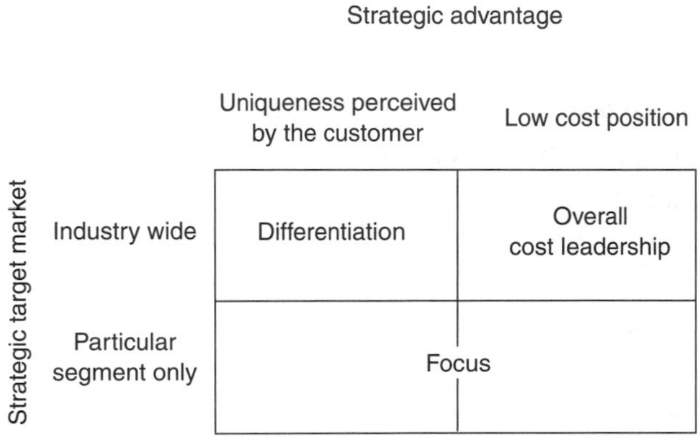

Strategic advantage

	Uniqueness perceived by the customer	Low cost position
Industry wide	Differentiation	Overall cost leadership
Particular segment only	Focus	

(Strategic target market)

Figure 3.1 **Porter's Three Generic Strategies** (*source:* Porter, M. (1980) "Competitive Strategy", Free Press, p. 39).

In terms of providing a strategic road map to disillusioned business managers, Porter provided the three generic strategies as the only paths a company could venture down in order to create a competitive advantage. In doing so he furthermore stressed that a company could pursue only one of these, as an attempt to do otherwise would result in being "stuck in the middle" leading to poor performance.

Although hugely popular, the work of Porter has attracted criticism that may point towards some deficiencies and limitations in this paradigm. First, Porter has been criticized for being too concerned with established big businesses by prioritizing these over fragmented and niche businesses, suggesting that the framework cannot be applied to more dynamic and evolving industries.[15] Second, the generic approach will invariably lead to a company copying the other players in the market leading to average performance. When everyone does the same as their competitors they can only hope to become equal to one another – never to beat them. Third, the notion of "being stuck in the middle" is being challenged by Kim and Mauborgne (2005) and Andersen and Poulfelt (2006) as they illustrate that the dual pursuit of both differentiation and cost leadership has been and is being executed successfully by a number of companies such as Southwest Airlines, Ryanair and Lidl. A fourth point of critique concerns the implicit assumptions on the identical nature of companies' resources and strategies and the lack of or short-lived heterogeneity that may categorize the resources of a specific company, which can also be termed a narrow focus on the external factors.

This comment is best illustrated by a quotation by Donald Hambrick:

The economics approach catalyzed by Michael Porter to strategy focused on industry structures, competitive dynamics, pricing, capacity decisions, vertical integration and so on. But there was no attention to managers. But in this instance, it wasn't because managers were deemed unimportant, but rather because they were presumed to be fully capable of figuring out all this neat economic stuff and arriving at the "right" strategic solution. My strategy friends and I used to joke that you could always tell if a case had been written by Michael Porter: It didn't have any people in it.[16]

Perceiving strategy mainly from an economic perspective seems insufficient given the complexity managers are facing. No wonder that the strategy field had to include other disciplines in order to be able to cope with the broad spectrum of strategic issues.

Strategy the Sum of Your Resources – Another Traditional Toolbox

Contrasting the external focus of the positioning school, championed by Porter, the resource-based view focuses on the internal factors of a company, its resources, and how these can be developed to form a competitive advantage. In 1991, Jay Barney published an article on "Firm Resources and Sustained Competit-

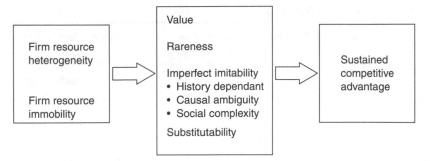

Figure 3.2 **The VRIN framework of the Resource-Based view** (*source:* Barney, J. (1991) "Firm Resources and Sustained Competitive Advantage", *JOM*, vol. 17).

ive Advantage" in which a framework for how a company's resources can lead to a competitive advantage is presented, as shown in Figure 3.2. Barney argues that if indeed the resources of a particular company are heterogeneous and cannot be easily transferred to another company (immobility) then the value, rareness, imitability and substitutability of these resources will determine the level of sustained competitive advantage.

The VRIN framework has since been revised to VRIO, ironically, substituting the non-substitutable character of a company's resources with the organization's ability to exploit the particular resource (the O).

With the likes of Wal-Mart, IBM, Sony, 3M and General Electric as examples, Barney takes the reader through the four main pillars of the framework and finally presents a table (see Table 3.3) detailing that all four pillars must be fulfilled before a resource can lead to a sustained competitive advantage.

With the goal of providing a framework for devising a strategy that could lead to sustained competitive advantage, the goal of the resource-based view is similar to that of Porter albeit of a more dynamic nature and with a clear focus on the internal resources. In addition to the VRIO framework, developed by Barney, the notion of core competencies was developed by Gary Hamel and C.K. Prahalad, which also rests on the resource-based approach. In their book, "Competing for the Future",

Table 3.3 **The VRIO framework**

Valuable	Rare	Costly to imitate	Exploited by organization	Competitive implications
No	–	–	No	Competitive disadvantage
Yes	No	–	–	Competitive parity
Yes	Yes	No	–	Temporary competitive advantage
Yes	Yes	Yes	Yes	Sustained competitive advantage

Source: Barney, J. (1997) "Gaining and Sustaining Competitive Advantage", Addison Wesley, p. 150.

published in 1994, the authors draw on cases such as CNN, Wal-Mart, Compaq, J.P. Morgan, Merck, British Airways and Hewlett-Packard to illustrate how these have managed to either reinvent their industry, regenerate their strategy or both.

As with the cases used by Barney these all represent big established businesses indicating a narrow focus on these over more fragmented and niche businesses and as with Porter this is cause for concern. When turning our attention to the case of British Airways (BA), they were faced with new and different competition in the form of new discount operators such as Ryanair and easyJet and found it very hard to fend off these competitors. One reason for this was that they were utilizing a different set of core competencies to offer a new low-cost value proposition to the customers. A value proposition that was not immediately possible for BA to offer on the basis of their core competencies, and which is why they established Go Fly, a new airline that would be run separately as a wholly owned subsidiary and compete in the European low-cost market. In 2002, only four years after it was established, Go Fly was acquired by easyJet.

This illustrates that the resource-based view is not free of flaws in the dynamic world of today's business where failure to continuously develop your strategy to either defend your position or expand the same is of great importance. To do so may not be a case of subscribing to one of the two conventional strategic approaches, the positioning school or the resource-based view, but more a question of mixing and matching in order to develop a truly unique strategy.

Some of the recent contributions to the field of strategy advocate for such an approach as well as for purposefully exploiting the dual advantage of low cost and differentiation, discarded by Porter as the certain way to mediocre performance.

Blue Oceans as a Toolbox without Competition

A main argument in the blue ocean perspective on strategy is that companies can completely bypass the competition by creating new markets.

The cornerstone of a blue ocean strategy is to simultaneously pursue low cost and differentiation, meaning to be "stuck in the middle" according to conventional wisdom. Porter is assuming that the structural conditions of an industry are given, whereas a blue ocean strategy argues that market boundaries and industry structure can be reconstructed offering the opportunity to create new market spaces. Table 3.4 lists the main differences between the conventional strategy thinking, labelled red ocean strategy, and blue ocean strategy as presented by authors Kim and Mauborgne.[17]

Table 3.4 **Blue ocean versus red ocean strategies**

Red ocean strategy	Blue ocean strategy
Compete in existing markets	Create uncontested market space
Beat the competition	Make the competition irrelevant
Exploit existing demand	Create and capture new demand
Make the value–cost trade-off	Break the value–cost trade-off
Pursue low cost OR differentiation	Pursue low cost AND differentiation

Source: "Blue Ocean Strategy", p. 18.

This distinction between red ocean strategy and blue ocean strategy and in particular the pursuit of low cost and/or differentiation is challenged by Andersen and Poulfelt (2006) as they argue that the very combination of low cost *and* differentiation can lead to disruptive and highly successful strategies in hyper-competitive markets. In the case of such disruptive strategies the competition is not rendered irrelevant, nor is a blue ocean discovered, but instead the red oceans become even redder through value destruction.

To back up the blue ocean strategy that will render the competition irrelevant, the authors offer a number of analytical tools to be used when crafting a blue ocean strategy. These include the strategy canvas, which is used to identify the range of factors a given industry is competing on and whether a company scores high or low on each of these factors, and the four actions framework, which is used to determine which factors should be eliminated, reduced, raised and created in order to break the existing value curve.

The idea is then to use the four actions framework to decide which factors a company should eliminate as competitive parameters thus reducing costs, which should be reduced below the industry standard, which should be raised above the industry standard and last but not least which new factors should be introduced that have previously not been offered. By doing this the authors argue that a new value curve can be established which potentially unlocks a completely new market or demand that is not catered for by any other company.

A number of companies, including Cirque du Soleil, Southwest Airlines and Yellow Tail, are used as examples of companies that have arguably created a new market. In the case of Cirque du Soleil they have managed to create a new value curve by offering a completely new kind of circus experience for the customer. By mixing traditional circus acts with a theatre experience, Cirque du Soleil has created a unique experience offering the fun and thrill of the circus and the sophistication and artistic richness of the theatre at the same time. Southwest Airlines is argued to have created a blue ocean by making high-speed transport available at low prices as an alternative to car transport by eliminating the larger part of the traditional added services such as meals, lounges and hub connectivity and instead focusing on low price, speed and frequent point-to-point departures.

Yellow Tail, a product of Australian wine maker Casella Wines, looked at the demand side of the alternatives to beer, spirits and ready-to-drink cocktails, and created a wine characterized as fun and easy to drink for everyone. They did so by eliminating or drastically reducing their focus on the traditional factors in the industry and instead introduced factors such as easy drinking, ease of selection and fun and adventure. This led to a different value curve for Yellow Tail, as shown in Figure 3.3.

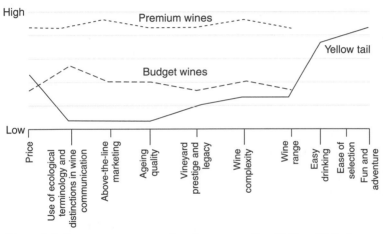

Figure 3.3 **Strategy canvas and value curve for Yellow Tail** (*source:* "Blue Ocean Strategy", p. 32).

By breaking the conventional boundaries of a given market, blue ocean strategy is argued to foster value innovation by unlocking new markets as opposed to value creation within a given industry.

As mentioned previously in this chapter, blue ocean strategy is very similar to the ideas presented by Lele in the book "Monopoly Rules". Here the term "situational monopoly" is used to describe a market situation where a company renders the competition irrelevant. One of the cases used by Lele, which is also used extensively by Kim and Mauborgne, is that of Starbucks which is argued to hold a situational monopoly.

Starbucks owns a situational monopoly, having capitalized on a situation in which no other company was meeting the need for a consistent, good-tasting cup of coffee. The packaged coffee players were too focused on selling coffee in cans; local coffee shops didn't have the money or the vision to expand aggressively nationwide. Starbucks stepped into the opening and exploited the potential monopoly for all it was worth.[18]

Given this, blue ocean strategy is argued to present the reader with tools to develop or identify pockets in the market that hold the potential of a monopoly. However, once a monopoly, or a situational monopoly, has been acquired or developed, the company must seek to defend this from new entrants thus turning the blue oceans red. Therefore the subtitle of the book "how to create uncontested market space and make competition irrelevant" could be interpreted as slightly arrogant.

As such the blue ocean strategy may not be sustainable over the longer term but does, however, provide the strategist with a toolbox for potentially spotting the next situational monopoly – the blue ocean.

Value Destruction Through Discount Tools

The last strategic perspective is discount or disruptive business strategy. Andersen and Poulfelt (2006) also challenged the idea of mixed strategies meaning "stuck in the middle" as a certain way to inferior performance.

In contrast to blue ocean strategy, a discount strategy is disruptive in its nature as it does not create a new market but competes in the existing red oceans by destroying value for the industry as a whole while creating value for the company executing the discount strategy.

At the centre of a discount strategy lies the discount product which is lean and unbundled, leaving room for transparency, and providing a contrast to the increasing number of peripheral services attached to conventional products.

Such a "no frills" product is accompanied by aggressive pricing, which is what drives the value destruction of a given industry. Examples of such value destruction can be seen in the telecommunications industry where fierce competition and the emergence of discount operators and new services, such as Skype, have driven the call charges dramatically down. The airline passenger traffic in Europe has also experienced significant value destruction by declining ticket prices due to the emergence of low-cost airlines, such as Ryanair and easyJet.

In addition to a lean and unbundled, demand-driven and very price aggressive product, the discount strategy contains three other building blocks, as shown in Figure 3.4. A good brand in terms of a discount strategy is one which pairs low cost with high perceived quality and communicates this through tactics defined by their conflicting nature. A good discount image is in many cases built by challenging the establishment head on as Ryanair has managed to do with considerable success. Technology deployed in a company pursuing a discount strategy is matched to the range of performance that customers can utilize. As such it rests on using proven technology as opposed to the latest and greatest, it is scalable and suited for simplicity.

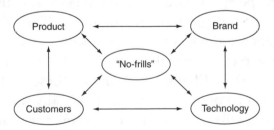

Figure 3.4 **The four building blocks of a discount strategy.**

Customers are viewed as co-producers of the service in question and on a mainly transaction-based level. As such there are no loyalty programmes and costs of relationship marketing are completely eliminated as every customer receives an equal treatment focusing on the value of the core product. Customers are seen as viral ambassadors for a company pursuing a discount strategy promoting the discount offering given its perceived superior price/quality ratio.

While also questioning the notion of being "stuck in the middle", discount strategy is markedly different from blue ocean strategy given its disruptive nature and focus on value destruction in highly competitive markets – red oceans.

A discount strategy, however, also has its limitations as this strategy is mainly targeted towards specific markets in which former monopolies and incumbents have lost their agility and flexibility and therefore are ripe for attacking. Companies competing in high-end markets such as those for luxury cars or customized products and services will be ill advised to follow a discount strategy in its entirety.

Mapping the Four Different Perspectives

Now that the four perspectives of strategy have been described, it is argued that the positioning and resource-based views represent conventional strategic thinking, whereas blue ocean and discount strategy represent a more unconventional approach to strategic thinking. Table 3.5 lists all four as well as their main characteristics.

These four strategic perspectives are argued to constitute the strategy landscape and strategic thoughts of today. They do, however, also represent a series of strategic perspectives that, to some extent, resemble recipes as is the case with the management literature discussed in Chapter 2. Many of these make extensive use of the same companies in order to justify widely different strategic perspectives. They leave little room for residuals or something unexplained and assume a perfect correlation between the success, defined mainly as maximizing shareholder value, and the given perspective. They offer little proof for the assumed cause-and-effect relation between the perspectives and such success and fail to acknowledge that best practice is difficult, in some cases even impossible, to transform from one company to another. Last but not least these strategic perspectives, as well as the literature discussed in Chapter 2, fail

Table 3.5 **The four strategic perspectives and their characteristics**

The positioning perspective	The resource-based perspective	Blue ocean strategy perspective	Discount strategy perspective
Compete in existing market space	Compete by developing strong resources	Create uncontested market space	Compete in hypercompetitive market space
Beat the competitors through a strong position	Resources should be Valuable, Rare, non-Imitable and exploited by the Organization: VRIO	Make the competition irrelevant	Own value creation while destroying value for others
Exploit existing demand	Utilize strengths in resource profile	Create and capture new demand	Both supply push and demand pull
Low cost OR differentiation	Leverage resources	Create uncontested value	Craft the strategy with disruptive effect

to explain the success of those companies that deliberately work in contrast to these, those companies that purposefully attempt to break the established rules, those companies that operate within the X-factor universe.

It is those companies that operate within the X-factor universe which will be explored further with the aim of identifying how unconventional strategies are formed, and how they relate to the above strategic perspectives. Why is it that some companies can disrupt conventional strategy thinking and be successful at the same time? What is it that makes up the X-factor in today's world of business and how is this identified? Did companies such as Google, Facebook, Hotmail and PayPal devise their successful strategies on the back of one or more of the above perspectives, or was it something else? In other words: What does it take to break the rules – and survive?

4

THE STRATEGY SYSTEM OR HOW TO COMBINE PERSPECTIVES

Successful attackers do not try to be better than their bigger rivals. Rather, they actively adopt a different strategy (or business model) and aim to compete by changing the rules of the game in the industry.[1]

(C.C. Markides, 2008)

In order to approach what is defined as indefinable in the X-factor context, it is necessary to draw up the competitive playing field. In the previous chapter, four strategic perspectives were discussed and argued to constitute a major part of current strategic thinking; when viewed in isolation the perspectives all provide the strategist with a recipe to follow. However, when the four perspectives are combined they provide a competitive map for the strategist to use to not only craft a strategy but to dynamically develop this over time.

This landscape, which is characterized by the ability to innovate and/or imitate in a competitive setting of monopoly or full competition, is mainly governed by market forces. The value proposition is what drives success. In addition to this market, an institutional market exists that is more regulatory in its nature. From a corporate point of view, this market concerns the ability to utilize institutional forces to gain a competitive edge and how these impact on those forces found in the traditional market.

Aside from these two markets, which are external in their nature, an internal market exists within companies in which

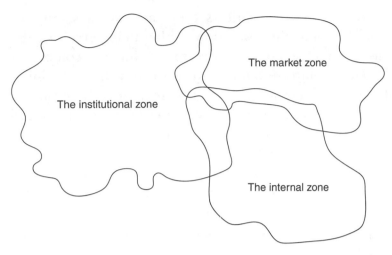

The market zone

The institutional zone

The internal zone

Figure 4.1 **The competitive landscape.**

various departments, divisions and the like compete for resources. Given this, three competitive zones can be defined in the strategy system, as shown in Figure 4.1.

Many of the X-factor companies are fully aware that the competitive battle is fought on multiple battlegrounds and also utilize forces belonging to the institutional zone in order to carve out a competitive edge.

The Institutional Zone – Neglected or Often Forgotten!

Traditionally, the institutional zone is considered to consist of external forces beyond the control of a given company which, however, must be taken into consideration when working with strategy. Examples of such forces are the political measures taken and the extent of government intervention, macroeconomic forces that influence the market zone, cultural and demographic forces that can change the preferences of consumers, environmental forces and the efforts to protect the environment and legal forces.[2]

Of these institutional forces, the political/economic forces constitute the primary drivers of the institutional zone. Contrary to traditional thinking, these factors can indeed be influenced by companies just as they can have a significant impact on the competitive situation. Rather than perceiving the institutional forces as a one-way stream of influence, companies in the X-factor universe tend to focus on how they can influence these forces in order to further their competitive position.

Regulatory measures initiated by political factors often interfere with market forces as is the case for industries where subsidies are given, such as alternative energy, or where regulatory restrictions are implemented, such as CO_2 emission impacting the auto manufacturing industry. Companies in the X-factor universe are fully aware of the impact regulatory measures can have and therefore spend a considerable amount of resources in order to influence these. Examples of this are: Ryanair, which has gone to considerable lengths to influence the liberalization of the airline passenger industry and airport regulations; easyJet, which supports restrictions on the age of an airline's fleet in order to curb CO_2 emission; and Vestas, one of the largest manufacturers of windmills, which is attempting to influence the subsidies given to alternative energy.

Aside from regulatory measures, the economic conditions can likewise impact a company's competitive ability. Many Chinese companies have gained a competitive edge due to their local economic conditions which facilitate a much lower labour cost base. This is to a large degree supported by initiatives such as government backed financing. When combined they provide a strong institutional, competitive fundament.

In times of crisis, political intervention and the resulting economic impact can be of a very significant size. When large government-backed subsidies are injected into the market in order not just to salvage certain companies but in some cases entire industries, the market forces and their invisible hand are effectively short-circuited. If it was not for such intervention, companies such as General Motors, Ford, AIG and Citigroup may have failed to carry on their operations in the wake of the financial crisis that began with the subprime crisis in 2007. These and many other companies in the US have received substantial subsidies in order to survive, which effectively influence the market zone. In other countries across Europe and Asia, similar subsidies have been given, thus underlining that the institutional market, or zone, is as global as the market zone.

In addition to the political and economic factors, cultural and demographic forces also impact the competitive situation as do the legal and environmental forces, but all these are to a lesser degree governed by the institutional zone that is characterized by governmental interference. Many of the companies analysed in this book place emphasis on how they can influence the institutional zone and the forces within this, which indicates the importance they can have on the competitive landscape in its entirety.

Given that companies are indeed able to influence the forces of the institutional zone, the competitive playing field takes on an added dimension which companies can utilize to their own advantage. What becomes of interest in this context is which institutional forces a company should seek to influence and how to do so. Companies in the X-factor universe, such as Vestas, have defined how they can impact the institutional forces in order to change the competitive situation.

This impact zone is naturally tied to the industry in which the company competes, but may also cover more general areas such as the government-backed financing that is utilized by, for example, Chinese companies currently invading the global competitive landscape.

As part of the competitive landscape the institutional zone can prove a vital competitive factor for some companies, whereas it holds less relevance for others, all depending on the nature of the industry and could therefore prove to be a force which should be taken into account when working with strategy. Another and more familiar competitive zone in terms of strategy is that of the market.

The Market Zone – the Traditional Zone at Work

As emphasized in Chapter 3, some of the strategy "schools" are said to offer an "outside-in" perspective on the company, notably the positioning school, but blue ocean and monopoly rules also operate with environmental contingencies. These two constitute a continuum, following the same underlying dimension and centred on the degree of competition in a relevant market space. Consequently, the archetypical strategy will be labelled "blue ocean" and the archetype itself "monopolist".

At the far end of the continuum we find some of the strategic notions from discount business strategy.[3] Companies following this type of strategy are often adopting disruptive views and actions and are not tied only to a discount profile. However, they typically act in a red ocean. Consequently, the archetypical strategy will be labelled "red ocean" and the archetype itself "disrupter".

Taken together, the monopolist/disrupter continuum constitutes the X-axis of our strategy system. The Y-axis is constituted by notions which mainly relate to parts of the so-called resource-based view on strategy, which means an "inside-out" perspective on strategy. In the resource-based perspective the starting point is the development and design of resources and competences internally in the company, and, basically, this may lead to either an imitator type of organization – "*we do not want to invent the wheel but simply mimic what others have already developed before*" or an innovator type of organization – "*as entrepreneurs we wish to build innovative power and execute accordingly*".

The implication of this is two new archetypes, namely the imitator and the innovator. When these are paired with the degree of competition visualized by the blue ocean and red ocean, the strategy system appears as shown in Figure 4.2. It is within this system that companies, those of the recipe universe and the X-factor universe, are placing themselves strategically and more interestingly move around over time.

When viewing the strategy system, four quadrants emerge as strategic areas in which companies can position themselves. Starting from the top right corner of the system and moving clockwise these are: (1) As an innovator in a red ocean, (2) As

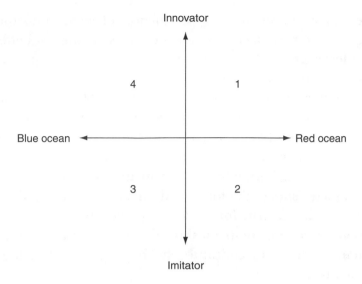

Figure 4.2 **The strategy system.**

an imitator in a red ocean, (3) As an imitator in a blue ocean and finally (4) As an innovator in a blue ocean.

Among those companies that successfully executed a strategy as an imitator in a blue ocean one finds the Japanese car manufacturers that grew their global market share by imitating existing technology – cars. Companies such as Toyota manufactured cars just as their American competitors did, albeit of a smaller size, and managed not only to conquer market share but also to create a situational monopoly by doing so. When turning our attention to those that manage to successfully execute a strategy of an imitator in a red ocean, discount companies fit the bill. By offering a product similar or better suited to the competitors but at a significantly lower price, discount companies are able to disrupt the market leading to potential value destruction for the market as a whole. The airline passenger industry is a prime example of this. Moving to those companies that occupy the position of an innovator in a red ocean, these are characterized by either offering an improved version of an existing product, such as mobile phones with MP3 player, or by innovating their production process to obtain advantages. The latter is what Samsung did when they innovated their production of semiconductors allowing them to manufacture semiconductors of equal or better quality at lower prices. This is also known as dual advantage or as being "stuck in the middle". Innovators in a blue ocean are characterized by their ability to open up new markets or create situational monopolies through their innovations. Classic examples of such companies are 3M, Apple Inc. and Google which are all argued to have created new markets by offering innovative products or by packaging known technology in an innovative manner.

The characteristics of the four quadrants remain static, which however is not always true for those companies that sail the seas of competition. Some companies move around inside the strategy system in order to continuously shape and seek a high Return on Strategy.

To illustrate the dynamic nature consider the cases of Saxo Bank, Ryanair and Huawei. Saxo Bank was founded as a traditional broker in the early 1990s offering services that were similar to other companies – the archetype of an imitator in a red ocean. Ryanair was likewise an imitator in a red ocean during its early years of operation while providing a similar service to that of the flag carriers. When Huawei was founded they focused on offering low-end and largely standardized telecommunications equipment at lower prices, which again fits the bill of an imitator in a red ocean.

Where are these companies today? They have moved to take on a different role, to become a different archetype.

Saxo Bank changed their strategic focus in the mid-1990s to become an IT brokerage focusing heavily on online investing, Ryanair rewrote the rules for European air passenger travel by adopting a discount strategy and in the process innovated the way in which customers book their tickets and, finally, Huawei has become one of the leading companies within the global telecom equipment industry through a focus on the low-cost R&D resources of China. When plotting the journey of these companies in the strategy system, the dynamism of strategy is captured as shown in Figure 4.3.

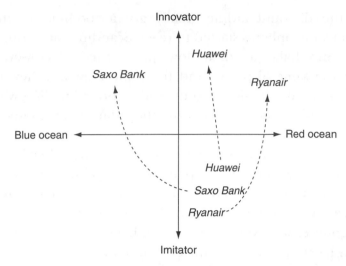

Figure 4.3 **The strategic journey of selected companies.**

The majority of companies are constantly moving within the strategy system in order to respond to the ever-changing market conditions. For some companies the movement is of a minor character by making small adjustments to a current strategy whereas others, as those depicted above, completely change their strategic focus. Certain moves fit conventional thinking and can be explained through one of the recipes, namely those moves made by companies belonging to the recipe universe, whereas other moves appear to deliberately work against the recipes and in some cases even redefine what can be done. Those are the companies that belong to the X-factor universe, which are able to utilize the X-factor to break the rules of the game.

The Internal Zone – Avoiding Internal Cannibalizing

In the book "The Rule of Three" Sheth and Sisodia discuss various patterns of competition. Their general observation is that there has been more and intense (fierce) competition in most industries. They also note that new aggressive players are entering in many, and even institutionalized, industries. Finally, they emphasize that many companies tend to forget the competition from internal cannibalizing.

When the discount airlines really got a foothold in the market many incumbents started to react. Scandinavian Airlines launched Snowflake as their low price carrier. However, they used the same airplanes and the same crew and flew to almost the same destinations. So instead of providing SAS with a new and additional business arm they started to compete internally.

The Australian airline Qantas did the same when they introduced Jetstar. However, this company, which is wholly owned by Qantas, is managed separately and operates independently and has apparently achieved a much higher success than its Scandinavian counterpart, which later was pulled out of the market.

Companies in the X-factor universe have avoided such kinds of internal cannibalizing in favour of working diligently with aligning their challenges and resources in their organizational design.

The X-factor Universe versus the Recipe Universe

As described in Chapter 1, the recipe universe and the X-factor universe are widely different. The recipe universe is characterized by companies that adopt the business book strategies of the positioning school and the resource-based view, discussed in Chapter 3, or fit one of the easy-to-understand recipes that are discussed in Chapter 2. In contrast to this universe stands the X-factor universe, which is defined by companies that cannot be explained by business book strategies or recipes but rather deploy unconventional thinking and deliberately work in contrast to these, utilizing instead the X-factor.

Whether a company belongs to the recipe universe or the X-factor universe is not determined by nature and as such it is possible for a company to break the rules of the game and successfully move from the recipe universe to the X-factor universe. This is exactly what Saxo Bank, Ryanair and Huawei have managed to do. Given this, the two universes and how companies move from one to another can be illustrated as shown in Figure 4.4.

The recipe universe	The X-factor universe
Saxo Bank, Ryanair and Huawei initially characterized as imitators seeking to position themselves in a red ocean. These can all be explained by the positioning school as either niche operators or leaders cost	Saxo Bank innovated the market for online investing and became an innovator in a blue ocean
	Ryanair adopted a discount strategy, innovated the ticketing process and became an innovator in a red ocean
	Huawei utilized the low-cost R&D resources of China and became an innovator in a red ocean

Figure 4.4 **Selected companies move from the recipe to the X-factor universe.**

However, it is not the move itself which is interesting albeit this underlines the dynamic nature of strategy, but rather how these and other companies have managed to enter the X-factor universe. This is due to the X-factor and how companies utilize this. But what is the X-factor?

As described in Chapter 1, the X-factor is defined as a critical yet indefinable element and as such it cannot be captured in a simple and generic recipe. It can, however, be approached by analysing those companies that have successfully applied out-of-the-box thinking to break the conventional boundaries of strategic thinking. By analysing a selection of companies from different industries located throughout Europe, America and Asia, a number of factors can be identified, which have assisted these companies' ability to develop their own X-factor and enter the X-factor universe.

The X-factor Universe as a Destination

How do strategists within a company approach the strategy making process? Do they plan their strategy as suggested by traditional strategic literature and stick to this? Are they working within confined industrial or market barriers when working on the strategy? Do they analyse a host of different markets and the value propositions currently offered by competitors in order to break the value curve and create a new market as suggested by the blue ocean approach? Are they looking to destroy value for the competitors while creating value for themselves through a discount approach or are they merely growing their resources to such a level that this will make all competition inferior?

It is argued that successful strategists look across these perspectives to lay their own strategic puzzle from the jigsaw puzzles that each of these strategies offer. In doing so they pick and choose a combination that fits their particular company. Some are even forced into changing their strategy and look beyond traditional measures by unfolding events that destabilize the system and call for new and different thinking.

When analysing a select group of companies from different industries and located across Europe, America and Asia, a non-exhaustive list of six key success drivers may be developed within which companies applied out-of-the-box thinking. Such thinking and the utilization of unconventional measures allowed companies to break into the X-factor universe and to remain within this.

These six key success drivers concern how the companies work with their customers and products, how companies utilize the financial circuit, organizational design and technology as drivers to enter the X-factor universe and achieve Return on Strategy. The sixth key success factor, which is leadership, cuts across all the factors with a view to balance and align for a greater Return on Strategy.

The customer attitudes and the attitudes of customers are addressed in Chapter 6. Not surprisingly, companies in the X-factor universe typically display a high degree of customer involvement and go a step further than other companies. The concept of the pro-sumer – the amalgamation of producer and consumer – is an invention which brings about both lower cost and higher satisfaction at one and the same time. Customer centric marketing supersedes product functionality marketing and the customers are generally regarded as viral ambassadors. In pursuing their goals, some companies, like Saxo Bank, do not see traditional channel conflicts as a problem, as well as the normal focus on expending many resources on traditional relationship marketing loyalty is relaxed considerably.

The product portfolio deals in Chapter 7 with how diligent work around products and services helps increase the Return on Strategy. First of all, this chapter provides ample evidence of how companies have used questionable toolboxes beyond their applicability and subsequently achieved a dissatisfactory low Return on Strategy. However, as cases with Huawei, Skype, Google, Novo Nordisk and Ryanair display there is also the possibility of entering into the X-factor universe. The likelihood of this increases, if the core product contains stickiness, if the company's supply side constitutes a new ecosystem, if products are viewed in the context of a coherent business model, if a demand pull is created and, finally, if life-cycle considerations are taken into the equation.

The financial circuit is the key driver addressed by Chapter 8. First of all, this key driver is very much overlooked in the current literature on management and strategy. The price killer aspect attributes to some of the very high Return on Strategy achieved by Skype, Facebook and Google, but also cost innovations play a major role. Ultimately some companies hit what is called zero-SAC, i.e. running the take-up of customers without any sales and acquisition costs (SAC). Another part of the financial circuit is the tendency for some companies to reverse the revenue streams, i.e. to gain revenues from other sources than the customers. Finally, financial partnering also opens up new avenues for a high Return on Strategy.

The organizational design issues depicted in Chapter 9 deal with the structure, values, people and the culture of a company. Establishment of particularly well-suited "wolf-culture" and dual-CEO structures are examples of how some companies have been attracted into the X-factor universe and thereby actively created a higher Return on Strategy.

The technology chain is addressed in Chapter 10 with a number of different ways to approach proven technology, groundbreaking technology, scalable technology and simple technology. Finding the right mix of these and avoiding technological exuberance is what characterizes companies in the X-factor universe striving for a high Return on Strategy.

The leadership genes are the core focus of Chapter 11, and it appears that the leadership genes actually work somewhat across the other five key success factors, the customer attitude, the product portfolio, the financial circuit, the organizational design and the technology chain. Many companies in the X-factor universe have top management possessing entrepreneurial skills. A leadership which is balanced, authentic, aligned for execution, passionate and focused on training the staff helps companies achieve a high Return on Strategy.

Prior to a company's utilization of one or more of the above described key success drivers, it often experiences a moment of crisis in the broadest terms of the word. A crisis that can be called a trigger event, an event which causes the company to deploy unconventional and out-of-the-box thinking which then breaks with the known recipes of the strategy world.

The framework containing the trigger events, the six key success drivers and the resulting Return on Strategy is illustrated in Figure 4.5.

Successful deployment of unconventional thinking within the identified key success drivers and the companies resulting inclusion into the X-factor universe has led to a high Return on Strategy for companies presented in the following. The overall Return of Strategy is defined as *strategic effectiveness* which may be further operationalized as *the degree to which a company meets with its strategic goals*. Obviously, 100% effectiveness is achieved if all goals are reached in time and at the allocated level of resources without substantial opportunity costs. Invariably, companies can either underperform or outperform. Strategic effectiveness includes too that companies meet their revised goals, as revisions and changes in strategy plans are typical ingredients

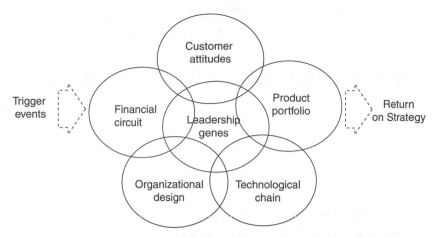

Figure 4.5 **Return on Strategy framework.**

in most companies. Companies in the recipe universe tend to underperform, at least in the long run, whereas companies in the X-factor universe tend to outperform.

This framework will be explored in greater detail in the following chapters. Chapter 5 initiates our journey by exploring the different trigger events that have formed the starting point for many companies' successful journey towards the X-factor universe as the destination. In this chapter, which focuses on different modes of strategy, it is argued that many companies do indeed bridge some of the four strategic perspectives when they develop their strategy. Furthermore it is argued that the process might be characterized by a planned effort as well as responding to the emerging events in the marketplace. In some cases, the initial strategy or idea has been completely altered due to unfolding events that may have led to the company in question facing a crisis. A crisis which has led to a new and superior strategy being put in place.

Following this, the six key success drivers and how they relate to a company's Return on Strategy will be presented and analysed in Chapters 6 to 11.

5

WHAT TRIGGERS STRATEGY?

All the best things that I did at Apple came from (a) not having money and (b) not having done it before, ever.[1]

Steve Wozniak, former CEO of Apple

Since its founding in the early 1990s, the strategic approach of Saxo Bank has been characterized by its flexible nature and ability to change according to unfolding events. When faced with a crisis in its early days, the company redirected its focus. The result became a new business model of an IT brokerage with a strong online presence as opposed to a traditional full service brokerage. Just after the turn of the new millennium the strategy was redefined further so that they also could be a facilitator in the market for foreign exchange through offering their award-winning proprietary technology to their competitors.

Such a strategic approach, which is characterized more by its flexible nature than by conventional strategy thinking, has been instrumental in shaping the X-factor of Saxo Bank. It is a strategic approach that provides Saxo Bank with increased manoeuvrability in the fast-changing marketplace of today allowing them to swiftly answer the changing needs of the market or tap into new opportunities. It also makes the company less vulnerable to fluctuations in the financial markets.

Aside from Saxo Bank's own flexible approach to strategy, the external environment plays an equally important role in the strategic direction of the company as the following quote from the two joint CEOs and founders underlines.

We value feedback from the marketplace above all else. It is our clients and our partners who help set the direction for our growth and strategy.[2]

Since Saxo Bank began their operations more than 15 years ago, the strategic approach has steered the company through planned strategic efforts as well as emerging strategic moves in response to a crisis. Had the company not been able to shift their strategic focus, they probably wouldn't have achieved such success.

Strictly following a devised strategic plan may lead to failure due to missed opportunities or lack of response towards competitors, whereas following no plan at all will likely lead to failure given the lack of common direction for the organization.

In addition to the ability to swiftly change strategic focus, Saxo Bank has utilized the entire strategy landscape to break new ground for how foreign exchange is traded and offered to private and institutional investors. By maintaining their flexible approach to both strategic direction and perspectives, along with other factors to be described in the following chapters, Saxo Bank has developed its unique X-factor.

Approaching the X-factor Universe with Value Creation or Value Destruction

The strategy approach as a trigger event that may lead a company towards the X-factor universe holds two main areas that are: (1) the events that lead to the development of a company's strategy and (2) the ability to bridge different strategic perspectives and thus make use of the entire landscape of how strategy should be performed as discussed in Chapter 3.

Virgin is often used as a classic example of a company following the strategy of a differentiator leveraging their strong brand to enter new markets and industries. Few can argue with the impact of the founder, Sir Richard Branson. The principles that Sir Richard Branson set out with in the 1970s still define the Virgin values of today that are: (1) Value for money, (2) Good quality, (3) Brilliant customer service, (4) Innovative, (5) Competitively challenging and fun.

The vision of Sir Richard Branson and the strategy approach of Virgin, which to a large degree is based on a first mover challenger effect, illustrate a relationship between the strategy approach and the ability of Virgin to approach the X-factor universe in a blue ocean fashion. Virgin did this in the UK both in challenging flag carriers and mobile incumbents.

The common characteristics of the markets in which Virgin operate are described as follows:

> *They are typically markets where the customer has been ripped off or under-served, where there is confusion and/or where the competition is complacent.*[3]

Thus, Virgin is an example of a company based on a value creation strategy.

At a later stage in the industry of flag carriers, when this industry turned to hypercompetition, Ryanair and easyJet emerged as disrupters, leading the industry towards value subtraction. Interestingly, both the strategies of Virgin and the strategies of Ryanair and easyJet have proved successful. If a market can be characterized by hypercompetition, and the traditional paradigm for how to attain sustainable advantages does not work any longer, this leaves space for disrupters to enter. Virgin is one example of a company within the airline industry that has crafted a disruptive strategy. Other examples within this industry include easyJet and Ryanair.

Discovering Your Strategy

The image of a dark room filled with strategists paging through Power Point presentations often comes to mind when thinking of strategy in the making. The picture of highly paid, and hopefully highly intelligent, employees, executives and often high paid management consultants devising the ultimate plan for competitive supremacy emerges. In many cases this could not be further from the truth.

A recent McKinsey analysis among top executives on strategy[4] showed that:

- More than half of 796 responses are dissatisfied with their strategy efforts,
- 80% view their strategic approach as "inefficient",
- 44% say their strategic plans do not "track execution", and
- 9 in 10 say organization speed and agility have become increasingly urgent issues for them over the past five years. Speed is a measure of how rapidly organizations execute an operational or strategic objective, and agility is the ability to change tactics or direction quickly.

As can be seen, the study supports the argument about the necessity to craft new directions on how to undertake the discipline of strategic management in practice. If more than half of the respondents are dissatisfied with their approach to strategy, there seems to be a real need for revising and redirecting modes for how to work with strategy.

But how does a new strategy then emerge? The research project behind this book has shown various contingencies. Some strategies that have turned out to be superior have been devised on the back of strategic failures and the need for a change of direction. Others have emerged due to a certain portion of luck and sheer stubbornness, while others again have been born out of a crisis facing the company. Finally some have come out of deliberate planning. Notwithstanding the fact that the last mode of strategy – deliberate planning – would be recognized as the "normal" mode in conventional literature on strategy, this mode is rarely seen within the X-factor universe compared with the three other modes. However, this does not mean that X-factor universe companies do not plan. It only indicates that the companies typically include much more non-conventional thinking in their approach to strategy.

The Crisis that Led to Supremacy

In the mid-1990s, Saxo Bank was faced with a crisis. At the time, the brokerage industry of Denmark was in the public spotlight due to stories of companies that were deploying questionable business tactics in an unregulated market causing large financial losses for individual clients. Despite being the first to gain a licence when regulation was put in place in 1995, Saxo Bank found it hard to generate sales leads through traditional channels because of general distrust with the market, and all the companies present had crept under the skin of potential investors.

> *It was a wake-up call for us, we looked at ourselves and asked is this what we want to do? Should we do business in Denmark? Should we do what we do or something else? I believe Kim and Lars at this point decide to really push the development of the online trading platform.*[5]

On the back of this, Saxo Bank changed their focus from operating a traditional business model towards investing heavily in the development of an online trading platform. This strategic move that looked beyond the existing industry boundaries, by effectively becoming an IT focused brokerage company, would prove highly successful in the years to come.

Another company that managed to successfully change strategic direction in the face of a crisis was Ryanair. Initially established as an alternative independent carrier to the flag carriers with the focus on a simple fare structure and better service, Ryanair was by 1991 facing financial collapse. As the CEO expressed it *"We had no control over money at all"*. It was then, on a winter night in Ireland that the decision was made by Ryanair to craft a disruptive strategy partly inspired by that of Southwest Airlines.[6]

In the coming years, Ryanair experienced tremendous growth and success and played no small part in redefining the passenger airline industry of Europe. From carrying approximately 650,000 passengers in 1991, Ryanair has become the largest European low fare airline carrying an estimated 52 million passengers in 2008 on 762 low fare routes covering 26 European countries.[7]

For the financial year that ended on March 31, 2008, Ryanair reported revenues of €2,713 million and adjusted profit before tax of €528.9 million up from €451.0 million for the previous year.[8] By comparison, Scandinavian Airlines reported profit before tax of approximately €178.5 million for the financial year ending December 31, 2007, while easyJet reported a profit before tax for the year ending September 30 of €260 million.[9] British Airways reported profits before tax of £883 million, generated on the back of revenues reaching £8,750 million and thus a profit margin of 10% compared with the 20% of Ryanair.

In the face of such growth and the impact Ryanair have had on the passenger airline industry, one can only wonder what would have been the scenario had they not faced near bankruptcy in 1991.

Apple, formerly Apple Computer, until they realized that they had expanded into other business areas, is a company that has experienced upturns and downturns. Apparently the learning curve has been especially steep during hard times, for as Steve Wozniak, former CEO, expresses it: "*All the best things that I did at Apple came from (a) not having money and (b) not having done it before, ever*".[10] This means, that especially tough times have fuelled the creativity and innovation capacity within the company. From a managerial point of view, it gives food for thought that rough water is often a trigger for innovations.

Crises are often defined as a catastrophe with fatal negative consequences. However, as just seen from Saxo Bank, Ryanair and Apple, a crisis may very well be the stepping stone to success in the next phase of the company's life. One may also put it the following way: Where companies in the recipe universe often use a crisis to explain or justify less than satisfactory performance, companies in the X-factor universe typically use a crisis as a trigger event for moving into the next (positive) phase. Often, this goes hand in hand with the creation of a sense of urgency which resembles the example (at the beginning of Chapter 3) regarding the military unit that lost their way in the Alps in a snowstorm. By just having a "strategic map", which they thought was right, they were both able and willing to continue the uphill struggle as everything made sense.

Concerning times of financial crisis this constitutes yet another example relating to the considerable differences between different universes. Many companies in the recipe universe are very keen to speak of market failure and lack of access to capital. Some of the companies in the X-factor universe seem to "exploit" the financial crisis to gain a stronger foothold and to accelerate growth. This is, for example, the case with companies such as Huawei, Facebook and Saxo Bank.

Saxo Bank is yet again an interesting model for exercise at least at the generic level. They are utilizing the financial crisis as a springboard to further penetrate the market with their trading platform. Moreover – despite financial results that are comfortably within the ballpark of their strategy – they decided to utilize the financial crisis as a means to cut costs, in particular staff costs, dramatically (by approximately one-third).

Failure(s) – A Vehicle for Success?

Successful strategies need not be born out of a crisis, but can just as easily happen due to a combination of an initial strategy failing and some pure luck. Going back almost half a century to 1959, the American Honda Motor Co. was formed in an attempt to crack the American market for larger, more luxurious motorcycles. The early years would prove disastrous for Honda with customers reporting clutch failures and leaking oil from the larger motorcycles that were thought to suit the American market. The initial strategy was failing.

While focusing on the sale of large motorcycles, the executives of the American Honda Motor Co. were driving around on the much smaller 50cc Super Cubs that had not been promoted to any great length. However, as these motorcycles attracted a considerable amount of attention in the communities around, the focus on promoting the efforts to sell these were increased. What Honda would realize was that even in America being big was not necessarily the key to success.

This shift in focus proved successful for Honda, which by the mid-1960s had grown their motorcycle sales to US$77 million representing a healthy 63% market share.[11] Honda thus discovered their American strategy on the back of an initial failure, some luck pertaining to the executives own use of the smaller 50cc Super Cub and their ability to rapidly shift focus to meet the demand for these smaller motorcycles and redirect their efforts to serve this market.

Back on European shores, the case of Naturhouse displays a similar path of failure leading to success. In 1992, the company Kiluva set up its first dietary retail shop in Vitoria in Spain with the objective of developing a business model for franchising. Having gained knowledge of the market working as consultants for Dietisa, a family-owned dietary products company, Revuelta initially distributed dietary products to independent retailers and decided to use this experience in setting up a retail chain of his own.

The initial strategy was to set up a shop in an upmarket location in a purchased space offering beauty products, massages, nutrition products and other health and beauty products.

We made every possible mistake with this first shop – we purchased the retail location in an area that was too upmarket, and we tried to do too much.[12]

With Spain going through a recession in 1993 and increased competition from both the market leaders and smaller competitors competing on price, the war for shelf-space was growing increasingly fierce. This forced Naturhouse to maintain a focus on opening their own retail outlets, albeit in a different format than the first attempt since this had failed.

By late 1993, the second Naturhouse shop opened in rented premises, located in a middle income area, offering only dietary supplements for sale and weight-loss advisory services given by trained nutritionists. Over the following years additional shops were opened and the business model was fine tuned allowing for the final strategy to emerge. Each shop would have two people, of whom one was a professionally qualified nutritionist, biologist or pharmacist providing advice to the clients and the other a sales person. The shops ranged from 50 to 100 square metres in size and carried a small inventory worth roughly €5,000, representing 200 stock-keeping units (SKUs). On the back of this strategy, Naturhouse managed to successfully establish a unique image within the dietary retail market based on trained professionals who gave advice to clients while maintaining their privacy.

From 1992, when the first retail shop failed, to 2003 Naturhouse opened 72 of their own shops in Spain and franchised another 444 of which 43 were international franchisees. They increased their annual revenues from €5.5 million in 1992 to €35.4 million in 2003, representing a compound annual growth rate (CAGR) over the entire period of 17%. When performing the same calculation for the period from 2003 to 2007, the CAGR comes out at above 25%. In 2006 they expanded further by buying a 5% share of the listed US company Neutraceuticals and informed the Securities and Exchange Commission that it wanted to reach 50%. At the end of 2008, Naturhouse had more than 1,700 centres worldwide providing advice to their clients.[13]

Failure of their initial strategic focus on a traditional health and beauty shop in an upmarket area has thus proved highly successful for Naturhouse.

Stumbling upon the Goldmine

In the previous sections, the discovery of a successful strategy has been catapulted by either a crisis facing the company or the failure of the initial strategy. However, this is not the only path for a turn in a radically different strategic direction. Other companies have achieved success by accidentally stumbling upon the strategy or by pursuing something of personal interest that had a mass appeal.

In 2004, when Mark Zuckerberg launched the original version of Facebook.com, called thcfacebook.com, it was in response to the existing facebooks at Harvard that were only produced for the different residential houses. Traditional facebooks were paper-based student directories containing information on other students such as hometown, high school and extracurricular interests as well as pictures of the person in question.

With the aim of developing an online facebook holding information on all Harvard students and being accessible to all regardless of which residential house you belonged to, Zuckerberg coded the online version of such a university-wide facebook. A few weeks after the launch of the web site more than 60% of the Harvard students were using the site and Zuckerberg was receiving enquiries from other schools on how they could obtain their own version of this, leading to the early expansion of Facebook.

Initially versions were developed for Yale, Columbia and Stanford as those were identified as the places where students of Harvard were likely to have many friends. This decision was purely based on intuition rather than number crunching and weeks of intensive analyses.[14]

Over the past four years this early, and to a large extent personal, need for a directory of your fellow students has grown into a network of more than 70 million active users. Facebook. com is the fifth most trafficked web site in the world and the second most trafficked social networking site in the world after

You Tube according to COM Score. The users view more than 65 billion pages per month and have made the photo application of Facebook the most widely used on the Web.[15]

From being a local US-based student directory it has grown to a global and people-wide vehicle to include a host of products such as Facebook Chat and Facebook Ads as well as numerous applications including Photos, Notes, Events, Video and Gifts.

By pursuing his own desire for a university-wide student directory, known as a facebook, Mark Zuckerberg stumbled upon a demand for a networking society of global proportions and as such the initial idea turned into a successful business, where the strategy has emerged and evolved along with the growth and success. Here there was no crisis or failure of the initial strategy, given that it was not thought of as a business at the outset, but instead a strategy that developed on the back of the discovered goldmine by way of a considerable element of luck.

Other examples of fortune pertain to the success of PayPal that was founded in 1998 by Max Levchin and Peter Thiel, and Hotmail which was launched in 1996 by Sabeer Bhatia and Jack Smith.

Before finally finding its niche as a web-based payment system, PayPal explored the avenues of cryptography software and the transmission of money through PDAs. PayPal grew to be one of the most secure methods of transmitting money over the web through a continued focus on security and the development of superior fraud solutions.

PayPal enables global e-commerce by giving consumers confidence and choices to pay online without having to worry about sharing financial information. PayPal users can pay from their PayPal balance, bank account or by credit card, and can easily send and receive money in 17 currencies across 190 countries in which PayPal operates. With more than 60 million active accounts, PayPal transacted US$47 billion in 2007. Every second, PayPal processes some US$2,000 in payments. PayPal payments represented about 9% of e-commerce globally and 12% in the US in 2008.[16] PayPal went public in 2002 and the same year the company acquired by eBay for US$1.5 billion.[17]

Sabeer Bhatia and Jack Smith were initially working on a web-based personal database when they luckily stumbled upon the idea of web-based email. Due to their employer's firewall they were hindered in accessing their personal email accounts when trying to communicate with one another and decided to solve the problem by developing an email account that could be accessed through a browser.

By offering free email to all people who had the opportunity to access the web, they managed to grow their user base at unprecedented speed, leading to Microsoft acquiring Hotmail less than two years after the first web-based email was born. A deal worth US$400 million, which would account for a decent return on the newly found goldmine over a two-year period!

The creators of the peer-to-peer file sharing service, KaZaA, Niklas Zennström and Janus Friis did not fail in their initial strategy of providing peer-to-peer file sharing but rather stumbled upon a series of legal issues that led to the demise of KaZaA and presented the goldmine of Skype. Taking their knowledge from this venture they created the peer-to-peer voice-over-Internet-protocol (VoIP) network, known as Skype.

Founded in 2003, Skype quickly grew to become one of the remarkable business successes of recent time. By 2005, when Skype was acquired by eBay for US$2.6 billion, it held 54 million user accounts worldwide. The number of user accounts has since grown to an astounding 309 million at the end of the first quarter of 2008.

On the basis of these accounts it may appear that managers and business leaders should only wait for the crisis to befall them, develop failing strategies or just put the success of a company and all the employees down to sheer luck. Naturally, this is not the case and not what is argued here. Instead what is argued is that managers must be open to a variety of inputs and events which can shape the strategy of a given company rather

than only put faith in miles of analysis and detailed planning
alone.

Planned Attacks that Conquered

In the early 1970s, Charles Schwab had a vision of a new type of
brokerage firm that focused on low commission rates, superior
customer service and salaried representatives. The idea of a discount brokerage was being introduced to a market where large
traditional companies such as Lehman Brothers and Morgan
Stanley had long held supremacy and where investment services
were offered in a traditional sense.

In 1975, the Securities and Exchange Commission (SEC)
allowed for negotiated commission rates on all securities transactions thus allowing for brokerages to establish their own
pricing.

While many of the existing brokerages decided to raise their
commissions, Charles Schwab decided to create a new kind of
brokerage – the discount brokerage.[18]

From 1975 to 1983, when Charles Schwab & Co. Inc. was
acquired by Bank of America, the number of client accounts
grew to more than 500,000. During the same period, the company introduced a host of unprecedented services such as seminars for its clients, which were introduced in 1977, extended
service hours in 1978, the first 24-hour quotation service in
1980 and the first 24-hour, seven days a week quotation service
by 1982.

The initial idea of creating a new breed of investment company – the discount brokerage – to battle the giants of Wall
Street had grown to become reality. The planned approach of
Charles Schwab that allowed him to identify potential in an
existing marketplace was indeed an intentional move aided by
the decision of the SEC in 1975. Therefore, this is also an example of how to disrupt the existing business logic and by this
challenge conventional wisdom.

Since the mid-1970s, Charles Schwab & Co. Inc. has managed
to create a new breed of brokerage through a planned

approach. This approach has obviously been of such a nature that unfolding events were welcomed and acted upon in order to strengthen the company. Examples of such events are the introduction of mutual funds in the 1980s and the company's ability to lead the online revolution of the 1990s. Over the past three decades the strategy of Charles Schwab has evolved from being primarily a discount brokerage to that of a hybrid between a full service brokerage and a discount brokerage.

Much of this success can be attributed to the early plan of Charles Schwab and the vision of a discount brokerage paired with their ability to navigate and take advantage of unfolding events. A planned attack that has catapulted Charles Schwab to the front of the brokerage industry reporting approximately US$1.4 trillion in total client assets and 7.0 million brokerage accounts by the end of 2007.

Another company which successfully planned their attack was the Japanese camera company Canon. In the 1970s, Xerox was widely regarded to hold the dominant position within photo-copying and few were expecting any competitors to attempt an attack on Xerox. Canon, however, decided to utilize their resources to develop new photocopying processes and targeted the demand for smaller photocopiers used in small offices, home offices or even used as a personal printer.

By developing an alternative to the technology of Xerox, which was protected by a vast amount of copyrights, Canon suc-cessfully invaded the territory of Xerox. The first copier to carry this technology, labcllcd the "new process", was introduced to the Japanese market in 1970 and was the first copier sold under the Canon brand. Throughout the 1970s, Canon introduced a number of product introductions, such as adding colour to the copier in 1973 and laser beam printing technology in 1975.

In the late 1970s, the top management of Canon began searching for a new market for the copier and discovered the segment of small offices, which Xerox had ignored. Believing that a low volume, value for money copier would satisfy the need of these small offices, Canon developed the concept of a personal side desk machine that could create a new market as well as aid in the decentralization of the copy function in many larger offices. It took the engineers of Canon three years to develop such a copier, a personal copier, which employed a cartridge-based technology allowing the users to replace the cartridge every 2,000 copies, thereby eliminating the need for maintenance.

In doing so Canon managed to take significant market share from Xerox and give birth to an entire new way of printing. Just as the personal computer grew in numbers so did the personal printer.

Four Triggers of Strategic Behaviour

Whether the discovery of a particular strategy, and a successful one, is down to a crisis situation, failure of previous strategies, sheer luck or due to more planned efforts, the approach that a company follows when developing their strategy and altering this over time is closely tied to the X-factor of that particular company and as such their ability to approach the X-factor universe.

The four triggers of strategic behaviour are summarized in Table 5.1. As can be seen, each strand can be characterized by various features that also indicate why the X-factor exists and emerges. Being forced to rethink a strategy can lead to the

Table 5.1 **Four triggers of strategic behaviour**

Crises	Failures	Luck	Planned
Launching a disruptive business model	Redirect business model	Reconstruct a concept, product or business model	Refining, leveraging and/ or diversifying business model
Revolution	Transformation	Emerging	Evolution
Top management	Management	Entrepreneurial	Managerial
Short term	Short term	No fixed time horizon	Various planning horizons

unlocking of new strategic ways and large market potential. Pursuing new and seemingly uninteresting avenues may lead to the creation of a whole new demand paving the way for successful strategic thinking. Accidents happen as we all know, but some can be a blessing in disguise leading to opportunities of great potential. Planning for such success can also yield result, particularly if the planning is combined with alternative and creative strategic thinking.

The four modes of strategy each represent different ways as to how one may rationalize strategy. Evidently, strategies related to crisis, failure and luck represent somewhat irrational, unpredictable modes of strategy which generally work well within the X-factor universe and achieve a high Return on Strategy. Strategy as planned goes well in conjunction with conventional strategic rationalism and would therefore tend to be more likely for companies normally operating within the recipe universe.

Bridge Building across Perspectives

When looking upon how the strategy of the above companies came about it may seem difficult to identify which of the four strategic perspectives, (1) the positioning view, (2) the resource-based view, (3) the blue ocean view or (4) the discount view, the various companies have adhered to. One explanation for this is that practice seems to be a mix of these in order to capitalize on the various characteristics and strengths that these strategies possess.

Given this, the notion of "stuck in the middle" as a certain way to mediocre performance can no longer be applied generically although some companies find themselves in trouble when attempting to execute such a strategy. Scandinavia Airlines did this when they introduced Snowflake as a response to the low price carriers, i.e. essentially mimicking others, thereby moving into the deep waters of the recipe universe and further away from the X-factor universe. However, as SAS used the same airplanes, the same pilots, the same staff and the same booking system, the customers had real difficulties in grasping the diligence of this initiative and to differentiate between the two services. They became blurred and SAS was to a certain extend caught in the middle of two different strategies, mainly caused by their attempt to craft a disruptive strategy by mimicking the recipe universe. No wonder that Snowflake did not become a success.

Not surprisingly, many companies do indeed use the entire strategic landscape when developing their strategy regardless of how they discovered this. Many companies can be argued to have positioned themselves according to the competition while also keeping a strong focus on developing their resources to create a competitive advantage. Other companies can be argued to work with elements of both blue ocean strategies and discount strategies in developing their strategy. Some are even argued to make use of all four perspectives.

Saxo Bank is seen to belong to the category of companies that make use of all four perspectives when developing their strategy. When the company was initially founded, the strategy was to be positioned as a niche operator servicing the needs of individual investors looking to invest in foreign exchange. At the outset, a planned approach according to the positioning school or as previously argued the strategy of an imitator in a red ocean. However, when asked about the strategy behind the development of their business at that time, the founders did not claim to adhere to a specific approach. As such their strategy was one without a strategy.

From an early desire to automate and thus reduce costs, Saxo Bank increased their focus on the internal processes and the technology of same while exploring the possibilities of an online presence. This is argued to represent the resource-based view given that the proprietary online trading platform of Saxo Bank was developed in-house.

Add these two together and Saxo Bank can be described as a company that was positioned in a niche and simultaneously focused on its resource base to continually develop the company's presence in online trading. From being a niche market, the market for investing in foreign exchange has grown substantially since the early 1990s when it became possible for private investors to trade in foreign exchange instruments. This indicates the advent of a blue ocean, albeit one which is turning red. Other features of the Saxo Bank strategy, such as their former aggressive pricing and viewing the customer as a co-producer, have the hallmarks of a disruptive strategy with discount features. It is the ability of Saxo Bank to mix all of these that has moved Saxo Bank into the X-factor universe where they currently fit the bill of an innovator in a blue ocean.

Given the above, it is argued that Saxo Bank is a prime example of how the four different strategic perspectives can be used for the purposes of one strategy. The strategy approach of Saxo Bank has not been focused on one specific perspective but rests rather on the belief and vision of the two founders. This approach has turned out to be instrumental in shaping the X-factor of Saxo Bank.

Building bridges across these perspectives is something which also characterizes the strategy of Samsung Electronics and their semiconductor division. From being second to their Japanese rivals at the end of the 1980s, Samsung Electronics managed to reinvent the production of semiconductors by creating internal competition among its research and development teams (R&D) – something which was highly unusual among companies in the late 1980s.

Positioned in an industry of declining margins and increased focus on low cost production, Samsung Electronics decided to focus their strategy on the development of superior production processes. By focusing on the production process and the development of semiconductors, Samsung Electronics was able to effectively pursue a strategy of differentiation and low cost at the same time.

The customers of Samsung Electronics were willing to pay a higher price for their products which, paired with the fact that Samsung Electronics had lower production costs, resulted in above normal margins. Above normal margins that was the result of the strategy which in Porter's terms would be "stuck in the middle".

The strategy and success of Samsung Electronics and their semiconductor business was made possible by focusing on the internal resources and how these could be used to simultaneously establish a differentiated position in the market and reduce costs.[19] Given this, Samsung Electronics was able to disrupt the market and execute a strategy of dual advantage, essentially moving from being an imitator in a red ocean to becoming an innovator in the same waters, thus abandoning the recipe universe for the X-factor universe.

Another company which can be argued to bridge various perspectives is Google. Google has successfully positioned itself as the superior search engine on the World Wide Web given their ability to deliver more relevant searches due to the algorithm initially develop by Sergei Brin and Larry Page.[20]

Since the early days, when Google was positioned in the market for online search engines and were competing face to face with Yahoo, Google has developed a number of additional products that are argued to have emerged from the employee ranks as opposed to stemming from any formal planning. These products include the web-based email, Gmail, and the application Google Earth to name a few. This has led to a continuously changing position for Google as they now compete with the likes of Microsoft, particularly the MSN of Microsoft, and eBay given that many of Google's advertisers are also using eBay as a sales channel.

Using their strong position within the online search market, Google has developed its product portfolio through levering their resource base, allowing the ideas of their employees to surface and potentially become successful products. In addition to bridging the positioning view with that of the resource-based, Google has gained its current position by offering its core service, searching on the web, free of charge to the users which in turn creates attractive traffic volumes for potential advertisers. This is argued to add an element of discount, albeit taking this to the extreme by offering a product free of charge.

As such Google can be argued to display elements across three of the four perspectives, and if one dares to consider the online search as a new uncontested market, Google effectively carries elements of all four. In terms of their position in the strategy system, Google started out as an imitator in an ocean with few competitors, but has evolved to become an innovator in various red oceans while simultaneously holding a near monopoly within the online search engine market.

Another example of companies that are characterized by elements of multiple strategic and even opposing perspectives is Southwest Airlines and Ryanair, although successful low-cost carriers in the US and Europe, respectively. They operate a business model that is equal to a blue ocean strategy in the case of Southwest Airlines, substituting road traffic with planes and a discount business strategy in the case of Ryanair pursuing head-on competition with traditional flag carriers.

When viewed in an American context, the low-cost business model that Southwest Airlines subscribes to is argued to represent a blue ocean strategy. It is widely used as an example of how a company can innovate the value curve and break the traditional boundaries of a given industry.[21] Southwest Airlines has reduced the in-flight amenities to a minimum and offers only point-to-point travel at very competitive prices, primarily substituting driving by car with flying. By this they have attracted and added a new market segment and developed a blue ocean.

Ryanair, which initially followed a similar model in the European market for airline passenger traffic, is widely used to illustrate the elements of a discount strategy.[22] They operate in hypercompetitive markets offering only point-to-point travel at very aggressive prices which to a large extent are made possible by the high involvement of the customer as a co-producer.

The traditional view that one perspective excludes another is strongly challenged by the strategies of the above and many other companies that manage to build bridges across the strategic perspectives by utilizing unconventional thinking. Building such bridges to develop a unique strategy based on the ability to mix and match is what the strategy approach is argued to revolve around. It is an approach where no recipe for success exists but instead is devised by the individual company and their ability to build bridges and to distil the right mix and dynamics over time when necessary.

Laying Down the Strategy to Approach the X-factor Universe

The strategy approach of a company is one of the factors influencing the ability of a company to utilize specific trigger events to break into the X-factor universe. For some companies the approach is characterized by accident, coincidence or by evading an unfolding crisis, and for others it is a more planned effort. Some strategies cannot be explained by existing strategic tools or individual strategic perspectives as they appear to include elements of various perspectives. Such strategies seem to build bridges across perspectives that are traditionally regarded as opposing views.

Once the boundaries between traditional strategic perspectives have been removed and the strategy formulation is seen as a process of crisis, coincidences, luck and evolutionary as well as planned or forced on by the environment, the strategy approach does indeed become a variable of indefinable nature – an X-factor that may lead to a successful migration from the recipe universe to the X-factor universe.

Where many contributions to strategy have sought to identify a narrow set of variables that would provide success, it is argued here that strategy should be viewed in a more dynamic context in order to unlock the potential of unconventional and out-of-the-box thinking. Once traditional boundaries between strategic perspectives are removed and new avenues of opportunities are embraced regardless of the mode through which they appear, the X-factor universe may become a viable destination for a company's strategy.

Companies may deconstruct the traditional strategy landscape and reassemble this in a fashion that is suited to their particular situation and core beliefs. They may do so in order to develop their specific and unique X-factor through their own combination of factors.

Saxo Bank managed to deconstruct the traditional landscape and deploy unconventional thinking when they decided to increase their focus on IT and the development of an online trading platform. A move, triggered by a crisis, that migrated Saxo Bank from the recipe universe to the X-factor universe and redefined their strategic position from that of an imitator in a red ocean to one of an innovator in a blue ocean.

Honda initially failed, but when the opportunity arose the company was quick to react by redefining their US strategy to offer small motorcycles. This move, which was triggered by failure, allowed Honda to migrate to the X-factor universe where they became an innovator in a red ocean.

Naturhouse is another example of a company that initially experienced a failure. But when they redefined the store concept to offer a very limited selection of dietary supplements and offered advisory services by trained professionals they effectively bridged the low amount of stock-keeping units (which is a treat of a discount strategy) with that of high personal service (a differentiator). As such they innovated the business model for offering dietary supplements and advice.

Canon utilized a planned effort of developing a different copier technique to conquer the market for small copiers and in doing so unlocked the market for desk top copiers. Those companies that have stumbled upon the goldmine, such as Facebook and Hotmail, managed to do so because they were trying to achieve other goals but as the opportunity arose they seized it.

Regardless of which strategic mode a company is experiencing, whether crisis, luck, failure or planned, it can act as a trigger event to redefine or optimize one's strategy – often such trigger events will allow for out-of-the-box thinking leading to unconventional strategies that bridge one or more of the traditional perspectives.

6

EXPLOITING CUSTOMER ATTITUDES

From the very start, Walt Disney envisioned Disneyland as a place where dreams come true.[1]

Customers are not least important as revenue generators for a company which would not normally be able to survive without customers. Sometimes, we see the opposite trend that some companies – like Google and Skype – were able to survive a considerable span of time with many customers albeit without a revenue stream from the customers, i.e. the consumers, in the first place. Thus, this chapter focuses on the customer attitude as well as the attitude of the customers. Google and Skype have diligently used selected customer means of measurements as bearing points, thereby facilitating their entering into the X-factor universe. However, also other companies have been keen to achieve a high Return on Strategy by ways of utilizing customer attitudes as a success driver.

The year 2007 was the "Year of a Million Dreams" at Disney. During that year, more than one million dreams were awarded to Disneyland and Walt Disney World customers. Some of the dreams included an overnight stay at Cinderella Castle Suite at Walt Disney World Resort and the chance to serve as grand marshal in Disney parades around the world. It became such a success that Disney extended it through to December 31, 2008 adding new dreams, such as a private stay at Disney's tropical island paradise, Castaway Cay, inside

Disneyland Park and spending New Years Eve at Cinderella Castle.[2]

In order for Disney to accomplish their vision of making dreams come true, new employees at Disney's resorts and parks begin their employment with a motivational course at Disney University in Orlando where they learn the amount of hard work that goes into fulfilling the dreams of customers. They also learn that they are not just employees in a global company but rather cast members in the Disney World show. Cast members whose main responsibility it is to serve Disney's guests.[3]

This notion of serving the needs of guests rather than customers is at the very core of how Disney perceives their customers. New employees are given courses on the subjects of the Disney language, history and culture to get a sense of the Disney factor. Employees are taught to show enthusiasm, to be helpful and friendly in order to make the experience of their guests as remarkable as possible. Each ride follows a strict script just like in a theatre or in a movie. And employees or cast members are taught to play on-stage and off-stage.

Disney has been in the business of making dreams come true for the better part of a century and has perfected their customer attitude to such a level that managers from other companies attend the Disney Institute to gain insight into their business magic.

I came to Disney Institutes' open enrolment program on "The Disney Approach to Customer Loyalty." In the middle of the first day of the 3½ day seminar, I knew I had finally found my solution.[4]

The above quote by Sue Boche, Director of Guest Relations in the Toys "R" Us corporate office, illustrates that the experiences Disney has created in terms of their customer attitude is of great use.

The position Disney has created for their guests is based upon experiences and continuous research on how to improve the parks for the guest. An example: In Disney World there is a garbage can every 25 steps, so litter will be tossed not dropped. Do you know why? The reason is quite simple. A Disney study years ago showed that people who were given hard candy with a wrapper at a theme park took an average of about 27 steps before tossing the wrapper on the ground. Hence the spacing of the garbage cans.

However, customer attitude is more than creating customer loyalty. It is a factor that can drive a company towards the X-factor universe and as such has been a key success driver for many companies that have broken into the X-factor universe. A company's customer attitude covers the perception a company has of its customers and thus how the demands of these should be catered for. Additionally, it also covers the attitude of the customers themselves and the dialectical relationship that occurs between the customer attitude and the attitudes of the customers.

What Is a Customer?

A customer is not just a customer! It depends on the attitude and the lenses through which you are looking on the most important asset of a company. A customer can be a customer, a consumer, a guest, a client and a business partner.

Stew Leonard, the founder and the owner of a retail store in Norwalk, Connecticut, puts it in this way:

> *True customers are like annuities – they keep pumping revenues into the firm's coffers. We should never let a customer leave the store unhappy because we look at each customer as a potential $75,000 asset. An average customer spends more than $150 a week on food shopping. That's more than $7,500 a year, and more than $75,000 over ten years. Customer service is big business when you look at the long-term picture.*

Customers of a given company can be characterized as belonging to either the consumer market or the business market. The consumer market, also known as the Business-to-Consumer

(B2C) market, is recognized by individuals or households who buy for personal consumption, whereas the business, or the Business-to-Business (B2B) market consists of organizations that buy goods for reselling or for use in producing other products.

In addition to these differences in buyer behaviour, the B2B market has several characteristics that are in sharp contrast to those of the B2C market. Examples of these are: few larger buyers, professional purchasing, several buying influences, multiple sales calls, derived demand and more direct buying.[5]

Customers, or how companies perceive these, are instrumental in developing a superior strategy for a given company as is the case with Disney. The perception of the customer, or the company's customer attitude, can prove a vital factor in a company's attempt to break free of the recipe universe. Given this, customer attitudes which comprise both the perception the company holds of their customers as well as the attitude of customers constitute a key success driver.

Customers Viewed through Different Lenses

Customers have become much more than merely consumers of a given product. The way in which companies perceive their customers has, for some companies, become a vital ingredient in the development of the companies' uniqueness and the success they have achieved.

Some companies, such as Disney, go beyond the traditional view of a customer and instead see guests looking for dreams to come true when visiting the parks and resorts of Disney. A view which is taught to new hires who are expected to treat every single guest with the utmost courtesy in order for their dreams to come alive and provide an exceptional customer experience. At Disney, the term customer service has been revised to become "customer's delight". This ability to provide guests with unsurpassed service and delight is a key component of Disney's distinctive uniqueness.

In the business model of Naturhouse, customers have become "clients" who make appointments to visit the store and receive free weight-loss advice from a trained professional, much like clients of health clinics who are also viewed as more than just customers. This advice is given in an office within the store while taking great care to ensure the customer's, or client's, privacy.

The look of a Naturhouse store is designed to emphasize this feeling of assisting clients rather than just customers. The fewer products provide a clean and uncluttered look which along with the brown wooden storage cabinets resembles the look of a pharmacy. Add to that the presence of a professional wearing a traditional white coat and the image of a doctor's practice springs to mind. Clients of Naturhouse are, however, not patients in a traditional sense but people battling with a weight problem. A problem which many face but are reluctant to discuss in a traditional dietary store among other customers. A problem which is not usually the reason for seeing a traditional doctor and thus not discussed with him or her but nevertheless is a problem.

Naturhouse has, through their customer attitude, which rests on providing professional advice in privacy to clients and on the basis of this recommending one of their 77 diets, created a distinctive image within their market space. This image is to a large degree based upon the customer attitude of Naturhouse. This is a customer attitude that sees clients not as customers, that sees clients looking for personal advice rather than just products and that sees long-term client relationships rather than one-off customers in a transactional relationship.

Such a customer attitude is naturally appreciated among the clients of Naturhouse and when this is coupled with advice and diets that produce results a success is born. Some of the testimonials given emphasize the impact such a customer attitude can have:[6]

Naturhouse has been the beginning of a love story.

I feel young, agile and encouraged thanks to Naturhouse.

My life changed in just 6 months.

Customers at Naturhouse are more than just transactional customers, they are clients who make appointments in order to receive personal advice and who enter a long-term relationship with Naturhouse. Naturhouse has essentially teamed up with their clients in order to develop the product that will satisfy the particular need of an individual client.

Teaming up with the customers has become essential for many companies and is also one of the themes in a recent IBM Global CEO Study (The Enterprise of the Future, 2007).

In the future, we will be talking more and more about the "prosumer" – a consumer/producer who is even more extensively integrated into the value chain. As a consequence, production processes will be customized more precisely and individually.[7]

In 1999, when Ryanair launched their web site, they effectively handed the entire process of finding the desired destination, the flight times and booking the ticket over to the customer. As such the customers of Ryanair became co-producers rather than customers, leading to increased customer satisfaction given the 24 hours a day, seven days a week availability of the Internet.

Including the customer in the actual production process did not only generate a greater satisfaction among customers but also resulted in significant cost savings for Ryanair which could be transferred to the customers in terms of cheaper flight tickets.

In terms of the customer attitude, the move to create the *prosumer* stands in contrast to the conventional marketing approach in which the customer merely consumes the products produced by the company. Another area where this differs from conventional thinking concerns the notion of tying the customer into the company through, for example, loyalty programmes and individualized relationship marketing. By requesting all customers to perform the booking via the web site and pay by credit card, a level playing field was created characterized by a "we" culture as oppose to an "I am special" culture.

The ability for Ryanair to break the conventional rules with such success hinges partly on the customer attitude of Ryanair. This attitude sees the customers as an equal and essential element in the production of services.

Egalitarian treatment and acting as a co-producer also characterizes the customer attitude of Google. In Google's statement of philosophy ten things (values) are listed which Google has found to be true and one of these is that "Democracy on the web works". Under this heading the importance of the users is communicated as follows:

> Google works because it relies on the millions of individuals posting websites to determine which other sites offer content of value. Instead of relying on a group of editors or solely on the frequency with which certain terms appear, Google ranks every web page using a breakthrough technique called PageRank.[8]

PageRank is the patented algorithm that is at the heart of Google's search engine. This technique evaluates all the sites that are linked to a given web page and by assigning these with a value, which is based on the sites linking to these, it is possible to determine the best source of information. Given this, it is actually the users of the Internet, those posting web sites, who are fundamental to the success of Google's search engine.

Another one of the ten values that Google has found to be true is that "Focus on the user and all else will follow". This philosophy, or value, stems from the founding days of Google and the customer attitude of the founders which rested on the fact that by placing the interest of the customer first, in this case superior search, it is possible to build a loyal audience without the need for marketing programmes designed to lock in the customer.

Continuing on the American continent, Facebook also represents a company taking the notion of customers as co-producers to its extreme. Initially developed as an online local social directory, Facebook has grown to become a worldwide network with the users producing the majority of the content.

Our mission is to increase the information flow between people and to help people learn what's going on in their world and express themselves.[9]

The above quote from founder, Mark Zuckerberg, goes some way in explaining the customer attitude of Facebook. A customer attitude which is built around the belief that when provided with the right tools, customers will provide content about themselves and seek that provided by others, thereby increasing the information flow. Thus, Facebook perceives their customers as people who are willing to share information with other peers in order to keep up with what is going on.

Facebook's core product is the platform upon which users design their profile and decide who to share their information with. It is equal for all and thus again an example of how non-conventional marketing can lead to success.

Moving from the "customer democracy" at Google over to the egalitarian "ombudsman" perspective at Ryanair and Facebook, we arrive at an even stronger role in other instances.

In the early 2000s the people in Procter & Gamble (P&G) were not oriented to any common purpose. The corporate mission "To meaningfully improve the everyday lives of the customers" had not been explicitly or inspirationally rolled out to the employees. Therefore, P&G expanded the mission to include the idea that "the consumer is the boss". The philosophy should be that people who buy and use P&G products are valued not just for their money but also as a rich source of information and direction. "The consumer is the boss" became far more than a slogan in P&G. It became a clear, simple and inclusive cultural priority for both employees, and external stakeholders such as suppliers.

The P&G efforts in the fragrance area are one example. From being a small underperforming business area P&G turned

the business into a global leader and the world's largest fine fragrance company in the world. This was done by clearly and precisely defining the target consumer for each fragrance brand
and identifying subgroups of consumers for some brands. P&G
still kept the partnerships with established fashion houses such
as Dolce & Gabbana, Gucci and Lacoste. The main point was to
make the consumer the boss, focusing on innovations that were
meaningful to the consumers including, for instance, fresh new
scents, distinctive packaging and proactive marketing. In addition P&G made an effort to streamline the supply chain and to
reduce complexity and thereby enable a significantly lower cost
structure.

"The consumer is the boss" also means that P&G tries to
build social connections through digital media and other forms
of interactions. One example is baby diapers. P&G used to use
handmade baby diapers for a product test. Today the product is
being shown digitally and created in alternatives in an onscreen
virtual world. Changes can be made immediately as new ideas
emerge and can be redesigned on the screen. As such P&G is
building a social system with the consumers (and potential consumers) that enables P&G to co-design and co-engineer new
innovations with the buyers. 'The consumer is the boss" has set
a new standard.

Other examples of how teaming up with customers in an
unconventional manner can lead to success are to be found on
both the European and Asian continents, for example, those of
Saxo Bank and Nintendo.

When Saxo Bank decided to focus on the development of an
online trading platform and online trading in general, their
customer attitude also changed. From initially viewing the customer as an individual with little or no expertise within the
world of investment, the perception changed to view customers
as tech savvy individuals who, when given the necessary tools,
were more than able to place their investments directly. Interestingly, this customer attitude coincides with the widely different strategic positioning of Saxo Bank, namely the change from

traditional brokerage in the era of being a red ocean imitator to a blue ocean innovator.

By combining this customer attitude with the development of an online trading platform, Saxo Bank effectively joined forces with the individual investor around the globe to lead the FX market in a new direction. A feature which in 2007 earned the two founders, Kim Fournais and Lars Seier Christensen, the prestigious Achievement Award, at the fourth annual e-FX Awards, sponsored by FX Week Magazine in New York. The award is given in recognition for making an outstanding contribution to the success of the e-FX industry.[10]

This award and the success of Saxo Bank would not have been possible if the customer attitude of the company had not believed in the abilities of the online investor.

On the Asian continent, Nintendo, the Japanese manufacturer of game consoles and games, was faced with falling market share in the early 1990s, and they then turned to their customers for help. Not by initiating traditional marketing surveys, focus groups or lengthy analysis, but instead by establishing online communities for gamers that became a platform for gaining invaluable customer insights.[11]

By offering incentives in return for customer information, Nintendo was able to successfully tap directly into the needs and preferences of the market. The information provided by their customers was subsequently used in developing new game offerings and product designs that would restore the position of Nintendo as a leading player boasting a 44% market share.

The above examples show how the customer attitude can be a major source of success for a given company and thus act as a key driver in migrating from the recipe universe to the X-factor universe. Moreover, it is illustrative that utilizing the customer is tied to a dynamic view of the link between corporate strategy and customer attitude rather than a static view. A change in the strategic positioning inevitably has to be followed by a change in the customer attitude as required and in some cases vice versa.

Customers as Viral Ambassadors

Customers who feel that they are receiving "a big bang for the buck" will be more likely to recommend other potential customers to follow suit.

Two effects are equally important here. They are labelled the WOW- and the WOM-effect, respectively. The WOW-effect was originally described by Mossberg[12] as a primarily event-driven effect very much tied to cases like entertainment, sports and cultural institutions. Precisely because of the "pro-sumer" trend, many customers experience a WOW-effect, a combination of surprise, admiration and satisfaction.

The WOW-effect has been very common with Google search, Hotmail's email service, Saxo Bank's trading platform, Skype's telephony software, the advanced e-ticketing system and the logistics of Ryanair or Facebook's "shared" platform. Combinations of accessibility, consumers as pro-sumers, consumer control, speed of delivery and price are some of the key components of this experience in the context of these companies.

Another example comes from Huawei, because the company is able to provide a WOW-effect in several respects. One is that the company is closely tied to governmental actions and may have a comparative advantage with respect to this. Another is that the company has developed very high implementation skills and therefore is able to turn the mobile operators' network equipment from, for example, Ericsson or Nokia very quickly and seamlessly.

These WOW-effects create the basis for the WOM-effect, the word-of-mouth-effect. It is a matter of fact that up to 80% of every purchase decision is based on the WOM-effect. However, it is also a matter of fact that the WOM-effect does not occur just because a customer is satisfied – something extra is needed. Thus, the WOM-effect attracts special attention when dealing with the aspects of the X-factor universe, because the WOM-effect revolutionizes the economics of a company by shrinking the cost structure radically.

Some business cases have even been "born-WOM" cases when the customers are destined to play an important role from the outset:

Think of eBay, which opened as an online store with no inventory, leaving it up to customers to fill its "shelves" with goods to sell. Or Wikipedia, which gutted the value proposition of 230-year-old "Encyclopaedia Britannica" by offering a free encyclopedia written and updated frequently by unpaid amateurs.[13]

Equally, the same type of effect operates with Facebook, Skype, Google and many others. Invariably, customers who play a strong part in producing the products and services will use WOM in their respective networks.

The WOM-effect leads directly forward to the notion of the viral ambassador. The viral ambassador materializes whenever WOM is in operation. Viral ambassadors have some of the same inherited characteristics as a "collective good", as the value of the effect increases exponentially with the number of ambassadors. The viral ambassadors may also go one step further and become volunteers. Companies displaying the ability to utilize these qualities have a good eye with regard to exploiting this voluntary enthusiasm in their daily production. One such example is to make customers/volunteers be part of a more formal contribution system.

An example of the power of a customer-driven contribution system is found at Procter & Gamble with their web site "Being-Girl". This web site focuses on teen and preteen girls, which is a very difficult target group to reach, and P&G therefore created forums where girls could interact with one another and share support and advice from others. P&G estimates that BeingGirl is a marketing tool four times as effective as television advertising.[14]

The example shows that there are more aggressive ways to create viral ambassadors than was originally invented by the "member-get-member" way launched by Hotmail in order to proliferate the number of customers and thereby increase the value to each customer. In the case of P&G, not only is the viral ambassador effect present, but customer service and customer care are taking a prominent place at the same time.

Customers Are no Longer Just Consumers!

Conventional theory advocates for perceiving the customer as mere consumers of a product produced solely by the company. As such the customer is the object of the marketing efforts performed by the company with the aim of tying customers into the company by offering augmented or peripheral services, loyalty programmes, relationship marketing, etc.

As illustrated in the previous sections and chapters, many companies break the rules of such conventions by including customers in the production of goods or service, by teaming up with them to grow the market as a whole or by asking them to provide valuable information used in product development.

Based on this, customers are no longer just consumers of a company's products or services but instead a vital part of the company's value chain.

The Break-up of Conventional Relationships

The customer attitude of a given company and in particular the attitude which includes the customer in its value chain has a profound impact on how the customers are approached.

Conventional theory is much concerned with the distribution channels of a given company and the conflicts that can arise among or within these. When viewing the entire supply chain as illustrated in Figure 6.1, the downstream activities, those that flow towards the end customer, translate into the number of channel levels a given company is operating with.

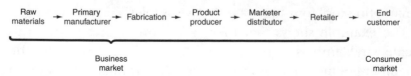

Figure 6.1 The B2B and B2C markets in relation to a simple supply chain.

Using the product producer of Figure 6.1 as a starting point the number of channel levels would equal three. The channel levels between the product producer and the end customer can vary from company to company within the same industry as some companies, such as Dell, sell directly to the end customer thus bypassing the traditional channels used by, for example, Hewlett-Packard and Acer Inc. This is illustrated in Figure 6.2.

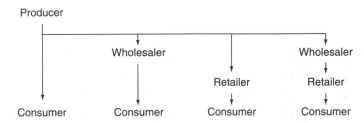

Figure 6.2 **Varying channel levels.**

In the traditional marketing literature the number of channel levels and particularly the potential conflicts that can arise between these are given substantial consideration. Two different kinds of channel conflicts may occur. The first, a horizontal conflict, arises when companies at the same level of the channel are in disagreement with each other. This would occur if, for example, a few retailers of Acer notebooks price a given product lower than agreed in order to steal customers from other Acer retailers.

The second and more common vertical conflict arises when companies at different levels, for example the product producer and the wholesaler, are experiencing conflicting interests such as the situation where both target the end consumer.

Conventional wisdom dictates that channel conflicts should be avoided as these can have a devastating effect on a company. Yet for Saxo Bank such a channel conflict is at the core of its success.

In 2001, Saxo Bank introduced their White Label Partner programme. A programme designed at offering other financial institutions the opportunity to gain an unbranded version of

SaxoTrader platform and offer this to their own customers. A move which, by conventional measures, signalled a potential channel conflict as Saxo Bank was distributing its products through a wholesaler as well as directly to the customers. Rather than having a devastating effect it catapulted the success of Saxo Bank onto a new level. In a matter of two years the trading income of Saxo Bank more than tripled. By 2007, the trading income had grown by a factor of 15 when compared with 2001. This growth is largely attributable to the customer attitude of Saxo Bank which was not hindered by conventional wisdom but rather driven by a desire to partner with both end customers and other wholesalers to grow the e-FX market as a whole.

Given this, conventional wisdom dictating that conflicts of interest will appear when the boundaries between the two markets, B2B and B2C, are blurred or even completely ignored is challenged by companies such as Saxo Bank. This proves yet again that Saxo Bank is able to utilize unconventional strategic measures which drive the company towards the X-factor universe rather than the conventional recipe universe. To some considerable extent, the same is the case for Disney, P&G, Google and Ryanair. However, they have not taken up the positive aspects of channel conflicts to the same extent as is the case at Saxo Bank.

When adding this to the notion of the consumer as a prosumer, the conventional wisdom is indeed challenged. Not only are companies, such as Saxo Bank, exploiting channel conflicts, but they are also including the consumer as an integral part of the value chain as in some cases the consumers produce the product/service, or a large part of it, themselves.

The Customer and the Brand

Thus far, we have dealt with the customer attitude viewed solely from the company's perspective. However, we also need to address the attitude of the customers for several reasons. First and foremost, several rule-breaking companies base their business cases on the social capital of customers, which clearly position such companies within the X-factor universe. Second, unconventional thinking with regard to the exploitation of the customers' attitude brings about interesting possibilities for any company. Third, the attitudes of the customers are important with regard to the brand of the company.

The Customer as the Social Capital Base of the Company

Putnam[15] has offered an interesting explanation as to why there is such a marked difference in wealth and financial strength between Northern and Southern Italy, a difference which years ago resembled the difference between the industrially developed countries and the developing or emerging economies.

He argued that individual trust has a positive spill-over effect into public trust, thereby lowering transaction costs considerably and paving the way for the so-called social capital approach, which may contribute tremendously to explain the difference between rich and poor, between success or failure.

It is widely acknowledged that financial capital, human resources, management, technology, raw materials and so on are necessary conditions in order for a company to produce an output. However, social capital does not seem to have a place in this equation.

Social capital is a production factor which the company can tap into centred on the confidence and the trust that the customer attaches to the company. However, the status of the customers may vary to some extent depending on whether it is the monopoly (blue ocean) or the disrupter (red ocean) from whom the customer is getting its products and services.

Generally, the monopolist (blue ocean) type of customers build confidence around the quality of the offering, whereas some of the disruptive business cases in hypercompetitive markets target the development of a collective consumer-based consciousness where the company will go a very long way not only to take advice from the customers but actually let the customers decide.

As is evident from Table 6.1, different types of trust are built up differently, according to the strategic mindset. Customers

Table 6.1 **Four types of trust**

Strategy/approach	Relationship marketing	Transactional marketing
Monopolist (blue ocean)	Stratification of customers, building individualized confidence within confined boundaries, i.e. *individual trust*	Egalitarian transaction (the transaction itself is at the same level playing field for everybody), i.e. *stratified trust*
Disrupter (red ocean)	Marketing to the customers as a collective entity, building collective confidence widely, i.e. *shared trust*	Egalitarian transaction plus equal treatment (all customers are subjected to the same price and have the same chance of achieving the same offering), i.e. *global trust*

subjected to a monopolist blue ocean strategy will inevitably tie much of their attention to the product itself. This is the case, for example, when Saxo Bank white labels its trading platform and sells it to Citibank on wholesale terms.

Yet, a completely different scenario is the case of the red ocean disrupters, like Costco, Ryanair, Skype, etc. By way of uniform pricing, cutting to the core, and facilitation of trusted behaviour through journalists, virtual chat rooms and special events, the pro-sumers manage to create a global trust which is evidence of probably some of the strongest collective trust that is possible. In the case of mass market retail services, this trend may be so strong that pro-sumers act as a kind of "ombudsman" in order to constructively influence the further development of the company's products and services.

This relationship is illustrated by the following example of a customers' reaction to the experience of travelling with Ryanair:

Dear Sir,

I would like to complain bitterly about the cost and service of your airline on a recent trip to Turin! Firstly the cost was £6 return and secondly, for this, we had to endure flights on a brand new 737–800. The cabin crew were totally efficient and friendly and the pilots utterly professional.

This is outrageous behaviour from a low cost airline!! How can people (who think they are better than everyone else) justify flying with BA paying hundreds of pounds more for the same services (minus a sandwich)??!!.

If you continue in this manner I will have no option but to report you to the CAA!!

Yours Sincerely
Jeff Swift, Leeds
17th of July 2001

Such feedback illustrates that the perception of Ryanair among the public is as the airline that attacks the overcharging establishment by providing exceptional value for money. As such, a case of not only acting as an ombudsman, but also as a viral ambassador.

Brandr and Brand

With "brand" we are yet again addressing an issue which is quite often regarded as something tied to the company or its management although it has much more to do with the attitude of the customers. The term "brand" originates from the Scandinavian "brandr" which means to burn. According to ancient history, branding livestock was common in order to retain ownership when animals roamed freely on the range. Livestock from a farmer with good reputation would then be more desirable and subsequently more expensive than livestock from a farmer with a less favourable reputation.

Although much has happened on the way from "brandr" related to livestock to "brand" related to today's mass market products and services, the underlying principle is the same: If the brand is considered attractive by the customer, the customer is willing to consume on terms that are also more attractive to the producer than they would have been alternatively.

The relative importance and design of the appropriate brand differs from archetype to archetype. A monopolist in the blue ocean does not face (strong) competition. Thus, the most successful monopolistic blue ocean brands like Gucci, Louis Vuitton, Porsche and similar can embark on a considerable consumer's surplus. Individualized relationship customers are willing to pay a considerable "surcharge", which may furthermore become galvanized by relationship marketing frills, like loyalty bonuses, extra services in addition to the core product, etc. The biggest threats for such a high-end brand are free riding (as seen with Asian imitations of Western-designed luxury goods) and that the situational monopoly disappears.

The disrupter, however, is very keen on bringing the prices down to zero or to a low price level, which is also justified in some cases by either the so-called zero-SAC philosophy (which will be further developed in Chapter 8) or by third part financing, see Appendix I. Zero-SAC means essentially zero sales and acquisition costs. When Skype launched their peer-to-peer VoIP product, they gave this groundbreaking product to the customers for free and attracted millions of customers with practically no sales or acquisition costs. Similar types of examples include Facebook, Google, Ryanair and the retail part of Saxo Bank. Customers generally do not receive frills and are consumers at a transactional level. This implies that the consumers regard the products and services almost as a common good which accelerates a kind of "free riding".

The main differences in relation to different branding positions are summarized in Table 6.2.

Customer-centric Marketing

In conventional marketing literature a given number of "P"s are often used to describe, or prescribe, what needs to be at the centre of attention for a company to achieve a competitive position. This is known as the marketing mix, which began with the 4Ps of product, price, place and promotion that was latter

Table 6.2 **Brands related to monopolistic and disruptive types of strategy**

Competitive landscape	Monopolistic	Disrupter
Brand	High-end brand	"Public utility" brand
Price level	Prices based on considerably more than full cost coverage	Prices set at zero or at a very low level
Sales and acquisition costs	High SAC	Zero-SAC (or relatively low SAC compared with incumbents)
Marketing approach	Relationship marketing frills	Transactional relationship and frills
Value of the customer	Consumer surplus	"Common Good"
Free riding	Avoid free riding	Accelerate free riding
Examples	Saxo wholesale, Cisco, Porsche,	Google, Skype, Saxo retail, Ryanair

revised to the 7Ps by adding presence, people and processes. One might argue that the customer is hard to identify as a key element in a conventional marketing mix.

The customer-centric approach of all the companies discussed in this chapter has been instrumental in shaping their strategy and competitive positioning. Rather than spending costly efforts on trying to second guess what the customers want in terms of product features, some companies actively involve their customers in the production of the goods allowing for competitive pricing.

Saxo Bank developed the online trading platform in order to provide individual investors across the globe (their customers) with the ability to trade directly in FX instruments without having to contact a broker by telephone. This approach, which was very customer centric at the outset played a key part in the subsequent strategic journey of Saxo Bank and their ability to migrate to the X-factor universe.

Ryanair introduced the discount concept to the European air passenger industry with great success by focusing on what the customers really wanted – cheap air fares from point A to B.

If you pile it high and sell it cheap, people will come to you.
(Michael O'Leary, CEO of Ryanair)

By involving customers in the production of the product through online ticketing systems and using word of mouth as a means of promotion, the customers became central to the success of Ryanair's low-cost business model.

Similarly US companies such as P&G, Facebook and Google use customer-centric marketing with great success. The last two hardly make use of any other type of marketing thus completely ignoring conventional wisdom. Rather than working with 4 or 7 Ps, Facebook and Google focused on what customers wanted and grew their businesses from this to become the largest search engine and social network.

In Asia, Nintendo applied tactics similar to those of P&G and their "BeingGirl" web site when they established online communities for gamers in order to tap directly into the needs and preferences of the customers. A customer-centric game plan which paid dividends as they gathered crucial information on what new games and product to produce resulting in the company re-establishing their position as a market leader.

As illustrated throughout this chapter, the customer-centric marketing approach of the companies discussed has played a key role in their ability to either migrate from a recipe universe to the X-factor universe or to instantly break into this. Applying a customer-centric approach will lead to more general competitive perspectives such as a company's position as an innovative disrupter or an imitative monopolist.

Attitudes as Part of the X-factor Universe

Companies that utilize unconventional thinking are able to redefine the ways in which customers have traditionally been perceived. They apply a customer-centric approach which contrasts with the marketing mix as we know it and some companies even incorporate channel conflicts as a central element of the strategy.

As illustrated with the cases of Disney and Naturhouse, seeing guests and clients rather than customers is a key success driver for these companies. The ability to involve the customer in the production of goods or services such as that demonstrated by Saxo Bank, Ryanair, Google and Facebook redefines traditional recipes and is a key success driver for these companies.

Just as P&G launched online communities to reach and involve teen and pre-teen girls with great success, Nintendo used a similar tactic of customer involvement to tap into what the market desired and as such created closer ties with their customers as these became crucial to their product development efforts.

From Europe to the US and across to Asia, the customer attitudes of companies in different industries are around to form a key success driver for those companies that successfully navigate in the X-factor universe. By utilizing unconventional thinking these companies have redefined the role of customers by involving them in the production of the product or the information gathering used as a basis for product development. Moving a consumer to become a pro-sumer effectively short circuits the traditional supply chain, which is exactly what some X-factor universe companies are looking to do.

Involving customers to a larger degree also allows for a customer-centric approach to marketing and competitive positioning in general, which contrasts with traditional thoughts on marketing mix in which the customer is hardly present.

Saxo Bank is an example of a company that has managed to utilize the customer attitudes as a key success driver, because they display unconventional approaches to many of the aspects raised in this chapter. Concerning customer attitude, Saxo Bank rely heavily on the pro-sumer advantages as both their private clients and their entire set up and technology is centred on self-service activation of transactions. Concerning the attitude of the customers, both rely on the transactional relationship based on a low sale and acquisition cost and subsequently low retail prices, and a more relationship marketing-based approach at the wholesale level and in the wealth management business line. Essentially, Saxo Bank has managed to take advantage of all the different customer modalities available.

Other companies have cherry picked a specific modality, such as Skype relying heavily on transactional-based relationships, Huawei relying on relationship-based attitudes and Facebook building the bridge between these two attitudes.

At any rate, the companies in the X-factor universe manage to apply out-of-the-box thinking to the customer aspects, which assist the companies in getting a high Return on their overall Strategy. One way they achieve this is by not only looking at the customer attitude as a standard element of the recipe universe but rather as a means to involve customers. They often receive an extra return because of the attitude of the customers where they manage to make customers ambassadors or even "ombudsmen".

The ways in which these companies utilize customer attitudes as a key success driver can be characterized as consisting of various bearing points that are used to navigate this particular key success driver.

Based on the above, salient bearing points are the following:

- Customer involvement
- Customer-centric marketing
- Customers as viral ambassadors
- Customers from conflicting channels.

As described, companies cherry pick from these bearing points to create their own unique utilization of the key success driver that is constituted by the customer attitudes.

7

REVISING THE PRODUCT PORTFOLIO

Most companies' experience with portfolio management was intense but short-lived. During its short life-time, however, portfolio management did heighten the demand for MBAs, skilled at the types of analysis strategic management required.[1]

(McGill, 1988)

In Chapter 6, working diligently with customer attitude was addressed as the first key success driver towards increasing the Return on Strategy. Invariably, any strategy must also comprise the supply side of the company, i.e. products and services. Thus, Chapter 7 addresses what companies actually supply as part of the strategy framework, starting off by addressing some of the strategic pitfalls and failures experienced by less successful companies.

The Rise (and Fall?) of the Product Portfolio Perspective

The conventional wisdom regarding the strategic management of a company's product portfolio stems from work that Mead Corporation in 1970 contracted Boston Consulting Group (BCG) to perform.[2] A major outcome of this project was to view a multi-market business as a product portfolio with the recommendation that each business (SBU – strategic business unit) or product in the portfolio demanded widely different strategies.

As yardsticks, market share and growth were identified, leading forward to the BCG four square matrix, in which "stars",

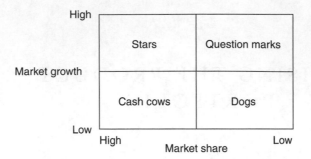

Figure 7.1 **The Boston Consulting Group matrix.**

"cash cows", "question marks/new ventures" and "dogs" were described comprising widely different characteristics and subsequently demanding widely different business strategies, see Figure 7.1.

The matrix has undoubtedly been a useful tool in some contexts. It has been used for classifying a company's SBUs and configuration of products. Once a company has classified its portfolio according to the matrix it must decide what to do with them. According to conventional thinking there are four options: Should the company increase the market share, maintain the position, harvest or divest?

As originally practised the matrix was a useful tool, but with certain limitations on how to get the valid data for its use. Later on, practitioners have tended to over-simplify its messages. In particular, the later application of the names in the matrix has tended to overshadow everything else.

But the most important danger is the assumption that there should be a balance of products or services across all four quadrants. Thus, money must be diverted from "cash cows" to fund the "stars" of the future, since "cash cows" will inevitably decline to become "dogs". There is an implicit assumption about the whole process. It focuses attention on and funding to the further development of the "stars". It presumes, and almost demands, that "cash cows" will turn into "dogs" following a life-cycle philosophy.

However, this tool did not work wonders for all who utilized it. For example, Texas Instruments used the BCG product portfolio tool for its consumer products with disastrous results in the watch, calculator and home computer businesses. Likewise, General Electric (GE) treated consumer electronics as a cash cow but was soon taught by Japanese companies that consumer electronics is a star market with a high pay off on investments in research and development.

Interestingly, while the product portfolios of both consumer electronics and automotives in the US have been very much tainted by conventional Michael Porter notions of avoiding being "stuck in the middle", Japanese and other Asian companies have tried to bridge both product differentiation and cost leadership at the same time, notably Samsung, Huawei, Toyota, Honda, Mazda and Nissan. To some extent, they perceived the Michael Porter-based forced choice for American companies between a differentiator and a cost leader type strategy to be counter-productive in the long run, since competitors were able to outperform by using mixed strategies that bridged generic strategies.

Focusing on the more recent problems in the US automotive industry, one has to take at least two deficiencies into account. First, a considerable part of the products in this industry has been specifically suited for the US home market. Today, many of these products are not suited for major segments of the market outside the US, owing to the current global focus on, for example, energy efficiency, safety issues and the size of the cars. This is a telling product story in its own right, because the increased globalization calls for renewed product strategies and products that are fully up to date with the changing demands from the global environment.

Second, US automotives have a long tradition of regulatory forbearance from the US government, whereby this industry is not only to be found with products in the market zone but also with products gaining interest in the institutional zone. A point of departure may be Charles Wilson's nomination in 1953 as secretary of defence by President Eisenhower. Charles Wilson was then president of General Motors, and he was asked during a Senate confirmation hearing whether he would be willing to serve as a secretary of defence also under contingencies where he was to make decisions unfavourable to General Motors. "Engine Charlie", as he was called, answered without hesitation, *"What's good for the country is good for General Motors, and vice versa".*[3] His answer was widely accepted and galvanized a helping hand under not only General Motors but also other parts of the US automotive industry.

This was visualized in a case in September 1979, when Chrysler Corporation was near bankruptcy. At that time, Chrysler was the fourteenth largest industrial firm in America, and Lee Iacocca, president of Chrysler, appeared before the Senate Banking Committee to petition the federal government for financial help. He argued that Chrysler was too big to fail with too many employees, too many stockholders and too many suppliers. Borrowing the logic of Charles Wilson, Iacocca successfully persuaded the senators, *"My problems are the problems of the country".*

Summarizing, US automotives have utilized the institutional zone in several decades to compensate for non-competitiveness with a partially or rather increasingly outdated or inadequate profile of products in the market zone. The general management of their products does not lead them into the X-factor universe, which would have required a radically different approach than mainly relying on special segments of, in particular, their US home market. Moreover, the Boston Consulting Group matrix has limited relevance with products (or strategic business units) displaying considerable internal synergy (whereas it may carry more relevance in cases of corporate conglomerates comprising widely different subsidiaries without synergy).

An interesting case in point here is the German firm Porsche, which was one of the very worst performers in the automotive industry in 1992–93. Not only did Porsche suffer from a large decline in revenues in 1992 but also in 1993, a total of 45% for these years. In 1991, profits had already fallen by almost 95%.

But Porsche survived and since this period Porsche management has taken decisive action to reduce the company's vulnerability towards such conditions, notably by way of a number of product development and diversification tactics, bringing Porsche's dependence away from the product focus on sports cars to new revenue streams from the Cayenne line of cars and from VW (Porsche currently holds a 42% ownership stake in VW which, however, has weakened their Balance Sheet). The German car industry does not have the same tradition for intervention as is present in the US automotive industry.

Seen from a product portfolio perspective, it is interesting that Porsche and VW jointly manage to have an interest in both the high-end and the low-end market, comprising distinct business models. When producing Porsche cars, a high degree of outsourcing takes place, whereas VW is based on insourcing.

During the escalating 2009 financial crisis it is also noteworthy that the German Government has excluded or showed extreme reluctance to discuss bailout packages, whereas this is a standard issue in the US automotive industry.

Competition in Various Zones

General Motors and the rest of the US automotive industry has already received considerable assistance from the US Government, and also a second bailout plan has been discussed, despite the fact that a number of analysts in 2008 had already warned that General Motors was in danger of ending up in bankruptcy regardless.[4] The company has chosen to downsize its product portfolio, although the company still wants to pursue products like Chevrolet, Cadillac and Buick. Time will show whether General Motor's product strategy has been sufficiently strong in order for the company to survive after help from the government.

The case of the American automotive industry is also a case of an industry not sufficiently aligned with the driving forces in the market zone. As such, they seem to have been ignoring the development in the institutional zone when it comes to climate and sustainability. For years they have been developing new and more advanced cars paying insufficient attention to the consumption of fuel and energy as well as to CO_2 aspects.

From GM's web site it says:

General Motors Corp. (NYSE: GM), one of the world's largest automakers, was founded in 1908, and today manufactures cars and trucks in 34 countries. With its global headquarters in Detroit, GM employs 244,500 people in every major region of the world, and sells and services vehicles in some 140 countries. In 2008, GM sold 8.35 million cars and trucks globally under the following brands: Buick, Cadillac, Chevrolet, GMC, GM Daewoo, Holden, HUMMER, Opel, Pontiac, Saab, Saturn, Vauxhall and Wuling. GM's largest national market is the United States, followed by China, Brazil, the United Kingdom, Canada, Russia and Germany. GM's OnStar subsidiary is the industry leader in vehicle safety, security and information services.

Although GM has had a dominant position in the market and especially in the American market, they have not been sufficiently profitable over the years and therefore they have not been able to sustain competitive pressure compared with some other car producers. In 2009, for instance, Tata Motor has announced that they will enter the US market with their new diminutive Nano car. This is being sold in India for US$1,980 although the price in the US might be slightly higher due to stricter safety and emissions standards.[5]

When Skype was launched it had created downloadable software to facilitate free peer-to-peer Voice over IP calls. However, the marketing gimmick was to make the software free of charge, which was unprecedented in the telecommunication industry, creating an exorbitant subscriber intake and much value for the customers, substituting US$1 calls per minute with free calls. Although it was easy to imitate Skype, the incumbent players in telecommunication were unable to do so, partly because Skype had already locked in a huge customer base with a zero cost, zero priced product (a detailed description of the underlying philosophy is offered in Appendix I), and partly because of their own revenue loss and subsequent cannibalization. Skype had created its own position in the market zone.

What Should Be the Product Scope?

The fundamental strategy of an enterprise is defined by answering the two questions: Where does the company compete and how does it compete? This question deals with the scope of the company's activities. Which should be the products and what should be the markets in which the company should compete? The second question deals with how the company should compete including what should be the business model of the company.

Deciding on the scope of products is a strategic choice. Should the company be highly specialized or should the product portfolio consist of a wide range of products and markets?

It is a sensitive and vulnerable decision. The toy company Lego that produces building blocks has learned this lesson. For many years, Lego was successful and expanded the business both geographically and conceptwise, among others developing Legoland theme parks. In early 2000 Lego diversified its product portfolio with merchandising spin-offs like Harry Potter and Star Wars. However, it turned out to be a failure. Lego experienced some major losses throughout 2002 to 2005. As the owner Kjeld Kirk Kristiansen emphasized "*We went into too many categories, and made too many different products without really being aware of what they were about, or what our brand stands for.*" After some harsh years, Lego with a new CEO, Jørgen Vig Knudstorp, is back on track again after a very successful 2008. The key components have been back to basics, off shoring of production, close relations with the customers and repositioning of Lego in alignment with its original brand, a strategy with some similarities to the strategy of Porsche.

The lesson learned by Lego is that scope and scale are important but still it is a question of accommodating the needs of the customers as discussed in Chapter 6.

Summarizing, the traditional product portfolio perspective as issued by Boston Consulting Group has very limited relevance for most companies, the positioning in the various zones carries importance, and that a too broad portfolio of products may be difficult to sustain. But what are the bearing points with regard to products and services, and how do they relate to this general introduction?

The Core Product Needs Stickiness

From time to time, companies drift away from focus on the core product, as was seen with Lego. The flag carriers did that in the 1980s and 1990s by introducing bundled offerings. They opted for not only delivering transportation from point A to point B, they also introduced gourmet food, porcelain plates, upgrades, proprietary hotel service and loyalty programmes such as bonus points, advanced flight magazines and gifts to their customers. However, the European challengers like the Ryanairs and easyJets introduced low fares, punctuality, electronic ticketing and very low turn rates – the time it takes to de-board and board planes – a much more attractive core product.

Likewise, as seen in automotives, some US car makers have been outperformed by Asian and European car makers who have focused on delivering higher customer value with the core product. Equally, Asian companies have been successful within consumer electronics by supplying products which are more competitive than the products of their American peers. Examples of expensive, even life-threatening, product differentiation also prevails in the telecom industry, postal services and the banking sector.

Interestingly, many of the recent successful companies, such as Ryanair, easyJet, Costco, Saxo Bank and Google expend lots of energy on making the core product attractive. It has come as a surprise to many incumbents that this approach also even comprises the notion of self-service. Introduction of self-service or rather the notion of the consumer as co-producer is very much in line with the concept of the pro-sumer as discussed in Chapter 6.

In many industries it seems that monopolies, former monopolies and otherwise complacent organizations drift away from the core product and miss out on the possibility of getting a substantial reduction in the cost base, whilst at the same time exploiting this as a means of differentiation. The problems of an incumbent and in particular the challenges in the internal zone when it comes to the production of the product may be illustrated by the following example.

Jim Schroth, founder of J.L. Schroth, Michigan manufacturers of rubber parts for automobiles, describes how his company responded to a request from Ford Motor Company:

> *I got a call on a Wednesday from an engineer at Ford who needed a little part shaped like a strawberry. I got the company next door, which does prototype stamping, to make part of the thing up. My toolmaker put all the people he needed on it, and I delivered the parts to Ford on Friday. It would have taken them weeks.*[6]

There is a long way from this example to the X-factor universe, where there is much focus on the stickiness of the core product. In the case of Ryanair, this implies a general cost consciousness as well as clear dedication to making the core product attractive based on proprietary production. This means that the Ford experience from the example would never occur in a Ryanair-like organization.

When Products Create Their Own Ecosystem

The concept of ecosystem has been part of the Cisco way of doing business. During the 1990s, the company leveraged partners for all business functions except for developing their core patented products and business strategy. Partners were used for sales, marketing, manufacturing, technical support and new installations. By this Cisco lived up to the motto "do what you do best and leave the rest for others to do".

When Google commenced its search engine they were not the first movers in that space but eventually became the biggest search engine on the Internet today. A main reason for the market penetration and sustainability of Google is tied to the constant development and subsequent creation of an ecosystem which seems to become more and more different from what its peers are doing.

First of all, Google quickly drifted into the X-factor universe when the search engine was paired with the world's largest advertising activity, known as Google AdWord and Google AdSense. Search and advertising activity formed the beginning of the new ecosystem which is emerging with gradual product development. This includes Gmail, paired with AdSense, Google Scholar, Google Earth, and Google's mobile activities, including the new operating system on mobile devices, namely Android.

The last activity, Android, may be viewed as an intelligent way to extend Google's activities with a strong foothold in the mobile communications space. Android is a software stack for mobile devices, providing the tools and APIs necessary for any third party to begin developing software applications to run on Android-powered devices. The openness resembles Linux's success, and it seems obvious that Google's successful ecosystem within the Internet space will now gain an extension into mobile devices and subsequently mobile communications.

As a company on the Asian continent, Huawei is likewise developing a proprietary ecosystem as the first mover with wholly IP-based offerings. But there is more to it than that. The product offerings are tied in with an admirable execution power, with financial engineering tools, with governmental assistance and so on, to an extent which has now in many instances moved Huawei from a second or third tier status, to the status of becoming equal among the best, and finally to emerge as the best among equals. In many cases, Huawei's ecosystem is impossible to match by competitors like Ericsson, Nokia-Siemens Network or Alcatel-Lucent.

The importance of the ecosystems is also in itself a way to explain the difficulties of the Boston matrix and the failures with the same in relation to portfolio management. Where the traditional portfolio perspective has no wider repercussions with companies pursuing a lean product line, the ecosystem perspective focuses on the synergy created between seemingly different activities. Hence, the header of Chapter 7, devising the product portfolio, does not relate to the BCG portfolio matrix, but rather to a series of products and activities which often constitute a new and in some (fewer) cases a proprietary ecosystem, difficult or maybe even impossible to imitate.

From Products to Business Modelling

Executives often raise the questions when it comes to products and services *"What should be the products and services our company should sell to our customers and what is the value proposition to these customers?"*

As discussed in Chapter 6, these questions are pertinent as many companies have widely similar core products or services. Within the airline industry, Southwest Airlines, Ryanair and easyJet are offering the same type of core services as the incumbents, namely transportation from one destination to another, but they have managed to package their service differently by emphasizing elements on how to position themselves differently. Starbucks, too, is selling coffee like many others, but managed to develop a competitive positioning based on much more than just handling coffee over the counter, thereby differentiating itself significantly from its competitors.

Therefore, when companies have to decide what to offer to the customers they should not only be concerned about the product or service. They should also ask the strategic question of "What do our customers really want and how can our products or services match this need?" Indeed the question is not only about products and services, but much more about the business model developed and used by a company and thus the value proposition offered to its customers.

Examples of various business models include Body Shop, Charles Schwab, Southwest Airlines and Amazon. When looking at the two last examples – Southwest Airlines and Amazon – it is not only about producing transportation and selling books, but much more the underlying business model. In both cases they reach out for the X-factor universe, because they are building their products into a business model based on substitution effects. In the case of Southwest Airlines, substitution of road traffic, in the case of Amazon, substitution of physical transportation when buying and selling books, and in both cases at substantial cost savings for the customers.

Gradual substitution also appeared to be the case with Skype as the proliferation of functionality implies that in particular the private consumer is able to substitute more and more of conventional telephony with Skype. The substitution effects of Amazon, Skype and others are important seen from a business modelling perspective, because substitution brings about the willingness to pay as consumers will compare the price (and quality) of conventional services with the price (and quality) of the new services. Obviously, Skype and others compare very well and the business modelling therefore works well. Arguably, the business modelling is more important than the product itself.

Demand-driven Products

When dealing with the supply side of the company as is the case with the product offering, conventional thinking often brings about supply push tactics. However, many companies in the X-factor universe have relied on the deliberate design of immensely strong demand pull effects.

Ryanair is one case in point. By cutting to the core, closing down expensive dealers, diminishing production costs by having only one type of plane, utilizing inexpensive airports, having high turn rates and letting the customers do the electronic ticketing, Ryanair became able to sell tickets much cheaper than the conventional flag carriers. By way of price elasticity, the demand grew exponentially and a very real pull was created in the market. Surveys show that low fares not only bring about substitution but 71% of the new demand comes from customers who would not have travelled otherwise.[7]

Obviously, the same is the case in other industries, for example with B2C offerings within the communications industry as pursued by Skype. Delivering inexpensive communication over the Internet and nothing else, Skype is a very simplistic product. However, only three years after the first user downloaded its software, Skype was sold to eBay for US$2.6 billion, one of the main reasons being the demand pull created. The demand pull was also helped by the ordinary consumers themselves, chat fora and WOM (word of mouth) and viral marketing à la Hotmail, see Chapter 6. The disruptive product was promoted even by the establishment as early as the beginning of 2004; for instance, the chairman of the Federal Communications Commission in the US:

> *I knew it was over when I downloaded Skype, Michael Powell, chairman, Federal Communications Commission, explained. When the inventors of KaZaA are distributing for free a little program that you can use to talk to anybody else, and the quality is fantastic, and it's free – it's over. The world will change now inevitably.*[8]

The founders of Skype were right from the beginning truly visible first movers aware of the demand pull they would create, as the following quote from Nicklas Zennström, CEO and co-founder of Skype, illustrates:

> *The idea of charging for calls belongs to the last century. Skype software gives people new power to affordably stay in touch with their friends and family by talking advantage of their technology and connectivity investments.*[9]

Skype managed to create a considerable amount of hype in the beginning, but users became subsequently aware that Skype was not hype at all but a very real demand-driven product at a high level of professionalism delivering value to the customers over and above their expectations.

Also, Huawei is creating some "hype" around its capability to take over vendor relationships almost overnight and Saxo Bank has also been recognized as the "best in class" with its IT-based trading platform. Such examples show that the demand pull effects are not only tied to the mass market but work well in the B2B segments.

The Relevance of the Product Life-cycle Thinking

Conventional wisdom in the strategy literature often emphasizes the importance of the product life-cycles comprising: (1) Market introduction stage, (2) Growth stage, (3) Mature stage and (4) Saturation and decline stage. It is based on the assumptions that (1) products have a limited life, (2) product sales go through various stages, with each posing different challenges and opportunities, (3) profits rise and fall at different stages of the product life-cycle and (4) products require different marketing, financial, manufacturing, purchasing, and human resource efforts in each stage.

As a conceptual map, the life-cycle is a valid instrument. However, even under the normal conditions, the most important aspect of product life-cycles is that, to all practical intents and purposes they often do not exist. In most markets the majority of the major brands have held their position for at least two decades. The dominant product life-cycle is that of the brand leader which almost monopolizes many markets, and is therefore one of continuity and should be understood as such. An example of a product life-cycle that is sustained through, for example, product developments or enhancements is shown in Figure 7.2.

As Dhalla and Yuspeh emphasize[10]: "... *clearly, the product life-cycle is a dependent variable which is determined by market actions; it is not an independent variable to which companies should adapt their marketing programs*". Marketing management itself can alter the

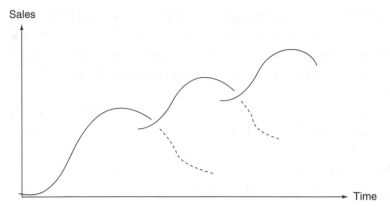

Figure 7.2 **Product life-cycle – sustained sales growth.**

shape and duration of a brand's life-cycle. Thus, the life-cycle may be useful as a description, but not as a predictor. The important point is that in many markets the product or brand life-cycle is significantly longer than the planning cycle of the company involved.

It is a matter of fact that 80% of the companies included as examples in the X-factor universe have an average lifetime from inception until today of less than ten years. Many are relatively young such as Skype and Facebook, and others are a bit older like Hotmail, PayPal, Saxo Bank, Cisco, Microsoft and Huawei. Even if the youngest companies – such as Skype and Facebook – are taken into consideration, these companies display a tremendous interest in constant development of their products, all centred on their respective core products from a life-cycle perspective.

One of the companies attaching considerable attention to life-cycle issues is the large diabetes company Novo Nordisk. Like other companies in the X-factor universe, there is much focus on product offerings, namely to help medicate people suffering from diabetes. Unlike the top five pharmaceutical companies, Johnson & Johnson, Pfizer, Bayer, GlaxoSmithKline and Novartis, which often tend to supply a suite of very different medications, Novo Nordisk is much leaner in their line of products. In the year 2000, the step was taken to divest all activities related to enzymes into a separate, stock-listed company, called Novozymes. This was an advantage both for Novozymes and for Novo Nordisk as the divestiture allowed both companies to focus and concentrate on their different lines of products.

In terms of market share on the attractive insulin market, Novo Nordisk now holds comfortably above 50%. For a long period of time, Novo Nordisk's stock has been traded at around double the level (measured against P/E) of its peers.

The long-term success of Novo Nordisk is not least due to it utilizing product development and product life-cycle management (PLM). Over time, they have developed a portfolio of modern insulin that is no longer based on human insulin, as well as having the market's most complete portfolio of insulin, when short- and long-term effects are taken into consideration.

Many other companies follow the same path or even adopt the same tactical weapon of staying focused, but very few have the ability to operate in such a disciplined manner as is the case with Novo Nordisk. Another example is Saxo Bank, expending many resources on the continued development of the IT trading platform. Just as Asian companies within consumer electronics outperformed many American companies during the 1980s and 1990s by way of high investments in research and development, Novo Nordisk and Saxo Bank are likewise in their respective industries models for exercise with regard to achieving Return on Strategy by way of high investment allocations.

Why Do Good Companies Go Bad?

Economy of scale is a concept often heard in business. The logic is that the average costs decline the more a company produces. Unfortunately it is not always a question of just pushing the volume button as other components also play a significant role. A Boston Consulting Group study of the personal computer industry showed that despite capacity expansion and assumed economies of scale, costs have not significantly declined. The reason was primarily that the majority of the cost came from procurement only leaving the total added value in the factory with 11%. This percentage could not create enough margin to support the business.

In the book "The Self-destructive Habits of Good Companies" (2007) the author Jagdish N. Sheth not only describes the personal computer example just mentioned, he also raises the question of *Why do good companies go bad?* In Chapter 2 on the recipe game, it was discussed that even if companies have followed a certain and successful recipe they apparently misbehave and later on go down the drain, as was the case for the majority of the companies in the "In Search of Excellence" study.

An interesting observation made by Sheth is that the average life span of corporations is declining, even as the life span of humans is rising. This certainly indicates that we cannot transform our human experiences of how to extend life to the corporate world. We might eat more healthily, we might exercise more often and we might increase our immunity towards diseases, but when it comes to the corporate world, the notion of "survival of the fittest" still exists.

Some of the reasons why good companies fail are quite obvious. When a company is developing successfully the top management sometimes start to believe that the success will last forever, meaning that they often become less focused. Also believing that the company is located in a blue ocean where "*the market is uncontested and where competition is irrelevant*", as the subtitle of the "Blue Ocean" book states, might be a dangerous route to embark on.

Sheth has identified seven reasons why companies fail. These are listed in Table 7.1.

The seven characteristics can easily be found in companies going down the tube. And in many cases more than one characteristic can be identified. When Digital and IBM hit the wall back in 1992, some of the reasons which could be traced were denial, arrogance and complacency. In both cases history shows that when companies are dominant in a particular business area they tend to exclude what is happening outside that

Table 7.1 **Seven reasons why companies fail**

The reason	Description
Volume obsession	Rising cost and falling margins
Denial	Cocoon of myth, ritual and orthodoxy
Arrogance	Pride before the fall
Complacency	Success breeds failure
Competency dependence	Curse of incumbency
Competitive myopia	Nearsighted view of competition
Territorial impulse	Culture conflicts and turf wars

Source: Sheth (2007).

domain. It seems that you are immortal and that competition can be ignored. Unfortunately, that type of myopia often has a boomerang effect.

Other examples of complacency can be found in industries where deregulation has taken place, as was the case within the US airline industry and the US post distribution system.

In the context of product portfolio as a key success driver it is noteworthy that a number of the characteristics are related to the product or the supply side of the company; for instance, volume obsession not justified by the line of products, arrogance and complacency based on a miscomprehension of the attractiveness of the products, and territorial limitations of a product in an increasingly global context. Part of the automotive industry is one case in point.

The Complexity of "Simple" Products!

Summarizing, five different product aspects seem to be important to address in order to arrive at an understanding of how to help move companies into the X-factor universe and to remain ahead of peers.

As evident from Table 7.2, products related to companies' supply side is a somewhat complex key success driver. This is evidenced by the way the companies within the X-factor universe work with this key success driver. If we look at Skype as an example, the company has undoubtedly invented a product offering, or rather a service, which is very much demand driven.

Table 7.2 Overview regarding different perspectives on product portfolio as a key success driver

	Stickiness of the core product	*Products as ecosystem*	*Products as business innovation/business modelling*	*Demand-driven products*	*Life-cycle considerations*
Why important?	Competitors tend to forget to develop the core product	New ecosystems change the game	The underlying business model is key	Most successes are based on strong demand	Over time, both winners and losers are created
Case examples	Ryanair	Google	Southwest Airlines, Amazon	Skype, Huawei	Novo Nordisk
Biggest risks or challenge	Not to reach regional or global economies of scale	No demand for the new ecosystem	No revenue streams	Time to market/timing	Underinvestment in R&D

This is visualized by the rapid take up of millions of customers at very low sales and acquisition costs (see Appendix I). Timing has proved important for Skype, because they seem to have launched and taken off at the right time, following the rapid increase of Internet usage from the inception of Skype and onwards, leaving earlier market entrants behind.

However, Skype also works with the other bearing points mentioned in Table 7.2. First of all, Skype has a very high score regarding the stickiness of the core product, which is their peer-to-peer VoIP. The software is very easy to download and is designed to utilize already existing PC and Internet capacity, thereby allowing for further exploitation of investments already expended by the customers. Many other software programmes have been used for the same purpose, but none other than Skype managed to reach global economies of scale.

Gradually, Skype is trying to develop its proprietary ecosystem by way of product development comprising calls in and out of the public networks, mobile telephony, video applications, and so on, thereby gradually creating a new ecosystem based on the already existing equipment and capacity. Naturally, there is a market for this new ecosystem because it substitutes services from the traditional telco incumbents. Many proponents of Skype have praised the voice-based peer-to-peer-product as "unconventional". However, it is a matter of fact that other similar-type programmes have existed decades prior to the launch of Skype. Thus, it is rather the invention of the ecosystem combined with diligent marketing which represents "out-of-the-box" thinking, leading forward to three-digit millions of customers enthusiastically "skyping".

The underlying business model was initially rejected even by many industry experts who did not see any viability or sustainability for Skype giving away peer-to-peer communication for free. However, this is precisely why Skype is developing the new ecosystem so that a revenue stream may be gained from other sources. Today, Skype is profitable, which furthermore galvanizes the sustainability of their business model.

It seems as if Skype is doing product life-cycle management (PLM), but it remains to be seen how the next generation of products will be configured and developed. The inherent risk here is equal to the risk of many other companies, namely underinvestment in research and development, in order to remain competitive and to ring-fence its current position.

As the example with Skype illustrates, the most salient bearing points are those addressed in Table 7.2, namely:

- Stickiness of the core product
- The creation of an ecosystem
- Business innovation/business modelling
- Demand pull-driven products
- Product life-cycle management.

All in all, Skype has a clear position with regard to all the bearing points, and later on, in Chapter 12, Skype will be benchmarked in order to illustrate how the product as a key success driver helped Skype enter and remain in the X-factor universe.

8

LEVERAGING THE
FINANCIAL CIRCUIT

We're proud to announce the public release of Skype Beta and the arrival of P2P Telephony! Skype allows anyone to experience free, unlimited, high-quality voice communication over the Internet.[1]

The above news was released on the August 23, 2003 and marked the beginning of what was to become one of the fastest business successes in recent time. The founders of Skype, Niklas Zennström and Janus Friis, became billionaires when eBay acquired Skype in 2005 for US$2.6 billion, the Skype community has grown to number more than 300 million user accounts worldwide as of August 2008 and the traditional telecommunications industry is faced with an entirely new type of competitor: the price killer.

By offering goods or services at significantly lower prices or in some cases entirely free of charge, such as Skype, the price level of the entire industry is likely to drop causing a subtraction of revenue equal to a value destruction, in particular viewed from the competing suppliers' perspective. In July 2008, Skype announced that since 2003, people around the world have talked to one another for more than 100 billion minutes using free Skype-to-Skype voice and video calls. Now imagine that these 100 billion minutes were previously offered by traditional telecommunications companies at an average charge of US$1 per minute, the value destruction would equal US$100 billion.

While the industry as a whole experiences such value destruction, Skype can report increasing revenues and deliver profitable results. In the first quarter of 2008, Skype posted total revenues of US$126 million, an increase of 61% over the prior year, while delivering a fifth consecutive quarter of profitability.[2]

The free of charge service has been fundamental to the success of Skype and as such the financial circuit of Skype stands as a central element of their strategy and the way in which they actively pursued entrance to the X-factor universe. In the case of Skype and other price killers, the pricing mechanisms become of great importance in the quest for competitive supremacy and as such become a key success driver of the company.

However, pricing is not the only factor within the financial circuit that may influence or even constitute the key success drivers of a given company and the strategy of same. The diligent way by which some companies have worked with the financial circuit has wider repercussions for conventional strategy recipes. Interestingly, the financial aspects and the financial circuit in particular were never adopted as part of the conventional recipes outlined in Chapter 3. Therefore, it can be argued that the financial circuit itself represents an X-factor at the general level at the same time as some of the salient elements represent valuable tactical weapons to reach and stay within the X-factor universe.

Consequently, we shall closely follow some key characteristics of the financial circuit, from pricing mechanisms to cost structures, from financing to lending through to how financial information is shared that can prove to be influential.

Chinese companies are capturing global market share through a value proposition that rests on cost innovations, other companies, such as Dell Inc., focus on cash flow and maintaining strong Balance Sheets as part of their strategy, while the strategy of yet others, such as Saxo Bank, focus on building partnerships with financial implications, such as revenue sharing.

The financial circuit of a given company and how this is put to use, can have a significant impact on the success of a company and thus the strategy of a company. The financial aspects represent an area that has not traditionally held a central place in the development of a company's strategy.

The Financial Circuit – the Overlooked Strategy Aspect

Conventional wisdom often views financial aspects as the outcome of a company's strategy as displayed through periodic financial statements and used for analysis by investors and stakeholders. It is seldom an integral part of a company's strategy – or at least perceived as such. Far less, financial aspects are viewed as an *input* to strategizing. However, much more attention has to be paid to financial aspects when working with strategy.

In the traditional view cost leaders are able to compete aggressively on pricing owing to a tightly controlled cost base and economies of scale, whereas differentiators can charge a premium based on product features that separate them from the competitors but require increased spending on, for example, R&D. Regardless of the chosen strategy the financial aspects were perceived as the outcome of the same rather than central or even direct *input*, to the making of strategy.

Challenging the conventions are those business models in which the financial circuit holds a central role. Business models that are based on reverse pricing mechanism enabling the company to offer their services free of charge to the end customer, business models that focus on leveraging low cost bases to aggressively move upmarket in their product offerings, or business models which are configured to eliminate steps in the supply chain in order to offer a superior value proposition to its customers are all examples where the financial circuit of a company is central to the strategy.

Facilitating a Success Free of Charge

At the top of Saxo Bank's corporate statement one will find the goal of the company expressed as follows:

To be the world's most profitable and professional facilitator in the global capital markets.

This goal, which emphasizes the financial circuit of the entire capital markets industry, has not been developed overnight but is instead the result of a business model that has been developed and refined over the years. The business model has been greatly influenced by the financial circuit of Saxo Bank and their ability to migrate into the X-factor universe.

Their early focus on establishing an online presence was partly due to the vision of the two founders, the crisis that Saxo Bank was facing and the cost reduction such a sales channel could lead to. Isolating the latter aspect of generating new sales leads by establishing an online presence as an alternative to traditional sales not only reduced sales and acquisitions but also presented Saxo Bank with the opportunity to service investors throughout the world.

Combining the online presence with the proprietary trading platform, the SaxoTrader, allowed for additional cost reductions as the investors were now able to place their own investments without directly contacting a Saxo Bank employee. Simultaneously it provided opportunities for Saxo Bank to differentiate their offering by adding features, such as news, analysis and charting functions to the platform.

Aside from charging a commission on trades executed, Saxo Bank offered the trading platform with all its built-in features free of charge, thereby redefining the industry which was previously characterized by limited access to the information necessary for making investments. In many cases, such information was only available to the intermediaries and not to the actual investors.

At the beginning of the millennium, the established online presence and an award winning trading platform was paired with an aggressive pricing strategy whereby Saxo Bank could fend off competition from the deep discount brokers while maintaining a highly differentiated product.

In 2001, Saxo Bank gained their banking licence, providing them with the opportunity to venture into more traditional banking products. However, instead of broadening their product portfolio with, for example, traditional lending activities to balance the income from commission with less fluctuant fee income, Saxo Bank remained true to their innovative IT-focused brokerage business model. They remained true to the financial circuit of generating revenue from trade commissions and foreign exchange adjustment while offering award winning, and cost efficient, technology to the investors free of charge.

This decision sheltered Saxo Bank from the faith that has befallen many of the giants within the financial services industry in times of crisis. The 2008 bankruptcy of Lehman Brothers was the most significant of them all topping the US chart for bankruptcies, holding assets at an estimated value of US$640 billion when filing for bankruptcy. This is more than the combined value of the following 15 bankruptcies put together. Other high-profile casualties include Bear Stearns which was acquired by J.P. Morgan Chase for a price of US$10, per share – the 52 week high of Bear Stearns at the time of acquisition was just above US$130 – and Merrill Lynch which was acquired by Bank of America.

Regardless of the financial situation investors will always trade, when share prices are dropping they will sell and reinvest in other instruments and vice versa when the markets pick up again and, with a business model that hinges primarily on the sales volume, Saxo Bank is able to navigate the crisis in a somewhat flawless fashion.

Immediately after gaining their banking licence, Saxo Bank extended their focus on the financial circuit to include external wholesale partners through their white label partnerships pro-gramme. By offering competitors an unbranded version of their proprietary trading platform on a wholesale basis in return for a share of the revenue, they effectively partnered with the com-petition to grow the market as a whole. Saxo Bank delivers proven technology which combined with the white label part-ner's brand is believed to increase the volume of trade in a par-ticular region.

This strategic decision and the partnerships Saxo Bank has entered with liquidity providers at the supply side has led to the positioning as a facilitator in the market. This positioning and the underlying strategy have been refined over time and made possible by the continued focus on not only their own financial circuit but also that of the players in the industry as a whole.

Saxo Bank's own financial circuit has predominantly focused on the ability to offer global private clients a superior and highly differentiated service at low cost with the external focus serving dual purposes. One is to improve on the value proposi-tion by partnering with liquidity providers that offer the actual products of foreign exchange, stocks and other financial instru-ments, whereas the other is aimed at growing the market by striking wholesale partnerships.

The Price Killer Model

As illustrated by the example of Skype in the introduction, the financial circuit and a company's focus on how to break the tra-ditional wisdom can lead to significant disruptions and effect-ively kill the existing pricing mechanisms of entire industries.

Skype did it in the telecommunications industry. Saxo Bank did in the brokerage industry. Google and Facebook developed entirely new business models centred on providing a service free of charge while others such as Ryanair, IKEA and Costco developed discount business models to disrupt their respective industries, albeit not by offering products or services free of charge but instead at a substantial discount and perceived price leadership.

The business model of these and similar companies contradicts conventional wisdom that pleads the case of pricing according to the demand curve, extracting as much financial value out of the customer as possible. In the case of the price killers, Skype, Google and Facebook, they have furthermore managed to untie the Gordian knot by both pricing their core products at zero and eliminating or considerably diminishing their sales and acquisition costs, see Appendix I.

Why is it that some companies, even those in hypercompetitive markets, can offer their products or services at significantly lower prices or entirely free of charge and still make a sound profit?

One explanation for this rests with the idea of a reverse charging mechanism in which a third party provides the revenue. Other valid explanations cover the ability to cross-sell other products or services, generating high-volume sales and finally building a brand value that can subsequently be capitalized.

Reverse charging mechanisms redesign the traditional financial circuit in terms of revenue generation, which consist of a manufacturer of goods or services that market these to the end consumer either directly or through intermediaries. Figure 8.1 shows such a traditional circuit when intermediaries are used. Price killers at the extreme end of the scale short circuit this in order to offer their core services free of charge to their end consumers by looking for third party revenues.

They redesign the traditional financial circuit in which a company produces a good or service and sell this to the end

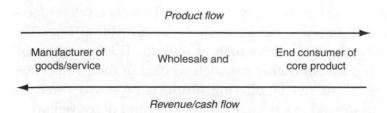

Figure 8.1 **A traditional financial circuit.**

consumer either directly or through an intermediary to focus on third party revenues. These revenues originate from sources that essentially are not using the core product or service such as companies advertising on various Internet portals. In doing so a new and unconventional financial circuit is created which stands in stark contrast to the traditional flows as exemplified by Figure 8.2. Such a business model is characteristic for many Internet services providing, for example, information free of charge to the worldwide Internet surfers, while creating revenues through banner advertising. One of the giants on the Internet, Google, has gained immense success by deploying a reverse charging mechanism.

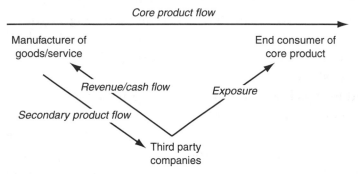

Unconventional financial circuit

Figure 8.2 **The financial circuit of reverse pricing.**

The Search that just Keeps on Growing

In 1998, Sergey Brin and Larry Page developed their PageRank algorithm as a fundament for the search engine that later became Google. From the outset, the end users of Google could perform their searches free of charge and by delivering more reliable results and presenting these in an uncluttered fashion on the web site Google.com, the usage grew at a steady pace. Until December 1999, Google's revenues came entirely from licensing their technology to Yahoo! and other third party sites with Google's own web site being completely free of advertising, offering nothing but search results. This was in stark contrast to other Internet portals whose advertising revenues were directly linked to the number of pages viewed and therefore offered additional content and tools to keep users from quickly linking to third party sites.

Overture, one of Google's early competitors and the market leader in the late 1990s, developed a new model for monetizing searches known as paid listings. Paid listings were text ads that appeared next to or within web search results for specific key words. These were essentially sponsored links where the ranking of the sponsored links depended on the amount that the advertiser offered in a bid. Advertisers only paid when users actually clicked on their sponsored links or listings, and the model thus became known as the cost-per-click model.

Google adopted a variant of this model and soon emerged as a serious threat to Overture despite hardly spending anything on marketing. By 2003, the market for paid listings had evolved into a near duopoly with Overture and Google holding a 90% global market share.[3]

The paid listings business model, or the price killer model of Google, depends on four factors: the coverage rate, click-through rate, average cost per click and revenue split. Coverage rates equal the share of queries for which at least one paid listing was sold, the number of sponsored links tied into a given search. The click-through rate depends on whether the sponsored link is actually clicked upon with the average cost per click being the price, or bid, paid by the advertiser.

Finally, the revenue splits that were agreed with affiliates, to whom the search technology was licensed, such as Yahoo!, MSN and AOL, also provided revenue streams.

With a business model that rested on offering the core product of web search free of charge to the billions of global World Wide Web surfers while generating revenue from third parties through reverse pricing mechanism, Google grew at a blistering pace to become the undisputed leader of online search. For December 2008, Google's share of the online searches was reported to be above 60% translating into nearly 5.5 billion searches.[4] This market share and Google's remarkable growth is reflected in the company's ability to grow their annual revenues from less than US$1 million to more than US$16 billion within ten years.[5]

In addition to providing free of charge search, Google has expanded its suite of products offered at no cost to the end user to include services such as the web-based email Gmail, the mapping application Google Earth, the picture application Picasa, and Google Docs the application for creating and sharing online documents, presentations and spreadsheets.

The development of these and other Google applications has broadened the scope of the company to reach across different industries. Given that many eBay sellers can also be found in the list of Google's advertiser, they effectively compete for the lion's share of their wallets. Even Microsoft may keep an eye on the doings of Google given their free of charge Google Docs, which allows the user to create documents, presentations and spreadsheets that can be shared online.

For Google, the unconventional notion of providing services free of charge to their end users makes perfect sense. Along with their PageRank search technology, the price killer model is at the very core of Google's strategy and thus a key success driver. Having reported revenues of more than US$5 billion for the three first quarters of the fiscal year 2008, Google just keeps on growing in success.

The price killer model helped Google become currently the world's most important advertising agent and quickly one of the most important content providers. It is quite interesting that in a recent global industry report of advertising agencies (the top 500) Google is not even mentioned although they are probably the company with the largest revenues from ads. This definitely illustrates the type of conventional thinking still prevailing in many industries.[6]

From a Paper Copy to a Worldwide Network

Another company which has experienced tremendous success by offering its services free of charge to the end customer is Facebook. In just four years, the number of active users has grown to more than 150 million and has become the most trafficked social web site according to comScore.[7]

In the early 2000s a facebook was a paper-based student directory containing basic information on fellow students at a particular university or high school. When Mark Zuckerberg, the founder of Facebook.com, launched the online version of a facebook in February 2004 at Harvard University it became an instant success. In a few weeks 10,000 users had registered for the web site and by March 2004, Facebook had launched at Yale, Columbia and Stanford.

The growth of registered users surpassed the 100 million mark in 2008, just four years after launch, as shown in Table 8.1.[8] According to comScore, the Internet market research company, Facebook holds the leading spot among social networking web sites, in terms of users, overtaking MySpace.com.

With end users able to establish detailed online profiles and use features such as create networks, messaging, post comments on a friend's profile or hunt for events, completely free of charge, Facebook is another example of the price killer model. However, a variant also included the added benefit of including the end user as co-producer of the content, which lowers cost but also provides access to the knowledge base of the end users who are developing applications on the platform. A total of more than 24,000 applications have been built on the Facebook platform of which the photo application is the most widely used photo application on the Internet according to comScore.

Table 8.1 **Number of registered users at Facebook.com**

February 28, 2004	*December 31, 2004*	*December 31, 2005*	*December 31, 2006*	*December 31, 2007*	*December 31, 2008*
10,000	1 million	5.5 million	12 million	50 million	>150 million

With revenues derived mainly from third party advertisers, Facebook is another example of a company that has adopted the price killer model. Reverse pricing, the end user as a co-producer and providing the platform for a network of developers are all factors that have influenced Facebook entering the X-factor universe and thus the strategy of Facebook.

Facebook, Google and other cases such as Hotmail and MySpace have all successfully exploded the demand and grown their user base by deploying the price killer model. Skype has likewise managed to do the same by offering some telephony at no cost while charging for additional services.

The very nature of a free of charge service will most often result in a significant change in the demand function for the product as it reaches the free of charge point as illustrated in Figure 8.3.

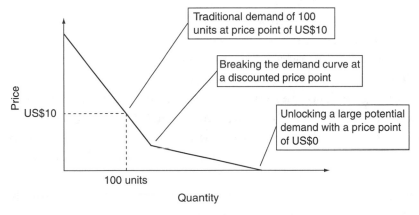

Figure 8.3 **Demand function at zero price.**

Facebook, MySpace and Skype have successfully unlocked the large potential demand with more than 100 million registered users for both Facebook and MySpace and more than 300 million for Skype. They have not only attracted large number of users but have also managed to do so at minimum or no sales and acquisition costs at all, another factor which contrasts with conventional wisdom. Sales and acquisition costs (SAC) are the average cost of signing up a new customer and are most frequently used by mobile telecom companies. Mobile telecom companies frequently pay incentives to retailers, who bring in customers to their networks as well as subsidize the costs of mobile phones. By avoiding such investments in bringing on customers and effectively having zero-SAC, companies can avoid negative initial cash flow, increasing the ability to reach profits quicker. (See Appendix I for an in-depth discussion of zero-SAC.)

Price killers that offer products or services completely free of charge are not the only companies that are able to unlock a potential and large demand. Prior to Google and Facebook, discount companies introduced a strategy of "no frills" products at low prices to unlock large volumes and successfully disrupted traditional industries such as passenger airline travel and retail.

As discussed in the book "Discount Business Strategy" (Andersen & Poulfelt, 2006), Ryanair successfully adopted a discount strategy in which a "no frills" product and an obsession for cost control were combined to offer customers point-to-point travel at low prices. In some cases even free of charge.

The focus on cutting costs included the introduction of productivity-based compensation, online ticket booking and harmonizing the fleet of airplanes spread throughout the organization and became a mantra. However, cutting costs to the extreme also led to greater performance on indicators such as turn time (the time the airplane is on the ground), on-time departures and cost of sales. A blend of drivers that was hugely influential in the success of Ryanair.

Other cases that have managed to deploy elements of a discount strategy to unlock large demand at low prices and disrupt traditional markets are Lidl, Costco, Southwest Airlines and IKEA to name a few. The price killer and the discount model are examples of how the financial circuit is used in defining a strategy that short-cut conventional wisdom by unlocking large demands at very low price points while doing so at little or no sales and acquisition costs (SAC). Table 8.2 illustrates how the price killer model differs from the conventional.

Table 8.2 **Conventional wisdom versus the price killer model**

Conventional wisdom	Price killer model
Prices are charged to provide full cost coverage	Prices are set at zero through reversing pricing
High sales and acquisition costs (SAC)	Zero or low sales and acquisition costs (SAC)
Price according to a linear demand curve	High volume by unlocking demand at low or zero price points

Neither economists nor business managers ever realized that it could be a win–win between the company and the customer that prices could be set at zero, until aggressive discount occurred and was further accelerated by diligent Internet-based companies such as Google, Facebook, Skype, Saxo Bank and others.

Cost Innovations

Another strategy, in which the financial circuit is central, is executed by Chinese companies who, through their focus on combining cost advantage and innovation, challenge traditional thinking. In the book "Dragons at Your Door" (Williamsom & Zeng, 2007), three main features of the strategy are argued to be (1) the ability to deliver high technology at low cost, (2) the ability to offer a wider choice at mass market prices and (3) the ability to transform speciality markets from low to high volume markets.

The Chinese Challenger

The Chinese telecom vendor, Huawei, has grown to become among the leading global players within industries dominated by companies such as Cisco, Ericsson, Alcatel-Lucent, Motorola and Nokia Siemens Networks by executing a strategy where the ability to develop best of breed technology at low cost is a key factor.

Huawei was founded in 1988 by Ren Zhengfei whose vision included the ability to develop strong in-house innovation capability. Due to this vision the majority of employees were employed within R&D from the outset.

By offering products at a price far below that of its international competitors, Huawei gained a foothold in the Chinese market, which up until 1995 accounted for all of Huawei's sales. When the Hong Kong government liberalized the telecommunications industry in 1995, Huawei went to great lengths to land their first international customer in the form of Hutchinson Telecom.

Hutchinson Telecom had decided to enter the Hong Kong market but was met with the, then novel, requirement that consumers were to be offered number portability. This requirement threatened to delay the launch of their services and potentially provide rival competitors with a head start.

Huawei came to their rescue. By committing to a shorter implementation period at a lower cost than the established suppliers, Huawei won the contract with Hutchinson Telecom and completed the task in three months. Hutchinson Telecom later went on to become one of the largest telecoms operators in the world through its "Orange" and "3" brands of which the first has been acquired by France Telecom.[9]

The contract with Hutchinson Telecom marked the beginning of Huawei's international expansion which initially focused on emerging markets such as Vietnam, Russia, Africa, Thailand and the United Arab Emirates.

By focusing on markets that many of the established companies regarded as peripheral markets, Huawei was able to gain a foothold in these through the ability to offer customized solutions at rock bottom prices. The low labour costs of China enabled Huawei to employ engineers at a fraction of the salaries present in international companies and allowed the company to combine low cost with innovation.

Having built volume in the emerging markets by offering low cost solutions, Huawei began to focus their efforts on high-end products and the markets of the developed world. Their chance to prove that they could develop high end solutions came when the company was pitted against the likes of Motorola and Ericsson in a parallel equipment trial staged by Etisalat, a United Arab Emirates operator.

By putting several hundred engineers on-site to work continually on improving the technology, Huawei outperformed the competition and in 2003 won the contract for full scale implementation of Wideband Code Division Multiple Access (WCDMA) technology.

Using the Etisalat contract as a reference, Huawei won additional contracts for entire 3G networks for operator SUNDAY in Hong Kong, Emtel in Mauritius and TM in Malaysia thus building their capabilities within state-of-the-art technology.

After gaining experience in these emerging markets, Huawei were well positioned to take their strategy of offering low cost high-end products that could be tailored to the needs of the customer to the mainstream markets of Europe and the US. In 2004, the first European contract to build a 3G network was struck with the Dutch company Telfort BV., who chose Huawei for their technological expertise and lower cost.[10]

By leveraging their cost advantage to develop customer-centric state-of-the-art products at low cost, Huawei has emerged as a serious challenger to the traditional and established players. They have grown their international footprint by partnering with more than 70% of the world's top 50 telecommunications providers and generated more than 70% of their sales from outside China. Focusing on R&D has led to the establishment of 14 R&D centres and 29 training centres across the world. Huawei currently hold 7% (152) of the essential UMTS patents worldwide placing them in the top five.

Huawei's continued focus on leveraging their cost advantage to develop high-end products has been instrumental in their rise and illustrates how the financial circuit can act as a central part of a company's strategy and facilitate entering into the X-factor universe. Other Chinese companies that are executing a similar strategy of cost innovation include Dawning (high performance computers), Teknova (medical diagnostic equipment) and BYD (rechargeable batteries).

Huawei has not only developed a complete solution as to how mobile network operators can switch almost seamlessly to Huawei's platform. They also offer the necessary financial instruments in order for network operators to gain some considerable additional financial benefits thus removing another barrier for the continued strong growth of Huawei.

The ability to use cost innovation is however not restricted to Chinese companies, or a novel phenomenon, as the case of another Asian company, Samsung Electronics, illustrates.

Innovating Consumer Electronics

In the late 1980s, Samsung Electronics was trailing its Japanese rivals within the market for semiconductors, but through a focus on R&D the company managed to short-circuit traditional wisdom and to manufacture a wide variety of DRAM memory products at low cost allowing the company to achieve higher than industry average margins on their memory products.

By continuously focusing on innovating the production and technology of DRAM, Samsung Electronics became the leading player, in terms of market share, in the DRAM industry by 1992. The company extended this position to eventually become the global market leader in more than 60 products covering memory chips, digital displays, home electronics, mobile devices, computing products and home appliances.

In 2005 Interbrand, the branding consultancy, rated Samsung as the most popular consumer electronics brand surpassing its Japanese rival Sony. In 2007, Samsung Electronics became the world's second largest mobile phone maker overtaking Motorola and recorded revenues in excess of US$100 billion placing the company among the top three companies in the electric appliances and electronics industry along with Siemens and Hewlett-Packard.[11]

One of the key factors to the success of Samsung Electronics has been their ability to combine their early cost advantage in the production of semiconductors with a continued focus on R&D and extending this into the development of other products. In many cases this is similar to the tactics deployed by the Chinese dragons given the continued focus to develop and manufacture high-end products at low costs. Whereas the Chinese dragons rely mainly on low engineering labour costs to develop high-end products at low cost, Samsung Electronics combined their early cost advantage with innovating the production process.

By initially entering markets for low-end products, Samsung could build volume that in turn would increase its scale advantages and accelerate the experience curve of its R&D. Subsequently this was leveraged in order to enter other markets with high quality products at low prices. This is a strategy which Chinese competitors have developed to fit their unique advantages and used to capture market share from Samsung.

Using the financial circuit to create strategies based on cost innovation led to not only lower prices but also differentiated and high quality products as another example of how this factor is used to draft strategies that differ from conventional wisdom. Table 8.3 lists the main differences between traditional thinking and cost innovation.

Table 8.3 **Conventional wisdom versus cost innovation**

Conventional wisdom	*Cost innovation*
R&D focused on developing high-end products charged at a premium	R&D focused on reducing costs for high-end products in order to sell these at low cost
High-end products restricted to speciality markets	Exploding speciality markets through low priced high-end products
Differentiation OR low cost	Low cost AND differentiation

By short circuiting conventional wisdom companies can utilize the strengths of their financial circuit to develop unique and winning strategies. Since the 1980s, Western companies have been faced with the competition of Asian rivals who successfully combine a focus on costs with that of manufacturing high quality products.

Cash Kings

As previously mentioned, the financial circuit is traditionally viewed as the outcome of a company's strategy rather than as an integral part of this. An outcome which is communicated and measured through the financial statements of a given company, typically the Profit & Loss account, the Balance Sheet and the Cash Flow statement. These are all designed to measure the financial health of a company and as such play a significant role in illustrating how a company is financially positioned to grow, take on new opportunities or defend existing ground.

From a company's point of view the financial health provides the platform for which strategic directions a company can take and how these are to be financed. When strapped for cash companies must raise funds to expand or fend off competition thus incurring additional debt that in turn may lead to a deteriorating financial health.

Cash flow is the lifeblood of any company. Without cash flowing into the company it will eventually cease to exist. However, cash flow is not just a matter of whether it exists or not but also a matter of timing. Traditionally, a company will incur the cost (cash outbound) of producing a product prior to generating a revenue by selling the product (cash inbound) and will therefore need to finance its operation from other sources for the period between producing and selling. Financing which will lead to increased costs that in turn must be passed on to the customers undermining the competitive strength of a given company.

All companies keep a keen eye on their cash flows. Some companies, however, do more than just that.

Reversing Cash Flows

The direct business model of Dell has turned the traditional flow of cash on its head by being able to bill customers for their purchases before suppliers are paid. As such the company realizes their revenue (cash inflow) prior to incurring the cost of producing the actual PCs (cash outflow) leading to strong financial health. For the financial year 2008, Dell reported a cash conversion cycle, the time between an outlay of cash for parts and the collection of payment for goods made of them, of negative 36 days.[12] In comparison Hewlett-Packard reported 27 days for the same fiscal year.

By a continued focus on optimizing the direct business model that rests on Michael Dell's three golden rules: "zero inventory", "never sell indirectly" and "always listen to the customer", the company became a leading player in the market for personal computers. The financial circuit played a significant part in the development and success of this strategy.

First, it was estimated that the direct model resulted in savings of between 25 and 45% in mark-up on every machine which could subsequently be passed on to the customer leading to a competitive advantage of cost leadership. Second, the zero tolerance for holding inventory and the company's ability to completely eliminate warehouses by 2004 allowed for further cost reductions and the ability to quickly market new breakthrough technology such as faster chips and hard drives.[13] The zero tolerance for holding inventory required Dell to apply the direct model to its suppliers as well as to customers, thereby creating an automatic and seamless process from when a customer ordered a product to the component requirement through to the actual delivery of the product.

With this in place, Dell created the billing system that underpins their ability to finance their operations at the expense of the suppliers adding to the financial health of the company.

By turning traditional cash flow thinking on its head, companies are able to positively impact the working capital of the company, the capital required to satisfy both maturing short-term debt and upcoming operational expenses, and thus improve the financial health.

One does not need to turn traditional thinking on its head in order to reach a position of good financial health. Many companies operating a traditional model report solid cash flows and healthy Balance Sheets every year.

Cash collecting Financial Health

A striking example of cash collecting is Cisco Systems, which for its fiscal year 2008 reported a net increase in its cash and cash equivalents of US$1.46 billion to reach more than US$5 billion in cash and cash equivalents. This further bolstered the current assets of Cisco Systems to a staggering US$35.7 billion, which is at a factor of almost one to three when compared with the current liabilities of US$13.9 billion. At the same time it was a sign of good financial health indeed.

One reason for this financial health is the continued focus on Days Sales Outstanding (DSO), the number of days it takes to collect cash from its customers, which was reported to be a mere 34 days for the fourth quarter of the fiscal year 2008. The ability to receive quick payment after invoicing a customer will have a positive effect on the working capital and thus lower the need for additional financing.

While the financial circuit of Cisco Systems cannot be argued as the sole factor for their success, the continued focus they have held on improving the financial health has influenced the strategy. A financial health which may be put to the test by the Chinese dragon, Huawei, that is executing a strategy in which the financial aspects play a larger part, as described previously in this chapter.

The cash kings, which are built from both traditional and untraditional thinking, are better positioned to weather any negative changes in market conditions such as the unfolding credit crisis of 2008 and the anticipated recession. A feature that may prompt more companies to let their strategy be influenced by the flows of the financial circuit given more turbulent times ahead.

Financial Partnering

Extending the financial circuit to encompass that of suppliers and or distributors, as Saxo Bank has successfully done within the market for online FX investments, is yet another way companies can include the factors of the financial circuit to their strategic advantage.

Distribution as a Financial Partner

In 1998, when the Hangzhou Wahaha Co. Ltd. (Wahaha), the largest Chinese beverage producer, decided to take on the giants of carbonated drinks, Coca Cola and Pepsi, they initiated their attack in the rural areas of China. Areas in which they believed they possessed a competitive advantage over the international giants due to the partnerships they had built with the distributors across the more remote locations of China.

Four years prior to the launch of the "Wahaha Future Cola", the company had developed a policy for how to tie channel members in over the longer term as a response to the growing problem of accounts receivable and bad debt. This policy introduced incentives for the channel members to focus on long-term gains. Distributors were required to pay an annual deposit in advance as cover for any potential future bad debt and otherwise operate according to Wahaha's payment policy.

In return the distributors would receive an interest rate from Wahaha that was higher than the bank rate. In addition discounts were offered for early payment and annual bonuses were awarded to distributors that met the criterion for prompt payment.[14]

Wahaha implemented this model over a period of two years effectively striking financial partnerships with existing distributors that led to a higher commitment among the distributors. This unique move became instrumental in the success of Wahaha and their ability to deliver products to the rural areas of China. These are areas where logistics are often difficult to manoeuvre. In contrast to many of the domestic and multinational companies that established their own distribution networks, Wahaha focused on partnerships with local distributors. By 2006, Wahaha had managed to capture a market share of 16% in the soft drinks market traditionally dominated by Coca Cola and PepsiCo.[15]

Cooperating with Competitors

In a press release from the March 13, 2002, Saxo Bank announced their plans to partner with the competition. Within that press release one of the founders and co-CEO, Kim Fournais, explains the underlying argument for doing so.

> Up to now, we have built our image as an investment bank oriented towards private investors. We now intend to market our trading platform to other investment banks around the world. The target group are essentially our competitors in the market. By offering them our unique trading technology, we can become part of their transaction flow and thus grow through partnerships.

This highly unconventional strategic move in which competitors would gain an unbranded version of the proprietary award-winning SaxoTrader platform in exchange for a share of the revenue would become highly influential in the subsequent growth of Saxo Bank. From 2002 to 2007, the number of white label partners grew to more than 100 while the revenue of Saxo Bank increased by a factor of ten.

Rather than competing with the other players in the industry, Saxo Bank chose a strategy of cooperative competition or co-opetition as it was termed by Brandenburger and Nalebuff when they introduced the concept in 1996.[16] Co-opetition is aimed at growing the market as a whole by utilizing the strengths of the competitors in the market. In the case of Saxo Bank they provide the technology whereas the partners bring local knowledge and brand to the table.

The strategy of expanding the financial circuit and entering into partnerships with the competitors achieved its seal of approval when Citibank announced that it had chosen to collaborate with Saxo Bank for the launch of their CitiFX Pro online FX trading platform.

Both Wahaha and Saxo Bank are examples of companies who have chosen to partner with external companies, distributors and competitors, in order to develop a unique and highly successful strategy. To a large degree such a strategy is influenced by their ability to utilize the financial circuit and the key success drivers inherent in this.

The Financial Circuit and Its Unique Influence

The influence the financial circuit can have on the development of a company's strategy is unique in many ways. As illustrated by the analysed cases, the influences do not merit a generic solution to the potential success a company's focus and inclusion of the financial circuit will lead to. Rather the four described influences all have unique characteristics as shown in Table 8.4. This figure illustrates that a successful focus on the financial circuit is not generic but rather dependent on other factors that are present for a given company. Thus the possibility exists for a company to apply their own unconventional and out-of-the-box thinking to develop the key success drivers that will bring competitive advantage to them.

Google and Facebook have gained tremendous success through their price killer strategies. Ryanair grew to be the largest discount passenger airline with a focus on a no-frills low cost service. The Chinese dragons have combined the jigsaw puzzles in a different way in which low cost engineering is central to

Table 8.4 **Characteristic of financial circuit influences**

The price killer	Cost differentiators	Cash flow kings	Finance partners
Reverse charging	Low-cost engineering	Reverse cash flow	Aim to grow the market as whole
Volume game – unlocking/ breaking the demand curve	Dual advantage of differentiation at low cost	Cash accumulation	Cooperation and competition

their strategy of offering high technology at low cost and moving into more and more speciality products or services in order to transform these into high volume markets. Dell has reversed the traditional cash flow cycle by getting paid prior to paying creditors, leading to a financially healthy business model, whereas Cisco Systems focuses on getting paid as fast as possible to maintain their financial health. Wahaha partnered with their distributors to battle bad debts and reach rural China, which enabled them to gain market share in markets dominated by brands such as Coca Cola and PepsiCo. Finally, Saxo Bank effectively joined forces with their competitors in order to grow the market as a whole by combining their technological strengths with the local knowledge and brand of a competitor.

Despite the diversity among the companies analysed, they share one common feature. They have all included the financial circuit as a central element of their strategy. They have all viewed finance as more than just the outcome of a strategy and successfully bridged the waters between short-term financial focus and long-term financial factors impacting the strategy of a company and the potential of the X-factor destination.

Yet again it is not a sufficient criterion of success to rest on the laurels of a well thought-out utilization of the financial circuit, in particular under contingencies of a "punctuated equilibrium":

> However, in the sustained disequilibrium of today's business environment, a paradox emerges. Although it's now easier to develop and deploy shaping strategies, it's also more difficult to protect them once they're established. Successful strategy now requires a series of shaping initiatives over time, rather than on disruptive big-bang effort to be exploited thereafter.[17]

Google is a foremost example of a company which short-circuited the search engine industry by creating its own ecosystem by bundling AdSense and search and now redefines the ecosystem by migrating into telecommunications also.[18]

The Financial Circuit as a Vehicle to a Higher Return
on Strategy

In many cases, X-factor universe companies include the financial circuit as a central part of their strategy despite this being a completely overlooked driver of strategic success in the existing literature. By doing just that they apply unconventional thinking, but the way in which these companies utilize the financial circuit is truly characterized by an out-of-the-box approach. Some use it to kill conventional pricing mechanisms by offering products or services free of charge, while others innovate their cost structures to gain a competitive advantage. Some turn traditional cash flows on their head, whereas others actively strike partnerships with their competitors to grow the total market and the potential cash flow.

As shown with the cases of Google and Facebook, their ability to redefine the financial circuit and utilize reverse pricing mechanisms has allowed for a business model in which the product offerings of search and social networking are free of charge to the customer. Hot on the heels of these price killers one will find discount companies such as Ryanair that seek to break the traditional demand curve by offering products at low prices aimed at unlocking large volumes. There is little doubt that these companies and similar, such as Hotmail, Skype, Costco and IKEA, demonstrate the ability to utilize the financial circuit as a key success driver in order to migrate to or remain in the X-factor universe.

The ability of the Asian cost innovators, such as Huawei and Samsung, to innovate the production process with the aim of offering high quality at low prices clearly contradicts the traditional view that argues this to be a strategy of being "stuck in the middle", leading to mediocre performance. By deploying unconventional thinking, these companies have managed to optimize their financial circuit allowing them to execute a strategy of low cost and differentiation or dual advantage.

The pursuit of dual advantage is not a characteristic that can be applied to Asian companies alone as the US computer manufacturer Dell has proved with their business model of selling directly. Dell's early focus on selling directly has allowed the company to redefine the traditional supply chain in order to cut costs and allow for not only lower prices but in many cases also higher quality. Add to this the fact that Dell has managed to reverse the cash flow in such a way that they are being paid by their customers prior to paying their creditors and the unconventional becomes clear.

Some companies look beyond their own financial circuit in order to utilize the financial circuit and do so in an unconventional manner. Saxo Bank has deployed a strategy of cooperative competition, or co-opetition, with great success by offering an unbranded version of its proprietary online trading platform to its competitors. Wahaha developed close ties with distributors of rural China though financial schemes and effectively used this to gain market share from Coca Cola and PepsiCo.

Summarizing, what allows the companies to utilize the financial circuit as a key success driver in an unconventional manner lead to the following main bearing points:

- Killing conventional pricing mechanisms
- Innovating cost structures
- Reversing cash flow mechanisms
- Co-opetition or financial partnering.

Whether it is the price killers, discounters, cost innovators or those that extend their utilization of the financial circuit to include external partners, they all demonstrate the ability to apply out-of-the-box thinking to reach the unconventional and highly successful use of the financial circuit. From the Far East to the US and across Europe, the addressed companies have all included the financial circuit as a key success driver in their efforts to create a high Return on Strategy.

There is no simple recipe for how to utilize the financial circuit in the pursuit of unconventional solutions and a high Return on Strategy. At this stage, the most guidelines that can be offered are not to overlook the financial circuit as a key success driver when working with a company's strategy. Far too often, financial aspects are taken for granted or just referred to a conventional CFO type of leader, and the importance of what is labelled the financial circuit in this book is far too great to do that.

Given this, it is up to the individual company to foster out-of-the-box thinking or deploy what appear to offer the best combination of key success drivers within the financial area.

9

OPTIMIZING THE
ORGANIZATIONAL DESIGN

An enterprise needs to develop a pack of wolves.
Ren Zhengfei, CEO and founder of Huawei

At Huawei all new recruits go through boot-camp-inspired training lasting up to several months in order to learn the culture of
the company. This culture can be attributed to the founder,
Ren Zhengfei, and his background in the People's Liberation
Army. It is a culture which eliminates individualism and promotes collectivism and the idea of hunting in packs. It is the
"wolf culture" of Huawei.

The Collectivistic Wolf Culture

The culture of Huawei is built on a sense of patriotism with
founder Ren Zhengfei frequently citing Mao Zedong's thoughts
in his speeches and internal publications such as the employee
magazine "Huawei People". Sales teams are referred to as
"Market Guerrillas" and battlefield tactics such as "occupy rural
areas first to surround cities" are used internally. In addition to
Mao Zedong, Ren Zhengfei has urged his employees to look to
the Japanese and the Germans for inspiration on how to conduct themselves, exemplified by the words written in a 1994
letter to new hires that states:

> *I hope you abandon the mentality of achieving quick results, learn
> from the Japanese down-to-earth attitude and the German's spirit
> of being scrupulous to every detail.*[1]

The notion of a "wolf culture" stems from the fact that Huawei workers are encouraged to learn from the behaviour of wolves, which have a keen sense of smell, are aggressive, and most important of all, hunt in packs. It is the collective and aggressive spirit that is at the centre of the Huawei culture. Combining the behaviour of wolves with military style training has been instrumental in building the culture of the company, which in turn is widely thought to be instrumental in the success of the company.[2]

In addition to the wolf culture of Huawei, the strong focus on building itself into an R&D powerhouse has shaped the organizational design of Huawei which at the end of the financial year 2007 employed 35,000 people, more than 40% of the entire workforce, within R&D. The company has 14 R&D centres around the world including centres in locations such as Silicon Valley and Dallas in the US, Stockholm in Sweden and Moscow in Russia. They are ranked as the fourth largest patent applicant under the Patent Cooperation Treaty (PCT) of the World Intellectual Property Organization (WIPO).[3] This and the commercial success the company has enjoyed over the past two decades, not least their ability to challenge Western giants such as Cisco, Lucent, Ericsson and Nokia, has made Huawei the place to be for young and ambitious men and women who are hungry for success.

A strong culture and recognizing the value of human assets stand at the core of Huawei and their use of the organizational design. This is perhaps best summed up by the following statement from their 2007 annual report:

> *Dedication is at the very core of our corporate culture. Providing the driving force for continuous innovation based on customer needs, our committed and devoted employees are Huawei's most valuable assets.*[4]

Contrary to the collective thinking that lies at the centre of Huawei's wolf culture, and can be argued to reflect the broader

Chinese culture, one finds the culture of Saxo Bank, which is built upon liberalistic ideals that characterize western cultures.

The Liberalistic High Performance Culture

The cultural foundation of Saxo Bank was formed in the early days of the company by the two founders and their beliefs, passion and drive. Through performance-based compensation schemes, the adversity that Saxo Bank experienced in the mid-1990s and the drive of the two founders a "can-do culture" was developed. A culture in which every last employee performed to the best of their ability and displayed flexibility that was instrumental in growing and developing the company during the early years. Despite not having a formalized culture that was communicated to employees, a common culture existed through the people that were employed in Saxo Bank.

> *When we first began, it was mostly uphill and I believe the way we survived was in large part due to the people we hired along the way. They had in them; they had Saxo in their blood.*[5]

Those employees that had Saxo in their blood also survived and thrived in the performance-based culture of Saxo Bank. This culture grew to encompass employees representing more than 70 different nationalities by October 2008.[6] Largely inspired by the novel "Atlas Shrugged", by Ayn Rand,[7] which portrays any form of state intervention in society as systemically and fatally flawed, seven virtues were developed by Saxo Bank and formalized as part of the Saxo Bank corporate value statement in 2005. These seven virtues are: rationality, independence, integrity, honesty, justice, productivity and pride.

Another source of inspiration for Saxo Bank and the performance-centric culture is the works of legendary Jack Welch, former CEO of General Electric, and his formula for constantly optimizing the workforce. The 20–70–10 formula states that 20% are top performers, 70% are average performer and the final 10% performing below par and thus a group of employees that is to be replaced. While not applying the exact mathematical formula, Saxo Bank makes no secret of the fact that underperformers will be replaced, comparing the company and its workforce to professional sports and arts organizations. A professional footballer who does not perform will be replaced in order for the team to compete as a whole.

In addition to this performance culture, the strong focus on IT and developing the proprietary online trading platform has been instrumental in how Saxo Bank has used the organizational design to their advantage.

Despite the fact that the underlying values and beliefs of Saxo Bank and Huawei are at opposite ends of the spectrum with Huawei emphasizing collectivism as a core value and Saxo Bank building theirs on the liberalistic idea of the individual, both companies have managed to successfully utilize their organizational design to stay tuned in the X-factor universe. This also indicates that diversity is a feature and an option of the X-factor universe.

The Organizational Design – the Engine or the Pulse of a Company

The organizational design of a company is more than the culture and values of the given company. It is to be understood in a broad sense albeit with a specific focus on people and knowledge. As such it comprises the structure of the company, i.e. how they are organized both internally and externally, the culture and values of the company as illustrated by the Huawei and Saxo Bank cases, and last but not least people.

In the article *Better strategy through organizational design*, Lowell L. Bryan and Claudia I. Joyce argue that research suggests that CEOs would be better off focusing on organizational design in order to prepare the organization for what lies ahead.

> *Strategic-minded executives may not be able to control the weather, but they can design a ship and equip it with a crew that can navigate the ocean under all weather conditions.*[8]

This quote captures how organizational design is to be an understood factoring term of entering and staying in the X-factor universe. It is the ship itself, the structure of a company and the crew of that ship, the very people and the shared values and culture of these.

Structure as the Backbone of a Corporation

As mentioned in Chapter 3, one of the early points that was discussed when corporate strategy emerged as a field of study in the 1960s was whether structure followed strategy or strategy followed structure. Alfred Chandler found in his work "Strategy and Structure" (1962) that managerial organizations developed in response to the corporation's business strategy. Corporate strategy is the long-term goals of the organization as well as the courses of action and associated allocation of resources necessary to achieve the goals.

Changes in the strategy would lead to organizational revisions. New organizational forms therefore become primarily a derivative of strategy according to Chandler. Since this thesis was explicated many have been discussing the correlation between strategy and structure as some will argue that structure in many cases is a determinant for strategy and not vice versa as argued by Chandler. Indeed for some organizations, structure is central to the executed business model and thus the chosen strategy.

According to Michael Goold and Andrew Cambell[9] most theories of organization contain a concept of "fit for purpose" meaning that organizations should be designed in a way that enables them to achieve their objective. As such this is not surprising. However, the key question still remains. Namely how to decide what should be the right design and what should be its contingents as there does seem to be one best way to design formal organizations. In the following we shall therefore discuss various organizational forms which different companies have chosen to fit their particular strategy.

Franchise Structure Central to a Healthy Strategy

The franchise concept of Naturhouse, the Spanish dietary company, has since the first franchise was opened in 1996 proved a remarkable success. The number of Naturhouse centres around the world has grown from only a few company-owned shops to more than 1,700 outlets, of which the majority are franchises.[10]

Having failed with their initial strategy, as described in Chapter 5, Naturhouse refined their business model of offering dietary advice and supplements in rented premises located in middle income areas to the point where it could be franchised.

To become a franchisee an initial investment of approximately €31,000 is required mainly to cover the costs of the interior and inventories. In addition to this an annual franchise royalty of €696 is paid to use the brand. Naturhouse claim that the investment is recovered within three years of operating with a typical store achieving annual sales of €72,000 in its first year, €144,000 in the second and €216,000 in the third year. The management of Naturhouse believes this presents an attractive alternative to paid employment for young nutritionists, biologists and pharmacists despite the hard work required. The amount of hard work is balanced by the amount of freedom and the regular income a franchise represents.

With this in mind, the strategy of Naturhouse is in fact the very structure and organization of all the franchise shops that make up the total footprint of Naturhouse. A footprint consisting of more than 1,700 shops worldwide which all have the same look and feel.

In the case of Naturhouse, structure and organizational design is central to the strategy that is executed and as such plays a significant role. Structure does not merely follow strategy but becomes an integral part of the same.

Structured to Exploit Channel Conflict

In 2000 when Saxo Bank announced their White Label Program (WLP) in which the proprietary SaxoTrader online trading platform is sold to competitors in return for a share of the revenue, the organizational design of Saxo Bank was influenced. From being primarily geared to servicing mainly private individuals through one direct channel, the organization now had to change to support the multi-channel approach in which both direct- and wholesale is pursued.

However, the decision to introduce the WLP programme was made possible by the award-winning nature of the SaxoTrader platform, which in turn was a product of the organizational design of Saxo Bank. An organizational design with a high degree of IT focus and approximately one-third of the employees being charged with IT-related tasks such as developing the platform and optimizing internal procedures through automation.

In the case of Saxo Bank and their WLP strategy one could therefore argue that strategy became a product of their early focus on IT, their structure, and not vice versa.

The success of the WLP strategy, however, did have significant implications on the organizational design of Saxo Bank, as the company from financial year end 2001 to 2007 grew by a factor of more than ten when measured in average headcount. Given this the WLP strategy and the subsequent growth of Saxo Bank had far reaching implications for the organization of the company thus supporting the notion of structure following strategy.

The organization and structure of Saxo Bank was not geared to such rapid success and as such the company responded to the growth by adding more employees. The higher number of employees combined with the lack of structure led to an organizational landscape of minor kingdoms within the company that were not necessarily working together but rather added to the complexity. Consequently the profit per employee experienced a sharp fall from 2005 to 2006 after previously growing, as shown in Figure 9.1.[11]

Responding to this development and the growth of Saxo Bank in general, the two founders and joint CEOs, Kim Fournais and

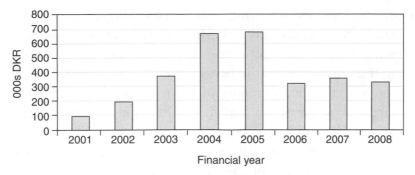

Figure 9.1 **Profit per average headcount for Saxo Bank** (*source:* Saxo Bank Annual Reports).

Note
The 2008 figure does not reflect the full effect of the dismissal of approximately 300 employees.

Lars Seier Christensen, hired the former CEO and CFO of Integrated Service Solutions (ISS – one of the largest facility services companies in the world), Erik Rylberg and Karsten Poulsen, to two new positions as Chief Executive Director and Deputy Chief Executive Director.

> *In choosing Rylberg and Poulsen for the new positions, Fournais and Seier Christensen focused on their established track record and extraordinary experience with streamlining and developing very efficient and profitable businesses.*[11]

On Friday September 26, 2008, approximately two months after the new management team was announced, their experience in streamlining was felt by a third of Saxo Bank's employees.

On this day all employees were informed that a number of positions were to be made redundant and as such they were all asked to be seated at their desks when the clock struck 15.00 in order to learn whether they were among those being released or not.

Those unfortunate employees made redundant were asked to clear their desks within 15 minutes, and hand over access cards and other items belonging to Saxo Bank before vacating the premises. In one sweeping move on a Friday, albeit not the thirteenth, Saxo Bank reduced their workforce by one-third. Not surprisingly, this gave rise to considerable "dialogue" among the unions and in the press.

Given this the development of Saxo Bank's organizational structure has played a vital part in the strategic direction of the company which in turn has impacted the organization. Whether this latest restructuring will increase the global competitive nature of Saxo Bank and further fuel the success of the company or lead to widespread dissatisfaction among remaining employees and impact the culture of Saxo Bank remains to be seen. Regardless of the outcome, Saxo Bank once again proved that they are prepared to tread untraditional paths in their quest for success.

Structural complexity and the reduction of same was also the case in September 1998, when Procter & Gamble (P&G) announced a six-year restructuring plan aimed at reducing the complexity of the organization by introducing a different structure that was to replace the existing matrix structure that had become too complex.

Throughout the history of P&G, which stretches back to when the company was founded in 1837, a number of different organizational structures had been implemented. In the 1920s brand managers of P&G were managing brands as individual companies thus creating a scenario of competitive brand management. Such competitive brand management was institutionalized in 1931 after which the organization began forming around product lines in order to facilitate faster and more customer-focused business decisions. When P&G established its first international sales division in 1948, it added complexity to the structure of the company as a whole as the large homogeneous US market was different to the heterogeneous markets of Western Europe. For the US, a structure of nationwide brand and product divisions was implemented, whereas a decentralized hub-and-spoke model was used in Western Europe.

In 1954, a divisional structure was added to the competitive brand management system in order to cope with the growing line of products. Within this structure, brand managers in the same division competed in the marketplace while sharing access to divisional functions such as R&D and manufacturing.

In 1987, P&G implemented a matrix organization thus replacing the competitive brand management system that had existed since 1937. In this organization, category portfolios were created in which various brands were managed (the category of, for example, soaps and detergents would manage different brands within this category). In the US, 39 category business units were created, each with its own sales, product development, manufacturing and finance functions. In this model functional leaders reported directly to their business leaders as well as to their functional leaders with, for example, sales people reporting to the category manager as well as the sales director and ultimately the vice president of sales. The European operations were by the late 1980s structured in a similar fashion with a European category division followed by country categories and finally country brand managers.

With growing opportunities in Asia and the developing countries, P&G merged the matrix structures of the US and Europe to create a global matrix. In this structure, regions were added as a layer above regional categories under which country categories and finally brand management was placed. In 1995 this structure was extended to the entire world with the creation of four regions – North America, Latin America, Europe/Middle East/Africa and Asia – each with its own president responsible for profit and loss.

While the global matrix structure facilitated early top and bottom line improvements through the pooling of knowledge, transfer of best practices, elimination of intraregional redundancies and standardization of activities, it ran into problems by the latter part of the 1990s.

P&G had become too complex, multiple reporting lines caused the structure to be asymmetrical, ultimately leading to each function developing its own strategic agenda that focused on maximizing its own power within the company as opposed to cooperating across the company to win in the marketplace. As a result of this, and the fact that competitors were catching up quickly, the sales grew by only 2.6% in 1997 and 1998 compared with an average of 8.5% throughout the 1980s. Given that full accountability could not be given to the profit centres as they did not manage the functional strategy and resource allocation, a culture of risk aversion and avoidance of failure was by many believed to be the cause of the declining performance. With over 100 profit centres, it just seemed like there were "*too many cooks in the kitchen*".[12]

It was in response to this that the six-year restructuring plan, known as Organization 2005, was put in place. A plan which called for voluntary job reductions of 15,000 employees by 2001 and the elimination of six management layers reducing the total from 13 to seven. A plan that ended the matrix structure as this was to be replaced by three interdependent organizations: Global Business Units, Market Development Organizations and Global Business Services. This new design when in place was believed to generate consistent sales growth of 6–8% and profit growth of 13–15% per year.

On January 1, 1999, Durk Jager was installed as the CEO in charge of implementing the restructuring and despite some immediate acceleration in business performance the results deteriorated over the coming year. After P&G issued four profit warnings in two quarters and lost US$70 billion in market value, Durk Jager was forced to resign on June 8, 2000.

His successor, Alan G. Lafley, has since implemented the restructuring programme which in turn has been instrumental in getting P&G back on track. For the financial year 2008, P&G recorded net sales of US$83.5 billion up from US$40.0 billion in 2000, which represents a compounded annual growth rate of approximately 8.5%.[13] The plan to simplify the structure of P&G has become a success.

The case of P&G shows that organizations can grow too complex and by doing so stimulate bureaucracy as the former global matrix structure of P&G did. In order to curb this effect, P&G

embarked on a restructuring programme which eventually proved successful.

As illustrated by the three examples of Naturhouse, Saxo Bank and P&G the structure can become a strategy in itself or serve as valuable input to a strategy. Naturhouse purposefully pursued a franchise concept aimed at young professionals as an alternative to paid employment for them. Saxo Bank's focus on technology and their structure to support this allowed them to develop their online trading platform to such a level that it could be offered as a white label partner solution, thereby successfully exploiting what is traditionally termed a channel conflict. A channel conflict that resulted in subsequent high growth for Saxo Bank which in turn led to a structure that became too complex.

For more than a century P&G developed their structure to become increasingly complex, leading to the company becoming increasingly risk-averse thus missing market opportunities that more agile competitors were quick to act upon. By reducing the complexity, P&G managed to turn this around.

Given this, structure should be seen as an important factor that can influence not only the strategy but also the X-factor of a given company. Thus structure becomes more than just a product of strategy as argued by traditional wisdom. It becomes a part of the strategy and thus contrasts with convention, as shown in Table 9.1.

The Search for Valuable Values

Value in today's world of business can be broadly categorized into two different categories. Those values that are quantitative by nature and those that have a more qualitative element.

Table 9.1 **Conventional wisdom versus structure as the backbone**

Conventional wisdom	Structure as the back bone
Structure follows strategy	Structure becomes the strategy
	Structure drives strategy

The first of these categories are common to all businesses as they relate to economic value generated by the company, i.e. for listed companies the focus has been, and still is, on shareholder value. The short-term focus of the stock markets and analyst has historically driven the concept of shareholder to the forefront of CEO's agendas whereas creating value for employees, customers and communities has taken a back seat.

This latter set of values, those characterized by a qualitative nature, is gaining more importance in the ever more dynamic marketplaces of today.

> *The only thing that works is management by values. Find people who are competent and really bright, but more importantly, people who care exactly about the same things you care about.*[14]
>
> (Steve Jobs, CEO of Apple)

The above quote illustrates the growing importance that some companies place on those values that do not immediately lend themselves to be quantified and measured in annual reports but however can have a significant impact on the performance of a company. In the book "Authentic Leadership" the former CEO and Chairman of Medtronic, Bill George, discusses the importance of among other things practising solid values. The subtitle of the book therefore is "Rediscovering the Secrets to Creating Lasting Value" (in the economic sense).

In the book "Leading through Values: Linking Company Culture to Business Strategy" (2006),[15] the authors argue that a shift in management focus has occurred over the past century leading to different management philosophies. They list the three management philosophies of (1) Management By Instruction, (2) Management By Objectives and finally (3) Leading Through Values as those overarching management philosophies that have emerged in response to the changing dynamics of the work environment and marketplace. This evolution is illustrated in Figure 9.2.

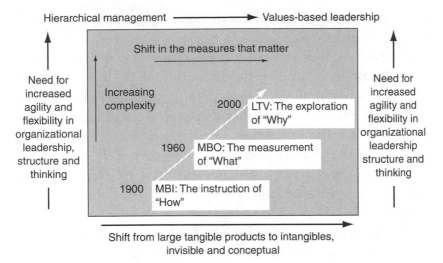

Figure 9.2 **The advent of values-based leadership** (*source:* Henderson *et al.*
(2006) "Leading through Values: Linking company culture to
business strategy". HarperBusiness, p. 43).

Having gone through the stages of "How" to perform a given
task and "What" to perform, today's employees are increasingly
considering "Why" they actually perform a given task, "Why"
is it they work for a particular employer and "Why" is the
company doing what it does. With this in mind the shared
values of a company become interdependent with the strategy
of same and as such of significant importance. In essence the
key driver is the question of sense-making and whether the tasks
and values make sense for the people involved in the
execution.

Externally Focused Values

As described earlier in this chapter, the success of Saxo Bank
has rested heavily on a shared set of values among its employees.
Although the seven values of Saxo Bank were not formalized
until 2005, the liberal values of the two founders and their
beliefs were effectively communicated throughout the organization by the two founders from the very beginning. With the
growth of Saxo Bank it became impossible for the two founders

to reach every single employee leading to the formalization of the corporate values.

The seven values of Saxo Bank – rationality, independence, integrity, honesty, justice, productivity and pride – are more than just words to fill out the corporate statement. They are the very way of life for the two founders and as such also expected to be that for the employees of the company. At Saxo Bank focus is on the performance of the employees. If you do not perform you are fired, if you perform well you are rewarded well and if you perform exceptionally you are rewarded exceptionally.

This focus can be traced back to the beliefs and values of the two founders, who advocate for a liberalistic society in which they believe the individual, when given the chance, will contribute excessively. Individualized value-based management is often considered a much stronger tool than some of current management tools, such as balanced score card and TQM. Even under a high growth scenario, Saxo has proved that they can retain a very homogeneous culture with core values matching those of the founders.

A similar performance-oriented culture and associated set of values can be found in General Electric. The values of GE were considered so important to the company that former CEO, Jack Welch, had these inscribed on small wallet-size cards that were distributed to all employees.

> *There isn't a human being in GE that wouldn't have the Values Guide with them. In their wallet, in their purse. It means everything and we live it. And we remove people who don't have those values, even when they post great results.*[16]

This statement illustrates the increasing importance of values in the modern business world. Not only must companies cater to those values that are shared by its employees, but employees are also judged against how they live according to those values. It is no longer just a matter of creating financial results.

The GE values that lie at the core of the company dictate that: "All of General Electric employees, always with unyielding integrity are:

- passionately focused on driving customer success,
- live Six Sigma Quality,
- insist on excellence and are intolerant of bureaucracy,
- act in a boundaryless fashion,
- prize global intellectual capital and the people that build it,
- see change for growth opportunities,
- create a clear, simple customer-centred vision,
- create an environment of "stretch", excitement, informality and trust ... reward improvements ... and celebrate results, and finally
- demonstrate, always with infectious enthusiasm for the customer the "4 E's" of General Electric leadership."

The "4 E's" are described as: "the personal Energy to welcome and deal speed of change, the ability to create an atmosphere that Energizes others, the Edge to make difficult decisions, and the ability to consistently Execute".[17]

Both Saxo Bank and General Electric have developed corporate values that are authentic to how these companies are managed and which are followed and even evangelized by the management of both companies. This is believed by both companies to constitute a vital factor of the success they have experienced.

Whereas the corporate values of both Saxo Bank and General Electric can be argued to revolve around what can be termed business-oriented factors focusing on the external environment and customers, other companies develop and implement values that are more internally focused. Two such companies are Apple and Google.

Internally Focused Values

Apple is by many credited with putting Silicon Valley on the map as well as creating the hard-working yet corporate-casual environment that characterizes many of the companies placed there.

One early example of the culture and values that have become characteristic of Apple is traced back to an off-site retreat the company held in Carmel in 1983. During this retreat, Steve Jobs offered three sayings intended to inspire the team and address the feeling that Apple was getting too large and bureaucratic. At this point approximately 80 people were employed by Apple. The three sayings were: (1) Real artist ship, (2) it's better to be a pirate than join the navy and (3) Mac in a book by 1986.

Inspired by the second of these remarks, programmers Steve Capps and Susan Kare made a pirate flag depicting a Jolly Roger (skull and crossbones) with an Apple rainbow coloured eye-patch with intent to hoist the pirate flag above the new Macintosh building that the company was moving into. Their mission was successful, leading to the pirate flag flying high over the building to greet the employees early on Monday morning after the retreat.

The Apple culture of today is characterized by its casual, relaxed and collegial environment as well as an intense work ethic. Apple workplace surveys often mention these characteristics in combination with the ability to embark on challenging projects. When Steve Jobs took over as interim CEO in the fall of 1997, he was known for walking around the Apple campus barefoot in cut-off shorts and a black shirt. His commitment to the casual dress code extended to executive meetings with external partners as he reportedly showed up barefoot to meetings with Microsoft executives.[18]

In 2008, Apple secured the top spot in the Fortune survey "America's Most Admired Companies". An achievement which is partly due to the culture and values of the company as well as the vision of Steve Jobs who has headed the remarkable turna-round of Apple from his return in 1997 to present day.

While Apple may be America's most admired company in 2008, according to Fortune, Google secured the top spot in the Fortune survey "100 Best Companies To Work For" for the second year in a row. This achievement is explained by the fast growth of Google and the fact that 99% of its employees hold stock option plans, the perks employees enjoy which include free meals, swimming, spa and free doctors onsite and finally the unique culture of Google.

The culture of Google, which is compared with that of a col-lege campus, rests on the ten things that Google has found to be true, its values, and a sense of pairing work with fun. The ten values are in the order they appear on Google's homepage: (1) focus on the user and all else will follow, (2) it's best to do one thing really, really well, (3) fast is better than slow, (4) demo-cracy on the web works, (5) you don't need to be at your desk to need an answer, (6) you can make money without doing evil, (7) there's always more information out there, (8) the need for information crosses all borders, (9) you can be serious without a suit, and 10) great just isn't good enough.

These values have all been instrumental in shaping Google to become what was stated in the first two sentences of the found-ers' letter that was distributed to prospective Google sharehold-ers before the company's 2004 IPO: "*Google is not a conventional company. We do not intend to become one.*"[19]

The authentic values of Google, Apple, General Electric and Saxo Bank have all played a vital part in their success and developed the notion of values from being primarily focused on finance to cover a broader spectrum.

By adopting a set of authentic and clearly defined values, a company can successfully brand itself to current and potential employees. When these values are aligned with the strategy of the company, it will render the communication of an organiza-tion's shared purpose and goals easier to understand, thus cre-ating a common sense of why they exist and why people should spend their time at this particular organization. Values-based leadership founded on authentic values thus takes the form of a longer term perspective as opposed to the more traditional short-term financial values that are still central to many companies' value statement as illustrated in Table 9.2.

Table 9.2 **Conventional wisdom versus values-based approach**

Conventional wisdom	Values-based approach
Focus on solely maximizing shareholder value	Focus on authentic values
Short-term perspective	Long-term perspective

Culture as the Binding Glue

Professor Edgar H. Schein from MIT Sloan School of Management, who is accredited with inventing the term corporate culture, describes organizational culture as:

the basic tacit assumptions about how the world is and ought to be that a group of people share and that determines their perceptions, thoughts, feelings, and, their overt behaviour.[20]

Furthermore, he identifies three distinct levels in organizational cultures which are: (1) artefacts, (2) espoused values and (3) basic assumptions and values. Artefacts in this framework are found at the surface and consist of, for example, visual organizational structures and processes, whereas the next level of espoused values relate to conscious strategies, goals and philosophies. The third level, the basic assumptions and values, are at the core of the culture and represented by underlying assumptions and values that exist at a largely unconscious level but provide an understanding of why things happen the way they do.

Given this, the culture of a given company forms the glue that binds organizational structure and values together with strategy and goals. With this in mind the culture becomes of great importance to a company.

Customer Service Culture

Since it was founded, Southwest Airlines has placed their culture at the centre of their business model and has developed this to a level where both employees and customers speak highly of the Southwest Airlines culture.

Southwest's Culture is what has set us apart from other airlines and companies since our start in 1971.[21]

A large part of Southwest Airlines' culture, which is known as informal, cheerful and fun-loving yet hard working, rests on living according to the Southwest way and its three main principles. These principles are known as: (1) The Warrior Spirit, (2) A Servant's Heart and (3) Fun-LUVing Attitude. The Warrior Spirit is characterized by attributes such as hard working, the desire to be the best, to persevere, and to innovate, whereas the Servant's Heart includes attributes such as to treat others with respect, to put others first, be egalitarian and to demonstrate proactive customer services. The Fun-LUVing attitude stresses the importance of having fun, not to take yourself too seriously, to celebrate success and to enjoy your work.

In addition to these principles, the Southwest culture emphasizes employees as the company's first customer and passengers as the second.[22] This is formally reflected by the company's mission statement, which was adopted in 1980 and includes a statement pertaining to the employees.

The mission of Southwest Airlines is dedication to the highest quality of Customer Service delivered with a sense of warmth, friendliness, individual pride, and Company Spirit.

We are committed to provide our employees a stable work environment with equal opportunity for learning and personal growth. Creativity and innovation are encouraged for improving the effectiveness of Southwest Airlines. Above all, employees will be provided the same concern, respect, and caring attitude within the organization that they are expected to share externally with every Southwest customer.[23]

Southwest Airlines has managed to create a culture of shared goals and values in which the employees, referred to as people by CEO Herb Kelleher, live by the Southwest Way and its three principles. Principles which have led to the extraordinary customer service levels of Southwest Airlines and the extent employees go to in order to please its customers. Examples of this include driving customers to their destinations when they have missed their flights, have customers stay at their home when they were undergoing medical treatment in an unfamiliar city and taking care of a customer's pet when they had no other alternatives.[24]

The culture of Southwest Airlines is indeed the glue that binds the structure, values and strategy of the company together in order to achieve its success. It is a culture that focuses on its own employees as much, or even more, as it does on the customers of the company and as such differs from many traditional cultures in which the focus is on customers and shareholders. It is a culture of 360 degrees service.

Another company which has created a service-based culture is Disney. At Disney customers are not just customers, they are guests, employees at Disney are not employees but cast members performing roles as opposed to job functions.

As described in Chapter 6, the customer attitudes, the notion of serving the needs of guests rather than customers is at the very core of how Disney perceives their customers but is also central to the Disney culture. At Disney theme parks quality service is defined as those behaviours the cast members exhibit in the presence of guests. Behaviours that add up to the personal touch which include smiling, making eye contact and using pleasant language.

The culture of Disney is based on the notion that they are in show business, something which is communicated to every cast member who is not hired for a job but rather cast for a role in the Disney show. Members of the Disney cast do not wear uniforms but costumes and play before an audience rather than serving the needs of customer. When cast members are facing guests, or are in a guest environment, they are perceived to be onstage, whereas the environment not facing guests is labelled backstage.

Thus, the culture of Disney is not merely to produce a service but rather to stage a play for its guests. A play which follows a strict script as mentioned in Chapter 6, and where the cast members must learn to play on and off stage.

The show business culture of Disney characterized by its focus on superior customer service has been through its ups and downs. Whereas the guests of Disney have continuously gained lovable memories of lovable characters and fun as well as a high degree of customer service, Disney itself experienced a period of lesser fun.

While the former CEO of Disney, Michael Eisner, was in charge a culture of control emerged in which unit heads were reluctant or unable to make decisions thus hampering Disney's ability to manoeuvre in the changing market. Disney became a centrally managed company with increasing levels of bureaucracy and declining trust. Despite recording remarkable results while in charge, Eisner was slowly causing the fun to evaporate from the Disney culture.

This led Roy Disney, the nephew of Walt Disney, to establish the web site SaveDisney.com with the aim of ousting Eisner and his supporters in order to revamp the company. Roy Disney criticized Eisner for mismanaging the company and instilling a corporate mentality in the executive structure that turned the Walt Disney Company into a "rapacious, soul-less" company.[25] On March 13, 2005, after more than a year of public pressure from the Save Disney campaign, it was announced that Robert A. Iger would replace Eisner as CEO.

One of Iger's first moves as the CEO of Disney was to reassign Peter Murphy as the company's chief strategic officer, and to disband the company's strategic planning division that was created by Eisner but charged by many inside and outside the company with stifling creativity under a superfluous layer of bureaucracy.

The assignment of Iger as the CEO of Disney signalled a change in the culture of Disney that has resulted in a higher degree of risk taking, management by consensus, delegation of more responsibility and less bureaucracy allowing Disney to react quicker to the wishes of its guests. It has also brought the fun back to the employees and cast members in a company where customer service is a central element of its culture. Culture is not a given factor but must be nurtured to develop into a competitive advantage as the case of Disney illustrates.

The Go-go Culture

In the book "Discount Business Strategy" (Andersen & Poulfelt, 2006), the go-go culture is introduced as an important part of the discount, or disruptive strategy. It is described as a young and efficient culture where employees can join to fight lazy competitors. It is a culture characterized by the pizza and coke environment, the focus on technology, company parties and a life style where getting the job done even during unusual hours counts more than the "let's do it tomorrow"-culture present at many incumbents.[26]

Such a go-go culture is at the heart of Ryanair and the success they have achieved in the European market for airline passenger traffic. The focus on low costs is central to the culture of Ryanair and expressed by the fact that employees are even encouraged to bring pens from home.

The job responsibilities of personnel at Ryanair cover multiple areas where, for example, the same employee will see to ticketing, boarding and in-flight services leading to higher efficiency and thus lower costs. The compensation schemes also reflect the focus on low costs as most of the employees are paid based on productivity.

However, it is not only low cost that characterizes the culture of Ryanair as the company's war with the establishment is also an integral part of the culture. A war that Ryanair has waged since they adopted their "low cost – no frills" strategy in 1991 and which has led to many public battles between the company and what they call the establishment. The employees of Ryanair identify with this stance in the market and are therefore willing to go the extra mile in getting the job done.

The go-go culture of Ryanair is different to the culture of Southwest given that Ryanair places little focus on the fun aspect of working or going the extra mile for the customer, but instead a keen focus on beating the incumbents on providing the cheapest fare possible. The customer service is also different given that Ryanair focuses on specific service parameters such as on-time departures rather than personal service.

Ryanair has achieved significant success by devising a cultural formula that drives the company to continuously lead the price war and execute their discount business model with significant success.

As is the case with Ryanair, Google is also characterized by having a go-go culture. The go-go culture of Google is however different to that of Ryanair given that a large emphasis is placed on the employees and the benefits of these.

The similarities between the go-go culture of Google and Ryanair lie in the hard working nature of the employees and their willingness to go the extra mile in order to get the job done even if this means long nights with pizza and coke. Pizza and coke may not be needed at Google as the employees at the Googleplex in Silicon Valley are offered three free meals a day at the company's restaurant. This is but one of many benefits that employees enjoy at Google. As described earlier in this chapter, Google does not perceive itself as a conventional company. In fact they go to great lengths to foster a culture that supports the unconventional.

At the Googleplex, which resembles a large university campus as opposed to a corporate headquarters, each bathroom stall holds a Japanese high-tech commode with a heated seat and on the inside of each stall is a quiz that asks technical questions about testing programming code for bugs. This quiz changes weekly.[27] Along the interior walls of the Googleplex, large whiteboards are strung together on which employees write random thoughts and ideas and all engineers are given 20% of their time to work on their own ideas and projects. Many of these projects have resulted in public offerings such as the social networking web site Orkut and Google News.

In addition to challenging its employees to innovate and pampering them with a host of benefits, which will be described in the following section, the go-go culture of Google has a strong element of "anything goes". This element of the Google culture is best captured by the words of Richard Holden, product management director for Googles's AdWords service, who states that:

If you're not failing enough, you're not trying hard enough.[28]

At Google they have created the position of a "Chief Cultural Officer" who is tasked with retaining the company's unique culture and keeping the employees, or Googlers as they are known, happy. One way to ensure this is to constantly find ways to maintain and enhance and develop the Google culture while keeping the core values the company began with – a flat organization, a lack of hierarchy and a collaborative environment.[29]

There is little doubt that the culture of Google is considered unique and stands in contrast to that of more conventional companies, but what is more interesting is that this culture, the Googley culture, is a highly competitive advantage for a company that seeks to constantly innovate and develop products: It is a culture that is fundamental to the positioning of the company in the X-factor universe.

As illustrated by the examples of Huawei, Southwest Airlines, Disney, Ryanair, Apple and Google, culture becomes a vital ingredient of the organizational design as this acts as the glue that binds the values of a given company to the strategy. Despite the fact that the above-mentioned companies all have their own culture that differs widely, they have all managed to instil a culture that drives the strategy and allows this to develop. A culture which is furthermore characterized by its extreme nature, employees at Southwest Airlines go to extreme lengths to serve their customers, at Disney employees perform for their customers, at Ryanair all employees are obsessed with costs and getting the job done in order to provide their customers with the cheapest possible flight.

Google fosters an innovative spirit by embracing a culture of risk taking and providing their employees with benefits and even free time to work on projects of their own choosing. And at Huawei they have developed the "wolf pack" culture. Culture is indeed the binding glue of these companies and something which they deliberately work with in order to utilize the organizational design.

People – The Real Gasoline

"It's all about people" is a frequently heard expression. Without people companies would not be able to produce their products or services and as such people, and particularly talented people, are essential in order to become successful. In 2000, McKinsey published an update to a 1997 survey among 77 companies from different industries to investigate the problems facing organizations in attracting talent.[30] Some of the findings from this research were:

- 75% of corporate officers surveyed said their companies had "insufficient talent sometimes" or were "chronically talent-short" across the board,
- 89% of the surveyed executives found it difficult to attract highly talented people,
- 90% of the surveyed executives found it difficult to retain all their high performers.

In addition to these findings the survey points to the fact that while the executive population is growing, the supply of talent measured by the number of 35 to 44 year olds is moving in the opposite direction.

Such findings illustrate the point that people are not just the real gasoline of the company but also a scarce resource that must be fought hard for in the marketplace of today. With this in mind, people constitute another important source of competition and one which was already in the minds of executives at the time of the original McKinsey survey published in 1998.

At the end of the day, we bet on people, not strategies.
(Larry Bossidy, former CEO of Allied Signal)

The first non-founding employee of Yahoo, Tim Brady, is a good example of the importance people can have on an organization. Having met Jerry Yang, one of the founders of Yahoo, at Stanford, Tim Brady was contacted at the end of 1994 by Jerry Yang who asked whether he would be interested in "...*doing some moonlighting after school*".[31] Shortly after, he became the first employee of Yahoo and spent eight years with the company as the Vice President of production effectively being the editor of Yahoo's site. The success of the Yahoo portal, which is argued to have won the portal wars, is largely a result of Tim Brady.

Despite not being the first employee but instead the 23rd, Paul Buchheit also had a significant impact on the organization in which he worked. Buchheit is credited with creating Google's web-based email system Gmail as well as coining the company's famous motto, "Don't be evil". In 1996, Buchheit began work on a little novel project characterized as a mix between a side project of his own and a project commissioned by Google, which became the email service of Google.

These are but two examples out of many in which the people of an organization have contributed to its success and illustrate the importance of recognizing the people as not just a resource but one which potentially holds the key to increased competitive advantage and as such the embedded X-factor of a company.

The People Design

In order for a company to fuel the organization with the gasoline that is made up of people these need to be attracted to the company and retained. In addition to this, the talents of the employees must be harnessed and leveraged in order for the organization to develop a potential competitive advantage. Lastly, the company must also be able to optimize its people resources by identifying those who do not perform to the desired levels nor fit the values and culture. These factors are what constitute the people design and as such the questions which become of great importance in terms of this are:

How do successful companies apply the people design to attract and retain talented people? How do they leverage these? How do they optimize the talent pool of their organization?

At Saxo Bank, three groups of stakeholders to whom the company exists and has significance are identified and included in the corporate statement. These three are: (1) Shareholders, (2) Employees and (3) Clients and Partners. Of these three, the employees are viewed by Saxo Bank as those that the company has the largest opportunity to influence, develop and not least to motivate. As such the role of Saxo Bank in terms of their employees is cited in the corporate statement as:

To motivate, challenge, fulfil and reward employees, and enable them to develop and excel in their professional careers and reach their personal goals.

This is highly aligned with the external and performance-based values of the company, which state that talented employees are rewarded whereas non-performers are released. A combination which is considered attractive to many professionals who thrive in performance-oriented organizations that seek to constantly optimize their pool of people resources. In a 2007 survey conducted by Universum,[32] a global leader in employer branding, Saxo Bank was among the top 25 companies that students in Denmark with a financial or economic focus mentioned as the employer they would like to work for.

The success of Saxo Bank plays no little part in this but the clearly communicated values and their performance oriented culture, which allows for graduates to quickly progress up the career ladder, as well as competitive compensation packages are of equal importance. Together these factors form the basis of how Saxo Bank manages to attract the talent of the future. Saxo Bank's ability to retain the talented people is, according to co-founder and co-CEO Lars Seier Christensen, due to the culture of the company and the fact that employees are proud to be a part of Saxo Bank. Aside from the formalized values that are apparent from the corporate statement, the tradition of celebrating success and having fun are mentioned as key factors in retaining talent. As Lars Seier Christensen notes: "*Saxo Bank parties are something very special*".[33]

With a formalized system of developing talent from the inside that was implemented in 2006, Saxo Bank seeks to leverage the talent by working with a model based upon six principles. These principles state, among others, that external recruitment is done primarily for entry level positions, that the potential of a person equals their future level of competence, that development mainly happens on the job and that the manager sees to the development of the employees. Given this, a very conscious effort is put into leveraging the talent of the company which is paired with an equally conscious effort to constantly optimize the talent pool.

Heavily inspired by Jack Welch, Saxo Bank carries out performance reviews on a regular basis during which the below average performers are identified and subsequently released in order to make way for hopefully new and better talent. As mentioned in the beginning of this chapter, Saxo Bank compares this to the mentality that is found within elite sports where underperformers are swiftly removed in order for the team to raise their performance. Moreover, discontinuation also takes place if there is a lack of alignment between the values of Saxo Bank and the employee.

In China, on the other side of the globe from Saxo Bank's headquarters, Huawei is considered the place to be for many young and ambitious men and women. This is also attributed to the success of the company, but their wolf culture, which focuses on collectivism and a sense of patriotism, plays an equal part in this. The fact that the company's headquarter in Shenzhen is often compared with the headquarters of Google, the Googleplex, owing to a similar feel of a university campus, also act as a factor of attraction for many young Chinese engineers.

Huawei also work with a highly competitive compensation scheme in which employees are rewarded on the basis of their performances allowing talented people to earn significantly more than they could elsewhere. In conjunction with this, a formalized career development model is implemented which caters for both the development of management and professional talent. Such systems allow Huawei to not only retain the talented people once they are hired but also to leverage their talent by offering progressive career development which is supported by formalized training programmes. With specific regard to training, Huawei view itself as a self-training organization due to their in-house developed online training and self-evaluation system, which is used by its entire staff worldwide.[34] This acts as another method for identifying and leveraging talent across the globe while maintaining the ability to instil the corporate values and culture into its potential and coming leaders.

Despite the fact that Huawei has a completely different set of values to those of Saxo Bank and General Electric, they also conduct regular performance reviews of their employees in an attempt to optimize the talent pool.

Although at opposite ends of the world and with widely differing cultures, it is interesting to see that Saxo Bank and Huawei are putting such an emphasis on the real gasoline of the company – its people. In many ways both companies use similar tactics such as branding itself according to its values thus attracting the people that will fit the culture, allowing for progressive career development based on performance and rewarding according to performance.

The fact that people can provide companies with an X-factor should be of little surprise given that the very definition is centred on a special quality or particular talent. However, to consciously focus on identifying and developing this is what companies must strive to do in order to tap into the potential that the real gasoline of a company holds and unleash the X-factor that may rest within its people. How to organize, inspire and free the potential of the people on board is a major challenge for entering and remaining in the X-factor universe.

The Organizational Design and Its Impact

The previous sections and their main characteristics are summarized in Table 9.3. These organizational factors have all been instrumental in the success of the companies described in this chapter albeit with some companies focusing more on certain factors over others.

Table 9.3 **The impact on organizational design**

Structure as the backbone	Values as a heart	Cultural glue that binds	People – the real gasoline
Structure as part of strategy not a result	Authentic values	Value-centred culture	People and passion
Structure as the driver	Long-term values explain why	Culture is aligned with strategy	People and performance incentives

Naturhouse and their franchise business model is utilizing the structure as a key success driver and as such goes against the traditional view which argues that structure follows strategy. Saxo Bank and P&G found their structures were hindering the Return on Strategy due to their growing complexity and as such also focus on the structure as a key success driver.

All the cases are working with their values emphasizing the authenticity of these as well as their alignment to strategy. They recognize that leading by values can provide for a shared understanding among the people employed and as such a clearer picture of what must be achieved. Whereas companies such as Saxo Bank and General Electric base their values on external factors pertaining to the competitive environment, the likes of Google and Apple are working with values of a more internal character focusing on the employees. Despite this approach being markedly different, the fact that the companies are all utilizing values as a key success driver is what can be argued unconventional as traditional companies do little to actively use values.

In terms of culture, the cases also display widely different approaches. Disney and Southwest Airlines have developed a customer service culture in which the employees will go the extra mile for their clients. The go-go culture is characteristic of Ryanair, Google and Apple albeit with differing characteristics given that the culture of Ryanair focuses on beating the establishment whereas the culture of the latter two revolves on allowing the employees to innovate. The performance-centric culture is characteristic for both Saxo Bank and Huawei despite these companies being headquartered in opposite parts of the world and emphasizing an individual and collectivistic culture respectively.

In the process towards the X-factor universe, some of the important bearing points are:

- Structural alignment
- Value driven
- Unique culture
- People oriented.

Despite the different ways in which they utilize the organizational design as a key success driver to achieve a high Return on Strategy, they all place great emphasis on aligning the structure, the values, the culture and the people to their strategy.

There is a considerable difference between companies as to how much value they are able to drive out of the organizational design. Arguably, a number of the companies in the X-factor universe are able to craft an organizational design which is much more efficient and effective than placebo.

Indisputably companies like Saxo Bank, Ryanair, Google and Huawei are all able to drive unprecedented value out of their organizations, i.e. they design their organizations in ways which lead to a higher Return on Strategy. Based on a longitudinal study of Saxo Bank, it seems as if each and every element – structure (the backbone), values (the heart), culture (the glue) and the people (the real gasoline) – all contribute to the Return on Strategy.

However, this is not a static picture. To remain within the X-factor universe, companies need to respond dynamically to changing contingencies and also to foster internal dynamics in order to keep agile. With Saxo Bank this is visualized by the fact that they took the role as a disrupter at one stage but moved to the monopolistic positioning of the blue ocean. They are not resting on their laurels as they initiated a major restructuring in 2008 with the introduction of a new management and the lay-off of one-third of a highly profitable organization. Companies who wish to remain in the X-factor universe are constantly in the mode of organizational change. Change becomes the engine of developing rather than merely a means to handle unpopular decisions.

10

SPINNING THE
TECHNOLOGICAL CHAIN

Anyone in the room could buy the same hardware that Google uses at Fry's Electronics.

Stephen E. Arnold[1]

For those not familiar with Fry's Electronics, it is an American chain of large retail stores offering software, consumer electronics, household appliances and computer hardware. This example illustrates that there are other ways to gain success in the X-factor universe than to overinvest in technology or move into the space of technological exuberance.

Taking all together, four different denominators characterize the technology chain, namely technology that is proven, scalable and standardized, simple and groundbreaking. However, before moving into the details of these key characteristics, the technology chain at Google is worth considering.

When Google was still in its infancy, the founders had to figure out how to extract enough computing power out of everyday computers to make their search algorithm run. Given this, the company's use of commodity hardware has been instrumental since it was founded in the late 1990s. This approach stands in stark contrast to that used by its competitors that make use of branded hardware from, for example, IBM, Sun Microsystems and Hewlett-Packard and has allowed Google to drastically reduce the costs associated with hardware. In addition to this, the operating systems used by Google are a combination of

Unix and Microsoft operating systems to which Linux and open source components are added. In order to maximize the performance of commodity hardware and reduce failures, Google developed software that could perform the specific task needed when hardware devices fail.

This combination of commodity low-cost hardware and in-house developed software has led to some significant characteristics for the technology behind Google. The Google data centres come online automatically and, under the direction of the Google File System, get work from other data centres. The computers placed in these facilities find one another and configure themselves with little or no human intervention. Each Google server comes in a standard case know as a "Pizza box", where the plugs and ports are placed at the front in order to make access faster and easier. The Google racks that hold the servers are assembled so that they hold servers on both the front and back side which allows for a standard rack to hold 80 compared with the normal 40. Each data centre, rack and server works in a fashion similar to "Plug-and-play" meaning that the network of data centres recognize when more resources have been connected allowing for these to go into operation without human intervention. Given this a Google data centre can get online in as little as 72 hours in comparison with more typical data centres that require a week or even longer for additional resources to get online.

The technology behind Google is a match between proven low-cost commodity hardware and in-house developed software that not only seeks to maximize performance and reduce failure but also allows for scalability. Add to this the patented search algorithm PageRank that was initially developed by the two founders and the technology of Google has elements of not only using proven technology that can scale to the growing needs but also that of technology that breaks new ground.

Perhaps the most significant feature of the technology behind Google is that it utilizes competencies in not only hardware engineering or software engineering but both. The technology chain is, given this, approached by Google from both a bits and bytes view and a soldering iron and screwdriver angle.[2] This is illustrated in Figure 10.1. This dual technological focus is aimed at using proven commodity hardware and develops company-specific software, based on readily available software in order to reduce cost, maximize performance and allow for scalability.

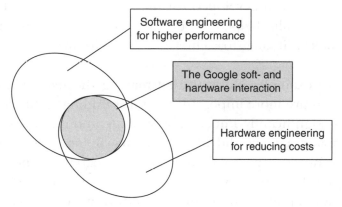

Figure 10.1 **Google's fusion of hard- and software** (*source:* adapted from "The Google Legacy", p. 58).

Google approached the technology in an unconventional and very talented manner. A talent which has led to the unique simultaneous utilization of commodity hardware and software development needed to power the PageRank algorithm and successfully grow at the rate of Google. In this way, they managed to utilize technology in an unconventional manner to gain a higher Return on the company's Strategy. Something which is typical for companies in the X-factor universe.

Skype is another example of a company that used existing technology with considerable success. Based on the software developed for the file-sharing service KaZaA, Skype uses a proprietary Internet telephony network. This operates on a peer-to-peer model which is different from more common client-server models.

With a completely decentralized user directory that is distributed among the nodes of the network, in this case the users' computers, the Skype model allows for easy scalability without the costs associated with a complex centralized infrastructure.[3] Skype, thus utilized an existing technology as the platform for their development of peer-to-peer telephony. A technology that was proven and allowed for high scalability became the starting point for the success of the company rather than a new and groundbreaking innovation. The ability of the two Skype founders to use a platform developed for file sharing to make Internet telephone calls helped them to utilize technology and out-of-the-box thinking to achieve a high Return on their Strategy.

These two examples illustrate that making the *right* technology decisions are more important than just finding technology as this can significantly impact the strategy and success of a given company. Google did not spend heavily on customized hard- or software to power their PageRank search engine but instead opted for a proven, scalable approach that allowed for in-house developments to optimize performance as well as costs. Skype used an already developed technological platform to offer their peer-to-peer telephony and gain success. A company's ability to approach technology in unconventional manners thereby driving an excess Return on Strategy helps such a company move into the X-factor universe.

Technology in a Broad Sense

When talking about the technology of a given company it is important that this is viewed in broad terms and not just the hardware and software that goes into producing the products or services offered but also how this can be used to drive the strategy of a company or even alter this. Furthermore, technology encompasses more than manufacturing technology as it also relates to the entire infrastructure of the company and their back office systems as well as production.

Some companies that have approached the technological chain in unconventional ways, thus utilizing their capacity for thinking differently – out-of-the-box thinking – and have managed to deploy their talent for doing so include Saxo Bank, Ryanair, Dell, Samsung, Apple and Google.

A Full Chain of Technology

When Saxo Bank changed their strategic focus from that of a traditional broker to that of an online broker, technology became a central factor in the development and execution of this. By developing the proprietary online trading platform, SaxoTrader, Saxo Bank effectively began their online strategic journey at the customer end of the supply chain. In asking what tools were needed for the tech savvy customer to place their investments in foreign exchange directly, Saxo Bank changed their focus on technology to also include the customer user interface as well as the back office systems and that used by suppliers of, for example, liquidity. In effect they began to view technology as a vital thread that integrated the entire value chain from suppliers to customers rather than a factor only relevant for the company's own value chain.

In doing so Saxo Bank developed their technological infrastructure to facilitate straight through processing (STP), allowing for an investor to place an order through the online platform that would immediately be routed through the system of Saxo Bank without human interference. When an order is placed, the system automatically sees to it that the investor's balance is checked and updated, that the trade is logged in the back office system and that the trade is executed with liquidity providers, brokers or online exchanges. A highly simplified illustration of this complex process is shown in Figure 10.2.

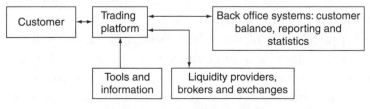

Figure 10.2 **The technology chain of Saxo Bank.**

As such, Saxo Bank has successfully developed a technological chain that allow for customers to place their orders
directly, thus including the customer as a co-producer of the
service, while automatically placing the orders with suppliers
and updating the back office systems of the company. This technology supports the strategy of an online brokerage providing
high levels of service in terms of tools and information allowing
investors to make informed decisions while securing transparency via the straight-through-processing.

Given this, Saxo Bank has managed to use the technological
chain of the company to support their strategy of a facilitator, as
discussed in Chapter 8, by applying out-of-the-box thinking to
expand the technology beyond the company's own value chain.

A similar case is that of Dell which used the emergence of the
Internet to further develop their technological chain to support
and grow the initial strategy of selling directly to the customers.
In 1996, ten years after Dell was founded, the company
launched their web site www.dell.com as the first step to establish a direct link with their customers through the Internet.

Initially the web site was nothing more than a simple product
and price list, but within two years it was further developed to
support customers configuring and ordering computers directly
via the Internet. Soon additional features, such as online technical support, order status information and online software
download, were added to the web site in order to provide customers with a comprehensive online purchasing tool.

This online purchasing tool was developed to work with the
company's existing system in a seamless fashion allowing for
real-time pricing and order status. In addition to this the seamless nature also allowed for a more agile internal response to
the ever changing needs of customers.

At the supplier's end of the value chain, Dell developed the
secure extranet valuechain.dell.com, which connected the suppliers of Dell in order to automate the information flow from
the time a customer order was received to the shipment of
required materials to build the system for that particular order.

Due to this, Dell was able to process a vast amount of customer orders and translate these into component requirements in an automated and seamless fashion.

Dell's utilization of the technological chain as a further enhancement to their direct sales model created a fully integrated value chain effectively facilitating a three-way information partnership with suppliers and customers.[4] This unconventional utilization of the technology and Dell's ability to integrate the various players to execute their strategy is what constitutes the X-factor of Dell in terms of the technological chain.

While Saxo Bank also deployed unconventional use of technology as a tool to integrate suppliers and customers, they did so in order to execute their strategy of a facilitator, whereas Dell used a similar approach to eliminate the middleman and execute their direct sales model. This is a similar approach but applied to different industries, each with a different strategic goal.

In Ireland a company operating in another industry has also managed to utilize the technological chain to integrate their customers allowing for a further development of their strategy.

> *Travel agents are a bloody waste of time.*
> (Michael O'Leary, CEO of Ryanair)

As the above quote clearly illustrates, Ryanair made no secret of the fact that they were aggressively seeking to cut out the middleman in order to further reduce the costs associated with point-to-point air passenger travel in Europe. Having already used more traditional means, such as establishing their own call centres, in their fight to circumvent the high fees charged by travel agents, Ryanair launched their web site www.ryanair.com in 1999. This made it possible for the customer to book a flight directly through the web site without the assistance of a travel agent, which along with the introduction of ticket-less travelling allowed Ryanair to leapfrog its competitors and the traditional flag carriers.

Within a year of its launch, the web site accounted for approximately 60% of sales and within two years this figure grew to more than 90%. By providing customers with the tool to book their own tickets online, Ryanair included their customers in the production of the actual product. Customers became co-producers of the service, which provided the company with the ability to further reduce costs given that the value chain had been freed of "bloody travel agents".

The suppliers of Ryanair are largely made up of The Boeing Company given that no in-flight amenities are offered, eliminating the need for catering. As such it would make little sense for Ryanair to extend their use of technology to their suppliers as the company itself holds all the assets necessary to produce all the service of point-to-point travel, they supply the airlines used for carrying passengers to and from European destinations.

Saxo Bank, Ryanair and Dell have all deployed technology throughout their value chain to not only produce their products and services but also to include the customers in the production of same. Given this, they have all managed to utilize the notion of the customer as co-producer, also described as a prosumer in Chapter 6, while maximizing the impact of technology. Whereas Dell and Ryanair have aimed at eliminating the middleman, Saxo Bank has filled the very position of a middleman by facilitating the flow between online investors and, for example, liquidity providers.

While Ryanair focused mainly on including the customer through the deployment of unconventional technology, Saxo Bank and Dell have managed to fully integrate the value chain to also encompass suppliers.

Common for all these is that they have actively utilized the technology to implement a full chain to support the existing strategy, allowing for seamless operation throughout the value chain or large parts of this. This stands in some contrast to conventional wisdom where silos of technology supporting different steps in the value chain are often seen and where technology seldom crosses the boundaries to encompass external players. This difference is illustrated in Table 10.1.

Table 10.1 **Stand-alone technology versus integrated technology**

Stand-alone technology	Integrated technology
Silos of technology supporting either production, back office or front office	Seamless technology throughout the value chain

While all three cases of Saxo Bank, Dell and Ryanair broke new ground for how to utilize the technological chain in order to move beyond traditional thinking, they all did so in order to support a chosen strategy rather than to just do it for the sake of technology.

Technological Exuberance – Pouring Resources into the Deep Water

Within conventional wisdom it appears that investing heavily in technology is often tied to a high Return on a company's Strategy, which is underlined by the many statements that are made by companies to illustrate their use of the latest and greatest technology. This however can lead to technological exuberance, which is characterized by a company deploying technology that overshoots the performance demanded in the marketplace or even internally in the company.

Consider the case of Concorde which can be argued to have overshot the performance demanded in the market for airline passenger travel, with its ability to travel at supersonic speed. This focus on providing what was essentially only demanded by a very limited share of the market and the continued investment in maintaining a highly sophisticated airplane eventually led to the closure of the Anglo-French project. Concorde flew its last flight on November 23, 2003 ending a 27-year history of overshooting the market and technological exuberance.

While the case of Concorde may be unique owing to its high profile, many companies are caught by the notion that the latest and greatest technology will ultimately lead to success despite the fact that no proof of such a relationship has ever been given. Not even the recipes offered by Jim Collins or

Nohria *et al.* state that technology in itself is a guarantee of success.

Pursuing a technology-based strategy can, however, be tempting for many companies given the potential return picking the technology of the future holds. The cases of Microsoft, Cisco Systems and Sony that have all come out as global leaders on the back of technology-based strategies provide further temptation for those who wish to become the next global leader by investing heavily in the technology of the future. However, focusing on the "wrong" technology can cause the demise of even the most successful companies. The case of Digital Equipment Corporation illustrates this as their continued focus on mainframe computers led them to miss the opportunities within personal computers and eventually caused their downfall.

The bursting of the dot.com bubble in 2000 is further evidence that technology in itself is not a guarantee for success as this ended the idea that any company which could muster a presence on the Internet would be successful for that reason alone.

Rather than pouring resources into deep water in search of the technology of tomorrow, companies must approach the technological chain from a different angle. They must view technology as a factor that can lead to success if, and only if, it is deployed in ways that support the strategy or if it is justified by a demand in the market. In many cases this approach will advocate for the use of proven technology as the case of Google and their use of commodity hardware illustrates.

This is not to say that new technology cannot provide companies with a source of competitive advantage, as the cases of Saxo Bank, Dell and Ryanair and their use of the Internet demonstrate otherwise, but rather that the technological chain of a company must be utilized to identify the right technology and use this to support or further enhance the strategy of a company.

As such, success does not stem from the technology itself but the ability to identify which technology, new or proven, provides the best option for a company to achieve its goals.

The Choice and Utilization of Technology

As argued in the previous section, the choice and utilization of technology is of importance with regard to the success of a given company. When considering the impact the choice of technology can have on not only the production of a product or a service but also on the entire value chain of a given company, choosing or developing and utilizing the right technology becomes of great importance.

When Saxo Bank embarked on the development of their proprietary SaxoTrader online trading platform, technology became a vital part of their strategy, but not their entire strategy, as this was to offer individual investors a platform through which they could trade directly without the use of an intermediary. While continuously developing the trading platform to increasingly sophisticated levels, adding more products and services such as analytical tools and real-time information services, the strategy remained focused on offering individual investors the opportunity to place investments directly.

The efforts to integrate the entire value chain were equally in support of this strategy as straight-through-processing would allow for greater transparency and better spreads for the individual investor to trade upon. Technology was utilized to improve the offering rather than for the sake of technology. While breaking new ground and as such being viewed as an innovator by not just the customers, online investors, but also by the industry, Saxo Bank's development of technology and thus their utilization of the technology chain remained fully supportive of their initial strategy.

By the early 2000s however, the SaxoTrader platform became a product in its own right when Saxo Bank chose to revise their strategy and offer the platform as a white label product to other financial institutions looking to offer their customers the opportunity of online trading. A shift towards a more technology-based strategy occurred as a result of the company's continued focus on developing the technology to fit their strategy as opposed to developing the latest and greatest technology regardless of strategic fit.

Likewise when Dell developed their online sales channel they did so to support an already existing strategy that focused on selling directly to the customer at low prices by eliminating the middleman. This initial strategy was also at the centre of focus when Dell integrated their value chain to include customers and suppliers as the automated process allowed for further cost reductions, given the reduced inventory, and a better service as customers were presented with the latest pricing and quick delivery.

While Dell was breaking new ground and utilized the technological opportunities the Internet provided before others in the industry did, or arguably in any industry, it was done in order to support the initial business model of selling directly. This is perhaps best illustrated by the quote given below:

> Dell, the company, seems to have been born and evolved with an anticipation of the Internet age.[5]
>
> (Andrew S. Grove, former chairman and CEO of Intel Corporation)

However, it is not only the Internet that has been instrumental in certain companies' ability to utilize the technological chain to great advantage. When Ryanair decided upon a low-cost strategy they began a series of cost cutting exercises that included the harmonizing and scrutinizing of the fleet.

In the early 1990s, Ryanair initiated a move to shift their entire fleet to consist of the Boeing 737 aircraft only, allowing for cost savings on training of personnel and aircraft maintenance. In addition to these cost savings, the flexibility of the staff was increased as all routes were served by the same type of aircraft. This did not constitute a groundbreaking development of a new technology nor did it utilize an emerging technology, but instead it was a technological choice that rested on keeping things simple and opting for an aircraft that had a proven track record.

This combined with Ryanair's utilization of the Internet to offer online booking and ticket-less travel is an example of how a different approach to the technological chain has been taken by the company. While opting for a proven and simple technology for their aircrafts, new and groundbreaking online booking and ticket-less travel was implemented at the customer end of the value chain. This illustrates that finding the right technology and utilizing this also includes the ability to combine aspects of new and proven, simple and complex.

As described in the introduction to this chapter this approach is also characteristic of Google, given that they use proven technology in terms of their commodity hardware while developing new software that allows this hardware to perform at the level required. Other examples of companies that use proven technology and break new ground to manufacture their products are the cases of Apple and Samsung Electronics.

In the case of Apple, the majority of components used in their products can be characterized as proven technology, such as touch screen and MP3 player functionality. However, Apple manages to combine and package these in new and innovative ways while also seeking to integrate the value chain as is the case with iTunes where suppliers of downloadable music are a vital component of the success Apple has enjoyed for their iPod series of MP3 players. Given this, Apple utilizes the technological chain to draw on proven technology and their ability to offer innovative combinations of these.

For Samsung Electronics the situation can be characterized as the opposite of Apple as they innovated the production process for manufacturing semiconductors, a product which is considered highly standardized and thus not perceived as an innovative and groundbreaking product by the customers within the business-to-business (B2B) market.

As a response to the challenge of fitting four million cells onto a tiny 4Mbit chip, Samsung Electronics adopted the stacking technology which involved replacing the previously common one-level construction on the chip with a structure similar to that of an apartment building. This technology was also adopted by Matsushita, Fujitsu and Hitachi, whereas other competitors such as IBM, Toshiba and NEC went with another technology, known as trenching, which involved digging below the surface of the chip to create floors below where the cells could be placed.

Stacking proved to be the technology that came out on top, which resulted in Samsung Electronics catching up to the industry leaders. This, however, was not enough for Samsung Electronics as they wanted the number one spot in the industry. Given this, they decided to further innovate the manufacturing process by increasing the size of the wafers used to cut the chips to eight inches. The required technology for doing so was at the time far from being proven viable, but despite this Samsung Electronics invested heavily in order to master the new technology.

This investment paid off as Samsung Electronics gained the number one market share in the market for DRAM chips in 1992 and maintained this leadership for the following 13 years.[6] By investing heavily in this new technology, the company was able to successfully execute a strategy of dual advantage where the costs of manufacturing were kept at a minimum while the chips were manufactured to a high quality, thus allowing for higher margins when compared with the competition.

Samsung Electronics subsequently used the earnings and expertise from their semiconductor division to invest in other technology products such as liquid crystal displays (LCD), flash memory, hard drives and mobile phones.

As such, Samsung Electronics deployed groundbreaking technology to produce a highly standardized product, DRAM memory chips, for the B2B market. A strategy which can be argued to be technology based but which when analysed further was implemented on the back of a desire to harness the dual advantage of low-cost manufacturing to produce high quality products.

The above examples illustrate that technology comes in many shapes and forms and as such it is not the technology itself which is interesting but rather the ability to utilize this in ways that either support the strategy or allow for the strategy to develop.

What is equally interesting is that the application of ground-breaking technology does not necessarily correlate with an innovative product offering, just as proven technology cannot be equalled to a standardized product offering. This is illustrated in Figure 10.3.

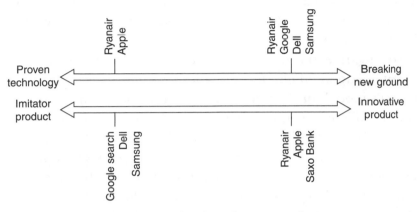

Figure 10.3 **Technology applied and product perception.**

The cases of Apple and Samsung Electronics illustrate that while Apple products are considered innovative these are in fact based on proven technology whereas the opposite is the case for Samsung Electronics.

In terms of Google and their PageRank search algorithm this did not translate into an innovative product as Internet search was known before Google was founded. Dell broke new ground for delivering computers but the Dell computer is not considered a groundbreaking product, whereas the online booking and ticket-less service of Ryanair can be argued to constitute a groundbreaking product when it was first introduced.

Given this, finding suitable technology and utilizing it to achieve the strategic goal of a company may not be as straight-forward as first believed, but instead presents a company with a complex jigsaw puzzle that can be pieced together in many different ways. The ability of a company to do so in an unconventional way is what constitutes the key success driver in terms of utilizing the technological chain.

The Technological Dilemma

The complexity that lies in finding and utilizing the right technology and how this can either support or drive strategy presents companies with a technological dilemma. When adding to this that the technology deployed by a company does not necessarily correlate to how a product is being perceived, the dilemma increases.

To illustrate the dilemma companies are faced with when deciding upon their technological profile, Clayton Christensen's model for disruptive innovation is used. This model, as shown in Figure 10.4, is developed to highlight how companies can overshoot the demand of the market when following a trajectory of sustaining innovations.[7] Often, companies may pursue disruptive innovations at a less sophisticated level than the most advanced level of groundbreaking technology. The performance that customers can utilize would as such become an indicator for the level of technology required to execute the chosen strategy with the range exemplifying the room in which companies can manoeuvre when deciding upon technology.

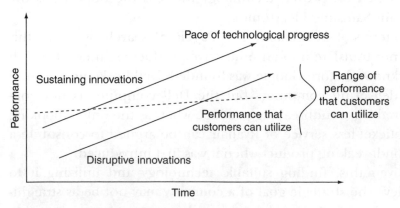

Figure 10.4 **The disruptive innovation model** (*source:* "The Innovators Solution", p. 33).

Arguably, the starting point for using this model to identify the technology profile would be the strategy range as this allows for a company to verify that they are in fact deploying technology which supports the strategy rather than implementing the latest and greatest without gaining a satisfactory Return on their Strategy. In the case of Ryanair, the harmonizing and scrutinizing of their fleet to consist of just one aircraft type can be used as an illustration of how a company reduces the performance, represented by latest aircraft type or variety of aircraft types, to match the strategy of a low-cost operator.

The emergence of the Internet and its use by Saxo Bank, Dell and Ryanair to offer new products/services or deliver these in new ways can likewise be compared with a disruptive innovation. Disruptive in a sense that it broke with the traditional sustained development of offering more personal service in the case of brokerages, offering more service at retail outlets in the case of computers and finally partnering with more travel agents to offer a better service when booking a ticket. The Internet allowed for a new technology trajectory to be formed which altered the technology profile of the company without colliding with its strategy.

However, the model fails to capture a company's ability to mix and match groundbreaking and proven technology as Google and Ryanair have done and to some extent Apple. In order to capture this, additional models must be used to determine the technology profile of a company within a given area. In the case of Google a model for determining the technology profile of their hardware could be applied, whereas a different model for the software would be necessary. Alternatively the vertical axis could be altered to cover other factors aside from just performance to capture what a given company is aiming to achieve with its technology profile.

As the cases discussed in this chapter illustrate, these factors differ among companies to some degree. However, common denominators can be identified which could prove useful when seeking to illustrate the desired technology profile of a given company through the adaption of the model of disruptive innovation.

The Denominators in the Technological Chain

The utilization of the technology chain hinges on proven technology, scalable technology, simple technology, groundbreaking technology or using technology to integrate the value chain. The ability to find the right match fitting their overall strategy supports a higher Return on Strategy.

Companies approach this from different angles with some companies, such as Ryanair, seeking simplicity in order to execute a strategy of low costs based on no frills, whereas Dell approached the technological chain from the angle of breaking new ground also to execute a strategy of low cost based on the direct sales model.

Similar to Dell, Samsung Electronics also broke new ground to innovate the production process of manufacturing semiconductors in the support of a low-cost strategy that was founded on economies of scale.

For companies such as Google and Skype, scalability is essential, which led Skype to purse a path of proven technology by using an existing platform to develop its peer-to-peer telephony, whereas Google deploy a mix of proven commodity hardware and in-house developed groundbreaking software to achieve a similar goal.

Apple is argued to approach the technological chain from a proven technology angle in terms of the components that go into the innovative design and packaging of products such MP3 players, computers and mobile phones and by doing so support a strategy of innovation. Saxo Bank broke new ground with their online trading platform and their ability to integrate the value chain to support their strategy of becoming a facilitator.

Summarizing, four overarching denominators can be identified within the technological chain as shown in Table 10.2. As can be seen from this table, the majority of companies used as cases do not necessarily subscribe to just one denominator

Table 10.2 **Four denominators of the technological chain**

Proven technology	*Scalable technology*	*Simple technology*	*Groundbreaking technology*
Skype, Apple, Google (hardware)	Google, Skype, Samsung Electronics, Saxo Bank	Ryanair, Google, Skype	Saxo Bank, Ryanair, Google (software), Dell, Samsung Electronics

but apply several of these in order to determine their technology profile.

It is exactly this ability coupled with the out-of-the-box thinking that has gained these companies entrance to the X-factor universe as they are able to utilize the technological chain in unconventional ways to execute their strategy with success.

The Technological Chain and Its Influence on Strategy

The companies that can deconstruct traditional thinking use the technological chain as another key success driver to increase the company's Return on its Strategy. Rather than implementing the latest and greatest technology, as many traditional companies choose to do, they opt for proven technology used in different ways or develop technology that supports the strategy.

Skype used the technology developed for file sharing to offer peer-to-peer telephony, whereas Google combined proven hardware with new software development to create a technological chain that was aligned to its strategy.

Companies such as Saxo Bank and Dell developed groundbreaking technology to gain a high Return on Strategy. For Saxo Bank this included the development of the SaxoTrader online trading platform as well as their ability to integrate technology throughout their value chain. Dell likewise developed technology for seamless integration throughout their value chain which effectively allowed them to offer products of high quality at low costs.

While Samsung Electronics did not develop technology for seamless integration, they did innovate the technology used for producing semiconductors, allowing them to execute a strategy of low cost and differentiation, thereby achieving a dual advantage. Ryanair broke new ground on the customer side of the supply chain when they developed their online ticketing systems, but at the same time opted for proven technology on the supply side.

Apple manages to package known technology in such a manner that the products of the company are perceived to be innovative and groundbreaking.

The ways in which the above companies utilize the technological chain to achieve a satisfactory Return on Strategy all constitute main bearing points on how to navigate this key success driver. Salient bearing points are:

- Using proven technology
- Deploying scalable technology
- Simple technology
- Developing groundbreaking technology
- Integrating technology throughout the value chain.

Companies in the X-factor universe display the ability to use the technological chain in order to execute their strategy by combining and utilizing these bearing points so they fit their specific purpose. There is no generic way to approach this as some companies have achieved a high Return on Strategy by developing groundbreaking technology whereas others have gone with proven technology. What can be said, however, is that the companies in the X-factor universe opting for proven technology tend to utilize this in new and unconventional ways. As such the unconventional and out-of-the-box thinking also becomes the driving factor when seeking to utilize the technological chain.

11

DRIVING THE LEADERSHIP
GENES

*My job is not to make business; my job is to ensure that other
people can make business.*

Jan Carlzon, former CEO of Scandinavian
Airlines System (SAS)

When Jan Carlzon was appointed the CEO of SAS in 1981,
he was faced with the task of turning around a loss-making
airline that had become known for poor service, an airline
with an on-time performance that had sunk to historically low
levels of below 85%, an airline with a fleet mix and a route
schedule that did not meet market demands and an airline that
carried one of the highest operating costs of any airline in the
industry.

From 1981 to 1983, Carlzon initiated three major changes at
SAS which constituted the so-called "first wave" of the company's turnaround. These were aimed at targeting the business
travel market as the airline's primary business, to make customer service a top priority and to reorganize the company
structure to decentralize responsibility. Within the first year of
Carlzon's appointment, the company returned to making a
profit and in 1984, SAS received the much coveted Airline of
the Year award. It was deemed superior to its competitors in a
number of areas such as passenger service, marketing and technology management. In that same year, the magazine "Fortune"
named SAS the world's best airline for the business-person and

Carlzon himself was named Sweden's most popular person by a major Swedish newspaper.[1]

The success continued for SAS with profits increasing throughout the 1980s leading to the company becoming among the top three most profitable passenger airlines in the world. For Carlzon the success led to the publication of his book, "Moments of Truth" for which Tom Peters, author of "In Search of Excellence", provided the foreword. This publication tells the story of how SAS under his leadership emerged from deficit to profitability through a strategic focus on the customer, encouraging a risk-taking attitude and by delegating more responsibility to front-line employees. It furthermore marks the height of Carlzon's career within airline passenger travel. Carlzon had become the king of the industry or at least perceived himself to be.

Carlzon lost sight of the passenger airline business and began to invest heavily in other businesses such as hotels, a move which he later admitted was mainly to satisfy his own needs rather than those of the company.[2] The acquisition of the Inter-Continental in 1989 and the Gulf War turned the profitable company of the 1980s into the red again. The losses of SAS grew in the early 1990s and after coming under increased pressure from shareholders and the board, Carlzon left SAS in November 1993 after 12 years of holding the post of CEO and providing leadership to the passenger airline.

The example of Carlzon and SAS illustrates the importance of leadership and furthermore that successful leadership is not necessarily a lasting trait. While Carlzon undeniably performed one of SAS' most astonishing turnarounds, he also spearheaded their subsequent downfall, which was arguably due to an increased focus on his own vision which overshadowed the dangers this held for the company as a whole.

Put another way, this is an example of a narcissistic leader. According to Michael Maccoby in his "HBR" article on narcissistic leaders, Jan Catlzon is a textbook example of how a narcissist's weaknesses can destroy the career of a successful businessman. As Maccoby puts it:

Carlzon's story perfectly corroborates the often-recorded tendency of narcissists to become overly expansive – and hence isolated – at the very pinnacle of their success. Seduced by the flattery he received in the international press, Carlzon's self-image became so enormously inflated that his feet left the ground. And given his vulnerability to grandiosity, he was propelled by a need to expand his organization rather than develop it. In due course, as Carlzon led the company deeper and deeper into losses, he was fired.[3]

As such there is often a delicate balance between the strengths and the weaknesses of the narcissistic leader. Practice shows that there seems to be a pattern: the more successful a narcissist becomes the more visible are the faults which can be observed. Therefore, the managerial challenge is to get leaders to realize their profile and to get them to act accordingly. Otherwise, the most creative and expansive leaders can ruin the organization.

The turnaround of Ryanair, spearheaded by Michael O'Leary, stands in contrast to that led by Jan Carlzon given the ongoing success of Ryanair under the continued leadership of Michael O'Leary. From facing a financial collapse in 1991, Michael O'Leary has managed to turn the fortunes of Ryanair around to become Europe's largest discount airline estimating that they will carry in excess of 50 million passengers in 2008 and posting profits for the latest financial year ending March 31, 2008 of €528.9 million.

The success of Ryanair was founded when the company decided to adopt a low cost – no frills strategy and promoting O'Leary from the position of Finance Director to CEO of the then struggling airline. His ability to focus on objectives was provided by others in the management team as the reason for his appointment, which along with his near obsession with costs allowed Ryanair to prosper. In addition to these traits, O'Leary soon showed a talent for mobilizing the employees at Ryanair to take an active part in the war against the established flag carriers. This ability was in no small part due to his own role as the face of Ryanair in their battle against the establishment.

The straightforward attitude of O'Leary and his controversial statements made to the press with regard to the established players achieved him icon status and fuelled the employees desire to go that extra mile for their CEO and the company as a whole. This behaviour and the visibility of O'Leary has clearly been instrumental in developing the perception among the public of Ryanair as the airline that has made travel available for the masses and thus the fundament for the company's success as Europe's leading low-cost airline.

In 2003, O'Leary was named the "Airline Personality" by Skytrax, a leading research advisor to the world airline and air transport industry, in a field of nominees that included the CEOs of British Airways (BA), Deutsche Lufthansa and even Southwest Airlines. The impact of O'Leary and his leadership is likewise recognized by his peers as the following quote from the chairman of BMI British Midland illustrates:

> *He is almost certainly one of the most successful leaders in the industry, with a unique business model, discipline and an extraordinary level of confidence.*
> (Sir Michael Bishop, chairman. BMI British Midland)

So where do the leadership genes of Michael O'Leary differ from those of Jan Carlzon? They both had initial and successful visions for their respective companies, they were both able to mobilize the employees to go that extra mile and they both showed a fierce determination for executing their strategy. However, where Jan Carlzon fell prey to complacency and competitive myopia and began to stray from this initial strategy, Michael O'Leary has remained committed to the low cost – no frills strategy since it was first deployed in 1991. The personality of the two may not differ that much, but where Carlzon lost sight of the overall company in order to satisfy his personal needs, O'Leary has managed to balance the two and maintain a winning formula.

Jan Carlzon and Michael O'Leary are but two examples of business leaders who have made a significant impact on the companies they were in charge of. If we turn the attention to the US names, such as Anne Mulcahy, CEO of Xerox, Robert J. Ulrich, Chairman and former CEO of Target Corporation, A.G. Lafley, CEO of Procter & Gamble, George David, Chairman and former CEO of United Technologies Corporation, Frederick W. Smith, Chairman and CEO of FedEx and Maurice R. Greenberg, former CEO of AIG, all spring to mind.

These have all been named as the Chief Executive of the Year by the Chief Executive magazine[4] and while some are still practising their leadership with success, others have been forced to vacate their position.

Anne Mulcahy, the 2008 winner of the award, launched an aggressive turnaround strategy for Xerox when assuming the position of CEO in 2001. The strategy not only resulted in returning the company to profitability but also reduced the debt and increased the cash while continuing to invest in research and development.

The 2007 winner of the award, Robert J. Ulrich is credited with crafting the unique brand and marketing image and focus of Target Corporation. This is widely considered one of the key elements of the company's success in the retailing industry. The strong performance of the company led Berkshire Hathaway, the holding company of Warren Buffet, to purchase a large portion of shares in a move that was considered a strong endorsement of the company's potential for continued success.

A.G. Lafley, who received the award in 2006, is credited with revitalizing Procter & Gamble by focusing on successful brands instead of trying to develop new brands and implementing a new customer attitude detailing that the "consumer is the boss" along with a restructuring of the company. The customer attitude and restructuring is described in greater detail in Chapters 6 and 8 respectively.

These three business leaders are all examples of business leaders who have maintained a successful leadership to this day, which however is not the case for all the previous award winners.

On March 15, 2005, the 2003 CEO of the Year, Maurice R. Greenberg, was forced to resign from his post as Chairman and CEO of AIG. The reasons, however, were not to be found in the company's performance but instead due to the allegations of fraud put forward by Eliot Spitzer, attorney general of New York State. These allegations materialized in a complaint that was filed in May 2005 by Spitzer alleging that Greenberg and Howard I. Smith, the former CFO of AIG, were conducting fraudulent business practice, securities fraud, common law fraud, and other violations of insurance and securities laws. However, all criminal charges were dropped after subsequent investigation and Greenberg was not held responsible for any crimes.

Martin Sullivan succeeded Greenberg as the CEO of AIG but only lasted three years in the position as disappointing results and the turbulent times of the financial markets prompted the board to request his departure. Whether or not Greenberg could have produced better results had he remained as the CEO is impossible to say but the fact that leadership is a key success driver for a company's Return on Strategy appears evident.

Leadership, however, is more than just the person at the top and his/her execution power in steering the company towards success. It is, or can be, the leadership style of an organization as opposed to that of an individual.

Leaving the US and looking to the Far East will reveal an Indian company that has built and developed its leadership style for more than a century. Founded in 1868, the Tata Group is a growing business group based in India with international operations in business sectors such as communications and information technology, engineering, energy, consumer products and chemicals. The combined market capitalization of the group's 27 publicly listed companies is approximately US$60 billion covering a shareholder base of 3.2 million.

The stated purpose of the Tata Group is to improve the quality of life of the communities they serve through leadership in sectors of economic significance. This purpose is backed by a belief in returning wealth to the society it serves, something which has evoked trust among consumers, employees, shareholders and the community. Such a purpose and belief has led to the formalization of five core values that lie at the heart of the Tata Group and which underpin the way they do business. These values are listed in Table 11.1.

These values, the purpose and a comprehensive document known as the Tata Code of Conduct have enabled the company to develop a leadership style that is central to the success of the company. This leadership style has become synonymous with the slogan that is used by the Tata Group and which is put on the very top of the main page of the company web site (www. tata.com):

Tata – Leadership with trust

Table 11.1 **Core values of the Tata Group**

Core values	Description
Integrity	Conduct business fairly, with honesty and transparency. Everything must stand the test of public scrutiny
Understanding	Must be caring, show respect, compassion and humanity for our colleagues and customers around the world, and always work for the benefit of the communities we serve
Excellence	Must constantly strive to achieve the highest possible standards in our day-to-day work and in the quality of the goods and services we provide
Unity	Must work cohesively with our colleagues across the group and with our customers and partners around the world, building strong relationships based on tolerance, understanding and mutual cooperation
Responsibility	Must continue to be responsible, sensitive to the countries, communities and environments in which we work, always ensuring that what comes from the people goes back to the people many times over

Source: www.tata.com.

The example of the Tata Group illustrates that successful leadership extends beyond the persons who are charged with the task of taking an organization to the next level. The style of an organization is an equally important aspect to consider when deciding on how to move forward, how to maintain or increase the Return on Strategy and how to utilize the leadership genes of both the people and the organization to do so.

As the examples of Carlzon, O'Leary, Mulcahy and Laftley illustrate, leadership is without doubt a key issue in the quest for achieving the strategic goals and for staying on the competitive edge, but how much is down to the leadership of top executives? How is leadership exercised and where does it come from? What are the characteristics of successful leadership?

Leadership – a Driver or an Obstacle?

Despite the importance of leadership within the corporate world a common definition is hard to come by and as Ralph M. Stogdill pointed out in his survey of leadership theories and research there are:

> *almost as many different definitions of leadership as there are persons who have attempted to define the concept.*[5]

Leadership has been discussed almost since the dawn of times but it is not until the twentieth century that theories of leadership began to take shape. In the 1920s the trait approach to leadership emerged which attempted to identify personal characteristics of leaders based on the assumption that leaders share certain inborn personality traits. However, as extensive studies concluded that good leaders tend to be more extrovert, more self-confident and taller than non-leaders, this theory was replaced by the theory of style in the 1940s. The theory of style is also know as the behavioural approach to leadership and revolves around the behaviour of leaders, which focuses on what good leaders do rather than who they are. Recent leadership thinking has introduced a new and dominant way of approaching leadership which is known as contingency theory. This states that leadership is dependent on a given situation which in turn leads to almost endless varieties of leadership.

When combining these three approaches to leadership, the traits or personality of an individual, the behaviour of same and finally the situation in which leadership is exercised can all be argued to impact leadership and whether this turns out for the better or not. Leadership includes the ability to align personality to a given strategic situation while displaying a behaviour that motivates, engages and directs the resources of an organization towards a common goal.

This includes that personality does matter as illustrated by the example of both Jan Carlzon and Michael O'Leary who can both be termed as rather extrovert and full of confidence with a fierce resolve. Behaviour is equally important, however, as the ability to motivate and engage the resources of an organization to a large degree hinges on the behaviour of the leader. Finally the ability to read the strategic situation is likewise of importance as the downfall of Jan Carlzon illustrates, given his failure to recognize that SAS was not geared to run a number of different businesses aside from its passenger airline business.

In addition to the three areas of leadership presented above, the notion of vision is also often viewed as a trait of a good leader. Whereas vision may not be necessary to become a good leader, it is essential for leaders who are transforming their businesses as it is often their vision which lies at the heart of any transformation. An example of this is the case of Louis Gerstner who managed to transform IBM from being a manufacturer into a true solution provider based on his vision, whereas the transformation of Ryanair did not rest on the vision of Michael O'Leary but rather his commitment to carry out the strategy.

Leadership is essential for the success of a company but it doesn't come in any predetermined shape or form. It is dependent on a series of factors as described above and is characterized by a certain personality and set of skills that provide the leader with the ability to lay the strategic jigsaw puzzle for his/her specific organization with the aim of gaining a superior Return on Strategy.

The Chicken and the Egg of Leadership and Strategy

In an article entitled *Leadership as the starting point of strategy* written by two McKinsey consultants,[6] the authors argue that many companies fail to recognize the leadership capacity that new strategies will require or fail to treat leadership as the starting point of strategy.

Even the best planned strategy may fail if there are no leaders who can translate this from concept to reality and execute it. Is it then a question of matching leaders to the strategy of a company or crafting strategies that match the capabilities of leader? Which is the chicken and which is the egg when it comes to leadership and strategy?

As illustrated by the examples of Carlzon at SAS and O'Leary at Ryanair, the question of which is the chicken and which is the egg depends entirely on the situation. Where Carlzon and SAS illustrate leadership as the chicken and strategy as the egg, Ryanair and O'Leary illustrate the opposite. Given this, leadership is not just a vehicle for revising or crafting new strategies but also a vehicle for executing existing strategies in order for a company to gain a high Return on Strategy.

WHEN LEADERSHIP BREEDS STRATEGY

In the early 1990s, the former giant and darling of the US computer industry IBM was suffering its worst time since it was founded. Despite recording an impressive US$64.5 billion in revenues for the financial year 1992, the company posted a record loss of US$4.97 billion leading to more than 100,000 employees losing their jobs at the company that had up until that point taken pride in its "job for life" policy. Strategic plans were drawn up for the dismemberment of IBM which in 1990 topped the Fortune 500 list as the most profitable company.

Although the plan to split IBM up was going forward, the board decided in January 1993 that is was time to make a change at the top. John Akers, the CEO and chairman, was asked to step down and leave the company.

After a long a hard search that saw candidates such as NCR's chairman Gil Williamson, Apple Computer CEO John Scully, Allied-Signal's chief Lawrence Bossidy and Motorola's George Fisker declining the position, the board decided to appoint Louis V. Gerstner Jr as the new CEO despite his lack of technological background. When the news of his appointment first appeared in the "Wall Street Journal" investors reacted by knocking a further 6% off IBM's already depressed stock price.[7]

"Newsweek" published an article covering his appointment with the title *Can he make an elephant dance?* referring to the task that lay ahead of Gerstner. It was widely recognized that IBM had misjudged the direction of the computing industry with its continued focus on mainframe computers, failing to recognize that much of the profit would move from hardware to chips and software.

How would it be possible for Gerstner to turn around one of the largest companies in the world? How could he make the elephant dance again?

> *The last thing IBM needs right now is a vision. What IBM needs right now is a series of very tough-minded, market-driven, highly effective strategies in each of it businesses.*[8]
>
> (Louis V. Gerstner, former CEO of IBM)

Much to the disliking of industry analysts, Gerstner approached the challenge by initially familiarizing himself with the company before deciding on what moves to make rather than announcing a grand plan or vision for the turnaround. One of the most significant decisions Gerstner made was not to carry out the plans for splitting up the company, which rested on his belief that customers valued the company's ability to integrate and service a wide variety of technologies.

Other strategic moves included an additional 35,000 job reductions, massive price reductions and technological reconfigurations on its mainframe computers, selling off non-core operations and realigning the company under customer-focused versus product-focused teams.

Gerstner, however, recognized that the turnaround of IBM did not only rest on implementing new strategic directions but equally on the company's ability to execute them and on changing the existing culture of the company. IBM was simply not executing properly, which to a large degree rested on the existing culture of the company which had become characterized by a deep sense of complacency and based on values that were established when Thomas Watson Sr had initially built the company.

By living and preaching a new culture in which execution, informality and cross-divisional cooperation were some of the main values, Gerstner managed to change the deeply rooted bureaucratic culture of IBM to that of a more casual company with a stronger focus on what customers required.

By 1994, the turnaround of IBM was becoming a reality as it posted a positive result and furthermore achieved its first revenue growth since 1990. The elephant had begun to dance. When Gerstner stepped down in 2002, the company recorded US$86 billion in sales and US$8 billion in net income and one of the most remarkable turnarounds in US corporate history was a reality.

The success of Gerstner can be attributed to his leadership skills which allowed him to change the longstanding culture of a giant rather than a grand vision. The strategy Gerstner implemented at IBM slowly took form during his first year with the company and was devised on the back of him learning the company from within.

As such Gerstner displayed what can be termed appropriate executive behaviour by balancing his own strategic insight with the needs of the organization, thus managing to align these to achieve the turnaround. Gerstner was able to breed the strategy based on his leadership and as such the latter became the starting point of the strategy, or the egg, which was made possible by the balanced leadership of Gerstner. A balance between the organization and his own ideas that was necessary in order to make the elephant dance.

Other high profile executives have been less fortunate when taking the reigns of global companies and attempting to formulate and implement new strategic measures. One such case is that of Carleton Fiorina, the former CEO of Hewlett-Packard.

WHEN LEADERSHIP AMBUSHES STRATEGY

In July 1999, Carleton Fiorina was appointed the president and CEO of Hewlett-Packard and thus became the first woman to serve as a CEO of a company included in the Dow Jones Industrial Average. Coming from a sales-oriented, non-engineering background and holding years of experience from the telecommunications sector, Fiorina launched a number of strategic initiatives aimed at creating the scale of economies that would allow Hewlett-Packard to become a low-cost supplier of commodity computers and servers. One of these initiatives was the hotly debated merger with Compaq Computer Corporation.

By taking these strategic steps and simultaneously expanding the corporate IT services of Hewlett-Packard, a two-pronged strategy emerged which was designed to battle Dell in the market for low-cost commodity computers and IBM in the market for corporate IT services.

In the nearly six years following the appointment of Fiorina, the market capitalization of Hewlett-Packard was drastically reduced, it incurred heavy job losses in attempts to restructure and curb costs, Fiorina had a public fall-out with board member Walter Hewlett (the son of co-founder William Hewlett) over the merger with Compaq and the company experienced an exodus of top managerial talent.

What Went Wrong?

Some of the reasons cited are Fiorina's failure in addressing the strategic fit with the internal environment of Hewlett-Packard and the culture that was built around engineering expertise and pride. Her leadership did not facilitate the change from a culture of product leadership and innovation towards a culture of low cost leaving employees unengaged and increasingly unmotivated. Her management style was in addition viewed by many as "flashy" and "imperial" seemingly lacking in appreciation for the engineering history of Hewlett-Packard.[9]

As such, Fiorina's leadership at Hewlett-Packard displayed elements of unbalanced behaviour by focusing too much on her own strategic vision while not paying attention to the strategic fit with the organization. This is similar to what caused the downfall of Jan Carlzon at SAS given his focus on implementing a strategy that seemed to satisfy his personal needs, equivalent to that of an overly narcissistic leader as discussed earlier in this chapter.

When Fiorina was asked to leave Hewlett-Packard in February 2005, Mark Hurd succeeded her and essentially executed the strategy already in place by deploying a different kind of leadership. With a much lower profile than Fiorina, Hurd set about aligning the culture and structure of Hewlett-Packard to fit the strategy and in the process paid more attention to explaining everyone's role in achieving success rather than selling the strategy. Hewlett-Packard quickly prospered following the appointment of Mark Hurd and overtook Dell as the top-selling computer maker in the world by executing the strategy that many credit Fiorina for laying the foundations to.

As such it was not the strategy, the two-pronged strategy of Hewlett-Packard, but rather the leadership of Fiorina that was at fault. Fiorina devised a new strategy for Hewlett-Packard but failed to lead the execution of same. In the case of Fiorina, leadership was the chicken and the strategy the egg, whereas the opposite was characteristic for Mark Hurd who managed to execute an existing strategy owing to his leadership skills that were better aligned to Hewlett-Packard.

The example of Fiorina and Hewlett-Packard illustrates that balanced leadership is key to the execution of a given strategy as even the best strategy can fail due to bad leadership. However, in some cases leadership simply forgets the strategy or leaves this behind.

WHEN LEADERSHIP FORGETS STRATEGY

Few executives will admit to the fact that they have forgotten the strategy of the company or that it fails during their shift although research indicates that this is exactly what happens in most cases.

A study conducted by Ernst & Young in 2004 revealed that a full 66% of corporate strategy is never carried out in real life. In their publication "The Execution Premium", authors Kaplan and Norton point to the fact that various surveys over the past two decades show that 60 to 80% of companies fail to implement and reach their strategy and strategic goals.[10] What this indicates is that the majority of companies fail to achieve a significant Return on their Strategy.

How can this be?

Many explanations have been offered which attempt to answer this question and furthermore provide a solution for how not to get trapped among the majority of companies failing to carry out their strategy. The topic of execution will be dealt with separately later in this chapter but, from a leadership point of view, a large proportion of the failing strategies are due to a lack of communication.

After spending long hours, or even days or months, crafting the superior strategy, many executives fail to create the commitment among the employees needed to implement a strategy. They fail to communicate the strategy effectively throughout the organization leaving employees stranded and in many cases unaware of the fact that a new strategy has been devised. In such circumstances the new and grand strategy will arrive with great fanfare only to live a short life after which it becomes yet another 50 page document kept in a desk drawer.

Aside from failing to implement new strategies, a survey conducted among executives shows another and equally alarming fact. Approximately 85% of the executive teams surveyed spent less than one hour per month discussing strategy and of these 50% reported they spent almost no time on strategy discussions.[11] Rather than monitoring and discussing how the company's strategy was faring, executives relied on more tactical operating systems, such as budgets and management by objectives (MBO) systems.

In fact they had forgotten the strategy or at least how to make the remainder of the organization embrace and commit to it.

BALANCING THE CHICKEN AND THE EGG

As illustrated by the three examples, leadership is an act of balance between, in particular, what the organization is geared for, the vision of the leader and finally making sure that it is all communicated and digested in a satisfactory manner by the organization. Based on this, balanced leadership is indeed a key success driver for getting a superior Return on a Strategy.

Leadership, however, is much more than just the executive levels of a company as leaders are needed at all management levels in order to execute the strategy of the company and even change the direction if needed. In addition, leadership must be governed; its practices must be overseen by those at board level. Leadership in a broader sense is therefore a question of recruiting, developing and practising leadership – in short the governance of leadership.

Governance of Leadership

As illustrated in the previous sections, leadership is indeed a key success driver for getting a Return on Strategy that outperforms the targets set. However, in order to fully utilize this driver companies must apply what is termed governance of leadership. This entails the ability to recruit and develop the top leaders of tomorrow while making sure that leadership is practised with a view to improve the strategic health of the company.

Leadership Throughout the Organization

The major focus on leadership is often concerned with the executive level. However, leadership should be viewed in a

broader sense. Leadership is practised throughout the organization and as such it becomes essential for a company's success
that not just executives but also senior and middle managers
display great leadership skills.

As discussed in Chapter 9, companies taking part in a McKinsey survey found it very difficult to attract talent with more than
75% of the corporate officers claiming their companies were
lacking in this department.

Asking the senior and middle managers of the companies
surveyed to report whether they had worked for an underper-
former or not, 58% answered yes and furthermore detailed the
following impact this had on their experience in the
company[12]:

- 76% found that it prevented them from learning,
- 81% found that it was hurting their career development,
- 82% found that it prevented them from making a larger
  contribution to the bottom line,
- 86% found that it made them want to leave the company
  in question.

Developing leadership talent can thus greatly influence the success of a given company as good leadership throughout the
organization will yield higher performance from managers,
executives and employees alike.

The Talent Factories

In 2007, "Fortune" magazine conducted research aimed at
identifying the top companies for developing the leaders of
tomorrow. In the global ranking, General Electric was crowned
as the number one company for developing the leaders of the
future. Other companies included in the global top 20 list
included Procter & Gamble, IBM and McKinsey from the US,
Hindustan Unilever, ICICI Bank and WIPRO from India, and
Nokia, BBVA and GlaxoSmithKline from Finland, Spain and
Britain respectively.[13]

We begin to evaluate leadership capability on day one of employ-ment.[14]

(John Rice, President and CEO General Electric
Technology Infrastructure)

The alumni of some of the above-mentioned companies include prominent names within the world of business. Hindustan Uni-lever has supplied more than 200 CEOs to other companies. Procter & Gamble has hatched the likes of Steve Balmer (CEO of Microsoft), Meg Whitman (CEO of EBay) and AOL founder Steve Case. The alumni of General Electric include James McNerney (CEO of Boeing), Frank Blake (CEO of Home Depot) and David M. Cote (CEO of Honeywell), which along with General Electric represents four of the 30 companies making up the DOW Jones industrial average.

Other companies highlighted as top companies for leaders in the research conducted by "Fortune" magazine are: L'Oreal, Lufthansa AG, SAP and BMW group, all with headquarters in Europe; China Vanke Co. Ltd, China Mobile Group, Tata Con-sultancy Services Limited and Lion Nathan Limited, all from the Asia-Pacific region; and finally McDonald's, Whirlpool Cor-poration and Medtronic Inc. from the US.

What characterizes many of these companies and their success in developing the leaders of tomorrow is not a generic model or recipe but rather a continued focus on developing talent. For many of the top ranking companies mentioned above, this focus extends beyond development programmes, formalized training and career progression. It involves the time of the CEO and many other executives. At McDonalds, the CEO personally reviews the development of the top 200 managers. At General Electric, CEO Jeffrey Immelt reviews the top 600, while Bill Hawkins of Medtronic spends nearly 50% of his time on people issues.

If any generic characteristics can be distilled from looking at the top talent factories it would be that the top executive man-agement, including the CEO, spend a great deal of their time on people issues.

In 2006, Saxo Bank decided to formalize their talent development and assign a high priority to this area of their business. This was partly due to the growth of the bank and the resulting lack of talented leaders to fill the increasing amount of managerial positions.

The results of implementing a formalized model for talent development led to approximately 75% of all new managers being recruited from within the company. Despite this percentage relating primarily to the recruitment at middle management level, the co-CEO of Saxo Bank, Lars Seier Christensen, firmly believes that this will extend to include developing the top executives of the future.

According to the current and former directors of Human Resources at Saxo Bank, Dion Sørensen and Erik Kjær, the development of leaders in Saxo Bank rests on six principles. These principles are:

1 External recruitment is done at the lowest level of the organization.
2 The competencies of leadership are working values, prioritizing your time and skills.
3 The level of leadership is decisive for the competencies of leadership.
4 Potential is equal to a person's future level of competence.
5 Development is done on the job.
6 The manager undertakes the development of tomorrow's leaders.

The above principles are what make up the formalized approach used by Saxo Bank to develop their talents into the leaders of tomorrow. This approach is known as the model of "Internal Supply".[15]

Developing leaders internally will further galvanize the culture of a company as those managers of tomorrow that come through the ranks of the company are highly likely to project the values and culture of the company.

Whether a company's culture rests on liberalistic values such as those deployed by Saxo Bank, which are discussed in Chapter 9, or focuses more on collectivistic values, the need for developing leadership throughout the organization is ever present. This is exemplified by the fact that Huawei, which is headquartered on the other side of the globe from Saxo Bank and holds collectivistic values at the centre of their culture, also puts a significant emphasis on developing leadership from the inside and throughout the organization.

With Huawei being considered the Chinese version of Google by the local workforce it provides the company with an added ability to attract local talent. This talent must, however, be developed in order for the company to breed the leaders of tomorrow and instil a sense of leadership throughout the organization.

Similar to the approach of Saxo Bank, Huawei also focuses on recruiting primarily at the lowest level after which the career development of an individual follows one of two paths. This can either be the path of management or that of professional development.

Moving from one level to the next is also characterized by the ability to obtain a certain set of skills which are obtained through the online training provided by Huawei to all employees and local management training.

Huawei makes extensive use of self-training and has developed an online tool which is used by its entire worldwide staff. This online tool is developed to offer each employee a platform for training and self-evaluation regardless of which career path is chosen, providing all Huawei employees with the same fundament of core competency and skills training. A feature which is well aligned with the collectivistic culture of the company.

Building leadership skills from a fundament of common competencies and skills has allowed Huawei to develop leaders throughout their organization which adhere to the wolf-pack culture and project the values of the company.

As such the ability to focus on developing the leaders of tomorrow is recognized by companies that embrace highly different values and are placed at remote ends of the known world.

There is little doubt that leadership is of paramount importance when seeking to achieve a high Return on Strategy. Many of the leading companies across the globe have recognized the development of leadership within the organization as an area of potential competitive advantage. Not least due to the fact that human capital is becoming an ever more scarce resource.

Leadership within an organization is a key success driver in gaining a satisfactory Return on a company's Strategy. At top level the cases of Fiorina and Gerstner illustrate this, whereas the survey conducted by McKinsey and the increased focus on internal development of talent underlines the importance of leadership throughout the organization. Leadership is, however, not just confined to the realms of developing the talent of the future but also how leadership is practised.

Practising Leadership

In the late eighteenth century Adam Smith published his work "The Wealth of Nations", which argues that the market forces provide an "Invisible Hand" that guides the free market to produce the right amount and variety of goods at low prices.

The "Visible Hand" would, in the context of Adam Smith, translate to unnecessary government regulation and influence on markets and it has been the dominant view in the Western world that the presence of such would lead to poorly functioning markets for goods and services.

Fast forward to the beginning of the twenty-first century and the financial crisis that swept the world with a global recession not seen since the Great Depression as the outcome, and the free market and capitalism appear to have failed. Due to this governments across the world have all been forced to deploy the "Visible Hand" in the form of subsidies, particularly to the struggling financial sector.

Many argue that greed and short-term profit was the trigger that led many financial institutions to take on high risk mortgages which subsequently had to be written off as many defaulted on their loans. With two of the leading mortgage lenders in the US being placed under conservatorship and other high profile financial institutions either going bankrupt, such as Lehman Brothers, or accepting a large governmental equity stake in exchange for access to liquidity, such as AIG, the ability to practise sound leadership indeed moves to centre stage.

While some of these companies find themselves in hard times, the same cannot be said for some of the executives who have been in charge as their compensation packages in many cases run into hundreds of millions of US dollars. Based on this, it would appear that practising sound leadership is not necessarily tied to the compensation, which in many cases depends on the stock price, and that new mechanisms for governing leadership are required.

Former chairman and CEO of Lehman Brothers, Richard Severin Fuld, Jr, is the prime example of an executive who received an astronomical compensation while practising questionable leadership, ultimately leading to the bankruptcy of the former financial giant. Over a seven-year period, from 2000 to 2007, Fuld, Jr received total compensation of no less than US$484.8 million.

Fuld, Jr was one of 12 former Lehman executives who received grand jury subpoenas in connection with three criminal investigations. During a congressional hearing testimony Senator Waxman asked Fuld, Jr:

You pocketed half a billion dollars while your company went bankrupt, I have a basic question to you, is this fair?[16]

The response of Fuld, Jr can be characterized as somewhat evasive. In his defence only US$6.4 million was paid out as base salary with the remaining relating to cash bonuses and stock options.

Lehman Brothers and similar companies that have fallen prey to the crisis illustrate that leadership at board level is equally important in order for a company to implement governance mechanisms that ensure the long-term survival of a company. As such it is not just a question of having the right leaders or the ability to develop leaders throughout the entire organization, but also a question of which guidelines and mechanisms a company implements to reward practising sound leadership.

One example of a company that has implemented specific mechanisms in order to secure its long-term health and the practice of long-term sound leadership is Novo Nordisk, one of the world's leading companies in diabetes care.

The Novo Nordisk Way of Management is a framework for how the company conducts its business and which consists of three elements. In addition to this framework, Novo Nordisk also works with a business principle known as the Triple Bottom Line that incorporates long-term and institutional competitive perspectives.

Beginning with the Novo Nordisk Way of Management framework, this consists of the elements: the Vision, the Charter and 13 global company policies. This framework is shown in Figure 11.1. The vision sets the direction for Novo Nordisk, including what it strives to achieve and how it aims to find the balance between commercial interests and responsible company conduct. Much of this is guided by the company's values that are described in the charter along with the commitments, fundamental management principles and the follow-up methodology of the company.

The values are developed to support the Triple Bottom Line principle, which seeks to balance financial growth with corporate responsibility, short-term gains with long-term profitability, and shareholder return with other stakeholder interest. As such all decisions made are subjected to the test of whether they are economically viable, socially responsible and environmentally sound as shown in Figure 11.2. The global company policies are

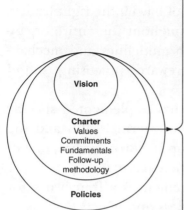

Vision
The vision describes what the company aims to achieve, and how:
- We will be the world's leading diabetes care company
- We will offer products and services in other areas where we can make a difference
- We will achieve competitive business results
- A job here is never just a job
- Our values are expressed in all our actions

Charter
Values
Each employee is expected to be: accountable, ambitious, responsible, engaged with stakeholders, open and honest, and ready for change.
Commitments
Novo Nordisk is committed to conducting its activities in a financially, environmentally and socially responsible way. This commitment is anchored in the company's Articles of Association. Any decision should always seek to balance three considerations. Is it economically viable? Is it socially responsible? Is it environmentally sound?
Fundamentals
A set of 11 management guidelines to ensure focus on efficiency and alignment in business direction, customer focus, organizational development, cross-functional cooperation and product quality
Follow-up methodology
Ongoing systematic and validated documentation of performance in all material areas of Novo Nordisk. Four components provide assurance to stakeholders of the quality of the company's processes and performance: financial and non-financial performance; facilitations; organizational audit including an assessment of "linking business and organization" as well as succession management; and quality audits.

Policies
In 12 selected areas greater mutual understanding and global standards are particularly helpful in guiding company operations: bioethics, business ethics, communication, environment, finance, global health, health and safety, information technology, legal, people, purchasing, quality and risk management.

Figure 11.1 **The Novo Nordisk Way of Management framework** (*source:* Novo Nordisk Annual Report 2008).

likewise engineered to support the Triple Bottom Line principle by providing operational guidelines within 13 specific areas such as bioethics, business ethics, communication, environment, finance, health and safety, and information technology.

These mechanisms, implemented to guarantee sustainable development and balanced growth, have been built into the corporate governance structure, management tools and performance measures in order to facilitate the sound leadership of the company.

Practising leadership at Novo Nordisk thus becomes more

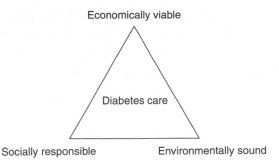

Figure 11.2 **The Triple Bottom Line business principle of Novo Nordisk.**

than looking to meet short-term financial goals as these are balanced with long-term perspectives and the interests of external stakeholders. The latter being a key component of the company's strategic leadership. The Novo Nordisk Way of Management has evolved since the 1920s when the first building blocks of the company were laid and the framework described above has been in use for several years.

Strategic Leadership

So far this chapter has discussed leadership and how this relates to the making of strategy and the ability to implement strategy as well as the governance of leadership, which form the fundament for discussing strategic leadership. In terms of strategic leadership, two distinct areas can be identified which will be described separately and these are: (1) the company's ability to drive the business and strategy and (2) the company's ability to align the company with external stakeholders.

Driving the Business

When attempting to define strategic leadership and how this may drive the business and its strategy, many point to the competences and skills that an executive must possess in order to make a company successful. In the 2007 article *Moments of truth* from the "Harvard Business Review", eight top executives were interviewed and asked to identify the most important leadership qualities necessary to provide leadership.[17] The eight qualities that were identified are shown in Table 11.2. These eight qualities are argued to be the most important constituents of the ability of an executive to drive the business and its strategy. In addition to these eight, the quality of authenticity should be included as a quality necessary for practising leadership. Authenticity in this regard covers the executive's ability to practise fundamental values, to lead with the heart, to establish relations and demonstrate self-discipline.

Table 11.2 **Eight qualities of leadership**

Quality	Brief explanation offered by the executives
Humility	Humility is a vital quality in a leader, just as it is for a company. If a company is to continue to prosper it has to be externally oriented. It must have the kind of humility that makes it listen to the customer and seek ideas from outside
Energy	It is important that a leader has the energy to not only make things happen in the organization but also to take difficult decisions
Intuition	As a leader it is necessary to trust your own feelings and instincts – your intuition. This however requires being hyperaware of your environment and learning to sense the vibes in the room
Vision	Vision is the ability to spot the possibilities the market offers and in some cases see those opportunities where no one else does
Perspective	As a leader one must be able to see beyond the system you are a part of. You must also be able to see the direction to take both in good and bad times regardless of the resistance at hand
Passion	You have to have passion to do something industry-changing and to overcome the sceptics and setbacks along the way
Conviction	Conviction is needed to make difficult and at times unpopular decisions, which may provide poor short-term results but over a longer period prove the right ones
Learning	Despite being successful, a leader must always be prepared to acknowledge his/her mistakes and learn from these

Source: "Harvard Business Review".

When viewing the executives of the addressed companies we have characterized as belonging to the X-factor universe, they all possess some, if not all, of these qualities. They do, however, tend to have one or a few primary qualities that characterize their leadership and thus also their strategic leadership.

For the two founders of Saxo Bank, vision, passion and conviction are argued to constitute their primary qualities and also those qualities that have enabled the company to not only venture down unconventional strategic roads but also to be successful in doing so. This is similar for many of the other entrepreneurial companies included in the sample of X-factor universe companies such as Google, Facebook and Naturhouse with the latter also being characterized by its ability to learn from its mistakes.

Although all display energetic qualities, none does more so than Huawei, which by its ability to mobilize hundreds of engineers with short notice relates a sense of energy to its customers, its competitors and not least the company itself.

For Samsung Electronics, its primary quality has been its ability to diversify its operations into consumer products where its lead in semiconductors could prove beneficial and as such reveals a high proportion of perspective in the strategic leadership. Perspective is also what characterized Wahaha as they engaged in financial partnerships with distributors in rural China in order to develop this market.

The ideal combination of what qualities the executives and the company itself must possess in order to enter and remain in the X-factor universe depends on the situation as no generic recipe can be given. This is also illustrated by the fact that the companies listed above all have different qualities that are essential to how they drive their business and strategy.

One thing, however, which can be argued to form a common thread among all the X-factor universe companies, is their conviction, as they have all been convinced that what they were trying to achieve made perfect sense. This conviction has been underlined by their authentic leadership, which also characterizes the companies of the X-factor universe, and is illustrated by their focus on values and aligning these to the strategy.

Strategic leadership is about what makes perfect sense for the company and the listed eight qualities as well as authenticity all contribute to the understanding of this. The qualities, however, must be distributed throughout the company in order to craft unconventional strategies that are understood by everyone onboard and to get the commitment necessary.

Strategic leadership is this ability to combine qualities needed for the organization to drive the business and strategy forward as well as the organization's ability to use external stakeholders in an optimal way.

Aligning to External Stakeholders

In addition to the internal stakeholders of a company it is surrounded by a number of external stakeholders, most notably the "Visible Hand" of government regulations and interventions. Top leaders of today are only too aware of how such regulations and interventions can impact their particular company or industry and furthermore how politics and regulatory initiatives can be used to position their company.

If you want cleaner skies, then ban old, dirty aircraft.[18]
(Andy Harrison, CEO of easyJet)

Contributing to the environmental debate, Andy Harrison of easyJet is calling on European governments to introduce legislation that bans aircraft over a certain age from flying. He suggests that any aircraft older than 22 years should not be allowed to operate within the European Union pointing to the fact that newer Boeing A319 aircraft are up to 15% more fuel efficient than older aircraft.

While such efforts position easyJet as an environmentally conscious passenger airline in the perception of the public, it also adds pressure on the competitors with a fleet of older aircraft. Considering that the average age of an easyJet aircraft is 2.2

years they are well positioned to suggest such legislative measures in order to gain a competitive advantage and as such provide a fine example of how leadership also involves influencing the external environment.

Ryanair is another example of a company that purposefully influences the external environment to gain exposure and a competitive edge. When Ryanair decided to make Hahn its Frankfurt destination despite it being more than 70 miles outside Frankfurt, its competitor Lufthansa decided to take them to court.

Ahead of the court case in Cologne, CEO Michael O'Leary decided to run a promotion on the Ryanair web site sending out the message that those who came to the courthouse in Cologne with a banner insulting Lufthansa would receive a free ticket on one of Ryanair's flights from Hahn. Although only a handful of Germans showed up, the riot police were positioned, leading to the media being alerted of the peculiar scenes and Ryanair gaining invaluable press coverage. As a former Ryanair executive explains it:

> *By the time the case was finished we were pursued out of the courtroom by six television cameras, ... And by the time Ryanair took its first flight from Hahn, there wasn't a German with a pulse that didn't know that there was a low-cost airline flying from this place that purported to be Frankfurt but manifestly was not.*[19]
>
> (Tim Jeans, Former executive at Ryanair)

Other examples of companies that are deliberately influencing or using external forces such as governmental regulations or negotiations are Huawei and Vestas.

When the Chinese government initiates negotiations, for example, oil contracts with Middle-east and African countries, Huawei uses this as an opportunity to offer the same governments telecommunications services. It effectively "piggy backed" on the efforts made by the government to open its own negotiations with government agencies.

In Vestas the position of political director has been created with the purpose of influencing the political issues on climate in a more structured manner. In a press release from 2006, Vestas states that it has hired a Vice President for Governmental Relations whose main task is to develop the dialogue with politicians, government officials and environmental organizations throughout the world.

Many other examples exist of companies that systematically and deliberately seek to influence the regulatory powers in order to gain a competitive advantage, which underlines the importance of this aspect. The companies and the leaders that are able to successfully exploit this to their advantage, such as easyJet, Ryanair, Huawei and potentially Vestas, hold an additional tool to maximize the Return on the company's Strategy.

The ability to drive the business and strategy of the organization forward while using external stakeholders to further position the company is arguably a large part of the strategic leadership that leads to the success of many X-factor universe companies.

Leadership Performance and Execution

Leadership is indeed about many things: The ability of the CEO to align strategy and culture, the ability of a company to develop leadership throughout the organization, the ability to govern leadership, the ability to drive the business and strategy of the organization while also using and influencing the external environment and the "Visible Hand" to execute all this.

As mentioned previously in this chapter under the heading "When leadership forgets strategy", somewhere between 60 and 80% of all companies fail to achieve the targets set out in their strategic plans. In other words they fail to execute their strategy.

The companies that manage to enter and remain in the X-factor universe are all characterized by a strong ability to execute their strategic goals and by doing so steering clear of the majority. But how do they do this?

In short, they deploy a sense of execution throughout the organization from the go-go culture of Ryanair, Google and Apple across the customer service culture of Disney and Southwest to the performance-centric cultures of Saxo Bank and Huawei. By deploying authentic values upon which the culture rests, the X-factor universe companies are able to align this to their strategic goals in order to create a commitment among the employees. A commitment which is essential when executing their strategy.

Aside from creating a commitment throughout the organization, X-factor universe companies are also able to successfully communicate the strategy to the entire organization thus providing everyone with a sense of meaning. The strategy makes sense to the employees who all understand where they fit in and why they are doing what they do.

Combining commitment and understanding of the strategic direction with the ability to act is what constitutes the fundament for how the addressed companies are able to execute. The ability to act or execute the strategy is in many cases a quality that the executives display and are able to instil throughout the entire organization.

Another important factor in terms of execution is the companies' utilization of the organizational design as a key business driver. As described in Chapter 9, the companies referred to hold a set of authentic values at the heart of the organization that provide a common ground for all employees which, when combined with the passion that characterizes the addressed companies, creates a good fundament for actually executing the strategy. Some companies such as Saxo Bank and Huawei add performance incentives to their organizational design in order to further boost the ability to execute and to stress the importance of this.

More specifically, research has shown that a company's ability to implement its strategy and translate it into the expected performance is in particular affected by three key factors (Holst-Mikkelsen & Poulfelt, 2008).[20] These are:

1   The strategy must *make sense* to the members of the organization. This means that the strategy should be perceived as appropriate, rational and necessary according to the situation the company is facing.

2   There must be *commitment* to the strategy. This means that the members of the organization must have the will and desire to work to realize the strategy and feel a personal commitment to it. It also implies that the members must be ready to take on new tasks as well as give up others in order to realize the strategy.

3   There must be the necessary energy and *execution ability* in the organization. This means that the members of the organization must have the necessary time and energy to contribute to the realization of the strategy and they must feel themselves capable of doing it. Actually putting the plans into effect is also part of having the ability to execute.

"Making sense", "commitment" and "execution ability" contribute each in its own way to implement the strategy and by this create business performance. This is illustrated in Figure 11.3. The figure shows that leadership performance has a direct impact on the business performance of a company. Further-

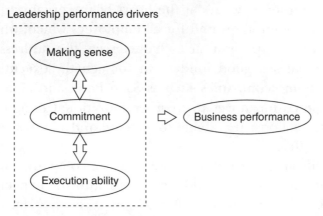

Figure 11.3 **Leadership performance.**

more, if a strategy makes sense to the members of an organization, it will have a direct impact on the organization's
performance and on the commitment to the strategy. Commitment has an impact on the execution ability in the organization
and as such the performance. The three areas of making sense,
commitment and execution ability are what form the leadership performance which impacts on the organization's overall
performance.

The Essence of Making Sense

"What are you doing here?" When the employees of a large
Scandinavian IT company began working on a sunny day in
August 2006 they were met with a sign on their desks with this
particular question. The newly appointed CEO had decided to
provoke all employees and invite them on a journey over the
following three years. He wanted people to participate in the
sense-making process and along the way make them decide
about their own role in the company's future. He did not want
people working in the company without the necessary dedication to the company's strategy. That was in fact a risky action in
a market with a high demand for people with the skills of his
employees. Fortunately for the new CEO and the company,
only very few people decided to quit their jobs, and the remaining felt compelled to participate with high enthusiasm.

The example of Louis V. Gerstner and his turnaround of
IBM also illustrates the importance making sense has on the
ability to execute a strategy. In contrast to Fiorina at Hewlett-
Packard, Gerstner went to great lengths to understand the company prior to developing the strategy in order to make sure that
the organization was ready and on board.

In a chaotic world the manager plays a central role as "sense
maker" but when it comes to developing a strategy one cannot
be sure that a "master code" of a certain nature exists or that
the key to the meaningful follows a certain logic (Weick, 1945).
When trying to make the world make sense under these conditions people must therefore look for a form of order without

being sure that such even exists. They must also decide how to represent this order and they must accept that they will never know if they have found a uniting order. There is rarely one true picture that fits a predefined reality.

Furthermore, people have the need to explain their behaviour in a way that makes sense and lies within some acceptable boundaries. This means that when people do something on a small scale they often do not have to justify it to a very large extent. But as the actions gradually become more important, people automatically seek to justify them in relation to a common purpose or goal. When this need arises in an organization there will often be a need to devote time to a dialogue where new issues get interpreted in relation to the existing mindset. In a strategy process this often takes place in strategy workshops or seminars, where the social interaction between the participants also plays an important role in the sense-making process.

The social interactions as well as the interpretation process contribute significantly to making actions meaningful, but in practice it is often only management who takes part in the strategic dialogue in strategy workshops and seminars. In return, employees are informed through top management's presentation in a kick-off meeting, through a presentation by their own managers in a department meeting, and through articles on the intranet, handouts or a DVD movie. The problem is that this is often far from sufficient and does not take into account that there are different needs at different levels of the organization.

Commitment as a Driver

Few who have seen Steve Balmer, the CEO at Microsoft, express his dedication for the company will argue against the fact that he is strongly dedicated to the company for which he is working.

Research shows that when people put their hearts and souls into realizing a strategy, it has better chances of becoming a success. More modestly, a personal interest and a will to contribute to realizing the strategy amongst employees is also a valuable asset for managers who aspire for better results. Committed and enthusiastic people are also much more likely to make other people feel the same way. Therefore, it can be a good idea to appoint a number of strategy ambassadors and ask them to communicate the strategy to all the other employees. That is what candidates running for a presidency are doing, and it is also what companies are using actively in order to out-manoeuvre competitors and achieve success with their new strategies. A typical strategy process therefore places a natural focus on creating commitment among the people involved, not least with the hope that afterwards they are able to pass on their commitment to the rest of the organization.

The concept of commitment can be related to basic motivational theories such as Herzberg's motivation-hygiene theory (Herzberg, 1968). People's commitment to a strategy can grow from "satisfiers" such as greater responsibility, recognition or interesting work assignments. This is under the assumption that "hygiene factors" such as job security, pay level, relation to colleagues and so on are satisfied. In addition, participation in the strategic work can contribute to a form of self-realization owing to greater personal prestige in the organization, more recognition, greater respect from colleagues and a promotion.

The importance of commitment is further emphasized by Pascal, who argues that commitment to a vision among people is more important than if a well thought through strategy plan has been made (Pascal, 1984). This is due to the fact that concentration and passionate dedication are necessary in order to develop specific competencies and success.

Ryanair and Michael O'Leary illustrate the impact commitment can have as O'Leary displayed a commitment to implement the strategy of a low cost – no frills airline, which bordered on the obsessive. A commitment or obsession that has been instrumental to the success of Ryanair and its ability to execute, as this commitment was channelled throughout the organization.

Focus on Execution

When a Super Hornet pilot flies at the speed of more than 1,200 miles an hour, it is essential that he feels confident regarding his capabilities towards the mission. He needs to make clear decisions and he also needs to know that sufficient support and backup exist throughout his entire flight from take off to landing.

The classical approach to execution is expressed by a formal written plan with a clear description of roles, tasks, responsibilities and deadlines. With this in place the next step is on the implementation, followed by a continuous monitoring and control of the activities and the results (Johnson, 2004).

Bossidy and Charan (2002) focus on how individual managers can contribute to a more effective organization. According to them, the discipline of execution has to do with how a manager can align people, strategy and operations, i.e. the three core processes of every business. In their quest for execution they focus on these core processes instead of formulating a "vision" and leave the work of carrying it out to others. With the right people in the right jobs, the idea is that a leadership gene pool will conceive and select strategies that can be executed. People will then work together to create a strategy in line with the realities of the marketplace, the economy and the competition. Once the right people and strategy are in place, they are then linked to an operating process that results in the implementation of specific programmes and actions and that assigns accountability.

Apart from the role that a manager can play in an organization's ability to execute, there are a number of "organizational dynamics" that can also play a significant role. These dynamics can, for instance, be the relations between the individuals, the organizational processes, the systems and tools used in the organization, and the organizational structure.

Many of the companies belonging to the X-factor universe appear to be aligned according to the three core processes in order to execute rather than working under a grand vision. This allows for greater dynamics, which is illustrated by the companies' ability to navigate the competitive landscape and change position when required. For some companies such as Saxo Bank, Huawei and Ryanair this positional change dramatically alters their competitive situation and placement as discussed in Chapter 4.

Given this, no specific recipe can be offered on how to support the execution of a company's strategy and achieve the goals set forth. What can be determined, however, is that all the addressed companies analysed throughout this book focus on execution and organize accordingly.

Where Does Leadership Take Us?

There is little doubt that leadership has a significant impact on a company's Return on Strategy or its ability to increase this. Top leaders map out the strategy of their companies, they motivate the middle managers and the employees all the way through the organization to excel and sanction tough decisions in times of crisis, they are the captains of the corporate vessels that sail the competitive waters of today's business world but take us to different seas, or universes. These captains must possess a passion for what they do in order to drive their organizations towards the X-factor universe.

It is, however, not just the captain who is of importance, but also the company's ability to attract, recruit and develop the required people in order for leadership to flow through the entire organization.

Such organizationally wide leadership is needed for a company to execute its strategy with success and maintain the sense of urgency. In short a company must be aligned to execute.

Successful leadership is furthermore characterized by a certain portion of balanced behaviour, which enables the ability of a leader to project belief and instil a sense of purpose. This is particularly true for those companies that enter the X-factor universe as entry into this is tied into the unconventional and the ability to apply out-of-the-box thinking. When such approaches are taken it is necessary to have a firm belief in one-self as a leader albeit always with a focus on balancing this to avoid irrational exuberance.

Leadership genes cut across a number of the other key success drivers identified. Already in Chapter 1, the question "Can entrepreneurial managers have their cake and eat it too?" was posed. And the answer actually appears to be a "yes" when the leadership genes help companies entering the X-factor universe. Consequently, leadership genes also make an impact on the other five key success drivers discussed, notably by way of lateral characteristics such as:

- Balanced leadership
- Value-based leadership
- Talent leadership
- Execution by leadership
- Aligning leadership.

Balanced leadership is what characterized Gerstner as he performed the turnaround of IBM and Michael O'Leary who has maintained a focus on his own ideas while balancing these with the strategy of Ryanair. There is little doubt that these two as well as the leaders of companies such as Saxo Bank, Google, Facebook, Huawei and the Tata group all possess passion in abundance.

Many leading companies have become talent factories by recognizing the need to recruit and develop the leaders of tomorrow. Among those companies discussed, Saxo Bank and Huawei have both formalized this and are developing their own leaders who in turn are familiar with the organization, leading to a better alignment for execution.

Leadership is about crafting a vision and shaping the expectations. However, the real test of whether this works is when the "rubber meets the road". For leadership is also about delivering according to expectations.

12

INROADS TO THE ACHIEVEMENT OF A HIGHER RETURN ON STRATEGY

Arguably, for most companies a prerequisite for achieving Return on Strategy is a return to strategy.

Far too many companies tend to put strategic development on autopilot, display a complacent attitude towards strategy or simply deal with strategy in only a symbolic or rhetorical fashion. Moreover, a considerable number of other companies deal with strategic development strictly according to one of the many recipes available. The implications are grave when – at the same time – external contingencies like increased globalization, recessions, market failures, financial constraints, and the gradual change from a unilateral to a vulnerable multilateral power system are taken into account. Thus, there is a growing need for a return *to* strategy.

The previous chapters discussed how companies deploy various ways of unconventional strategizing to break into the X-factor universe, this final chapter will discuss how to bring the jigsaw puzzles together as well as to offer road maps as to how companies can achieve a higher Return on their Strategy. So this chapter presents a résumé of the findings in the research project and toolkits in order to facilitate the efforts towards achieving a higher Return on Strategy.

The Recipe Universe Revisited

Initially, Chapter 1 provided a clear distinction between the recipe universe and the X-factor universe, and most of the focus in Chapters 2 and 3 was expended on exploring the recipe universe. The recipe universe consists of companies adhering to the business book recipes. Most common are the recipes that list five to eight variables or recommendations that companies ought to follow in order to quickly achieve success.

However, a look at the most successful books on strategy is a telling, albeit sad, story. The game for finding the right recipe in order to do the "quick fix" has been intense. The analyses presented in Chapters 2 and 3 portray a less favourable picture than one would expect with regard to the applicability of various recipes. In short, eight major flaws were identified in the quest for finding the right strategy, as shown in Table 12.1.

Consequently, the conclusion is that companies run a considerable risk if they just follow the business book recipes. The probability that the board or the top management adopting and executing one of the recipe strategies will end up as a fail-

Table 12.1 **Eight major flaws**

1 An unacceptably high number of the companies listed in the recipe management books eventually fails

2 Some of the same companies are used as models for exercise to justify widely different recipes

3 The recipes leave no room for residual factors or something unexplained

4 The recipes expose perfect correlation between the recipes and success as otherwise assumed

5 No proof has been issued to justify the assumed cause–effect relation between the recipes and success

6 Hidden and even unhidden problems in many of the successful did companies not addressed

7 The delusion of the so-called halo effect takes over

8 Best practice is difficult, from time to time impossible, to transform from one company to another

ure is definitely there. Invariably, it does not seem advisable for companies to follow the recipes in the literature, because the risk of failure is too high. Exactly how big this risk is remains impossible to assess precisely, but far too many companies end up trying a "quick fix" based on one of the traditional recipes and eventually fail or are otherwise left with a dissatisfactory low Return on Strategy.

One of the first inroads to gaining a high Return on Strategy is to stay out of the recipe universe – or at least be cautious – and to reject the idea that a "quick fix" is possible as a successful solution to the strategic challenges of the company. Before the inroads are outlined, the notion of "success" as dealt with in the recipe universe will be explicated.

What Is Success?

In the book "Outliers" (2008) the author Malcolm Gladwell poses the question:[1] Why do some people become successful and live remarkably productive and impactful lives, while so many more never reach their potential?" In the book, he examines the lives of various individuals from Mozart to Bill Gates, and he builds a convincing case for how successful people rise on a tide of advantages which some did deserve, some not, some did earn, and some were just lucky. Along with talent and ambition, the outliers enjoyed an unusual opportunity to intensively cultivate a skill that allowed them to rise above their peers.

The notion of success as dealt with in the recipe literature is questionable. Viewing the recipe as the independent variable leaves us with "success" as the dependent variable. Success is often measured by the stock performance at a glance or over a limited span of time. This conforms to what is typical in the recipe universe, namely a static view of the sample companies. At any rate, success seems to be closely tied to financial performance. But is that a fair means of measurement?

We know from the accelerating global crisis in 2009 that even companies who had performed reasonably well according to usual value criteria, suddenly ran into deep trouble, principally because of being cash strapped. It is a matter of fact that the so-called recipe literature has never addressed solvency issues as part of the financial definitions of success. Strangely enough it is very obvious to every reasonable onlooker that solvency issues are a matter of life or death when it comes to business failures, as was the case with the beginning of the 2008/09 financial crisis when first companies like Lehman Brothers, Fannie Mae, Freddie Mac, then other parts of the banking sector and later on other industries, such as automotives, ran out of cash. As the financial parameters are important in times of business failure, why should they not be important when looking at the background of business success?

Consequently, this book defines success differently, allowing for a broad range of parameters, including, but not limited to, a subset of financial parameters – and not only the usual stock listing and profitability criteria – to play an important part of bringing companies away from the pitfalls of the recipe universe and into the roads to the X-factor universe.

"Return on Strategy" and "Success": They Are Not One and the Same

Generally, this book tries to avoid using and advocating the term "success". Rather, the new umbrella terminology of "Return on Strategy" is extensively used as a first stepping stone to develop more fine-tuned means of measurements than was the case with the binary nature of "success" (and "failure"). Furthermore, success often goes together with a subjective perception of performance as evidenced by Rosenzweig's halo effect. Finally, stock performance and similar types of measurements have not proved a satisfactory degree of validity.

Conversely, Return on Strategy focuses on the actual achievement of the company compared with its strategic goals. Initially, one can pose the question: did the company fulfil its strategic goals? However, this would typically only lead to a binary answer, i.e. a "yes" or a "no". The terminology around Return on Strategy is therefore taken several steps further than this. In the intended mode, a company achieves full (or 100%) effectiveness if it fulfils all its strategic goals on time and with the resources allocated. Achieving exactly 100% Return on Strategy will rarely be the case. Most companies will obtain a lower Return on Strategy. Others may easily obtain a higher Return on Strategy, if the management and the Board play sand-bagging tactics and display mediocre strategic ambitions by setting the goals unrealistically low in order to be able to demonstrate overperformance when the moment of accountability (and maybe even bonus payments) ticks in. Others might be overoptimistic and outline very high ambitions and then later blame institutional elements in the environment for preventing the company from achieving its goals.

However, companies in the X-factor universe rarely use tactics concerning the level of ambition with regard to strategic goals. Such companies often outperform and do better than even their own strategic goals.

What is suggested here are some key qualitative and limited quantitative means of measurement, and this book certainly does not put a stop to the development of measurements, which is a virgin field for many companies. Additionally, this book advocates for comparative assessments, for example, paired comparisons between a given company and its peers. This means that not only is the company's own Return on Strategy addressable, also its relative performance adds to the picture of whether a company is fit for the X-factor universe.

Much literature on strategy seems to overlook the fact that many companies do not have a shareholder's criterion of maximizing the stock value in a limited span of time as their primary goal. A considerable number of very successful companies are not even stock listed, and other companies do not have profitability as the foremost criterion of success on the agenda. Some examples from this book may illuminate this particular point.

Skype is a type of company which was declared a success early on despite the fact that it burnt money from the very beginning and until a considerable span of time after they were acquired by eBay. They were not stock listed and would therefore not qualify for featuring in the usual business books. However, Skype was a tremendously satisfactory business case in that the founders managed to come out of their KaZaA venture, achieved an impressive amount of downloads of their software, and disposed of their shares at a much more attractive level than they had actually dreamt of themselves. In short, they were hugely successful as they had overperformed their strategic ambitions.

Another example is Hotmail. The founders neither had the time, nor resources to strictly follow a strategy. They were – like the KaZaA predecessor to Skype – in a crisis and had to invent a mail system which they could access anonymously. Once invented, they had fulfilled their strategy, yet they discovered a need and a utility beyond their expectations for their product, which subsequently was strongly demanded in the market. Thus, Hotmail is an innovation or business development case much more than a case of profitability and stock development.

These examples illustrate that the conventional method of measuring success has no applicability with regard to such business cases where the initial goal may not be tied to profitability and where stock listing never occurred. Arguably, there is a need to (re-)define the success criteria. Rather than stock listing, profitability and similar criteria, success in the X-factor universe depends on whether companies fulfil their strategic ambitions and deliver accordingly in a way that is attractive compared with their peers.

In summary, a major inroad to Return on Strategy is to deal with the "comparative effectiveness", comprising the two components addressed earlier in this chapter, namely the internal part of Return on Strategy assessment ("effectiveness") and the external component of Return on Strategy ("comparative"). This leads the company to the following questions: Do we have 50% Return on our Strategy or do we have 100% or almost 100% return? And how is our performance compared with our peers?

In the cases of Lehman Brothers, Fannie Mae and Freddie Mac the Return on Strategy was low or 0%. In the cases of Skype and Hotmail, the Return on Strategy was over and above 100%.

Beginning to Unfold the X-factor Universe

The X-factor has been explained as containing an element of something indefinable. Every business case and the strategic stewardship of any company contain elements of something indefinable. It is thus intellectually impossible to set up an equation or a recipe which includes a definition of the indefinable. That was precisely one of the reasons why the existing recipes failed.

Thinking "Out of the Box"

However, this book has consistently tried to approach the indefinable and seek definitive explanations as to how some companies manage so well in the X-factor universe. Contrary to companies seeking the recipe universe, many of the company stories told in this book are characterized by thinking *out-of-the-box*. One example is Steve Wozniak, the former CEO of Apple, when he said that all the best that he did at Apple came from (1) not having any money and (2) not having done it before, ever.

By not having any monetary resources, Apple had to think "out-of-the-box" and it is then hardly surprising that Apple ends up with business innovation based on "not having done it before, ever". The Apple innovations comprise a well-known suite of product successes, more recently with iPod, iPhone and iTunes, whereby Apple has created a new ecosystem with a number of unprecedented market tactics.

Their innovations have been brought to the market in the spirit of Steve Wozniak. By way of thinking "out-of-the-box" they have managed to cross the chasm[2] several times, not least with their hotly discussed iPhone. They managed to create a considerable amount of hype by way of building up expectations and, from time to time, underinforming the market. As one among several examples this was the case both at the 2007 and at the 2008 3GSM world conferences, when around 60,000 participants could find all mobile terminals and other equipment and services exhibited but had to look vainly for Apple. It appears that Apple built up much more trust, expectations, WOM (word of mouth) and so on by staying away from this number one yearly event in the industry.

All the Key Success Drivers as Part of the Strategic Engine

When reviewing all the key success drivers that have been discussed in Chapters 6–11, the notion of trigger events and key success drivers for entering or remaining in the X-factor universe become particularly important for a good start to the strategic engine. As is the case with an engine in real life, it can be started and turned off several times, run at different speeds and change over time. Likewise, there are numerous ways in which the strategic engine can be started and, once started, may change dynamically over time.

Trigger Events – the Opportunity

Trigger events as discussed in Chapter 5, "What triggers strategy?", are those events that present a company with an opportunity to redefine the current strategic situation and kick off the strategic engine. Companies facing a crisis are forced to rethink, but can do so in many ways, and when unconventional thinking is applied it can lead to new and prosperous strategic opportunities. When a strategy fails, it may in some cases lead to unforeseen opportunities as companies are once again forced to rethink and in many cases apply out-of-the-box thinking to approach the X-factor universe. Similarly, planned efforts, when these include a conscious element of unconventional thinking, and lucky breaks often lead to strategies that migrate a company from the recipe universe to the X-factor universe.

Saxo Bank is a prime example of how a crisis can act as a trigger event which will lead to a successful entry into the X-factor universe. If plotted along the strategy system, this migration becomes evident as Saxo Bank, prior to its crisis, was pursuing a strategy involving a large component of competing in a red ocean and imitating the competitors combined with a small component of blue ocean activity and innovation. After changing its strategy to become an IT-focused brokerage, the profile of Saxo Bank changed radically as shown in Figure 12.1. Using the strategy system in this way will allow companies to identify opportunities that either assist in the migration towards the X-factor universe or allow them to stay tuned to the changing dynamics of the marketplace.

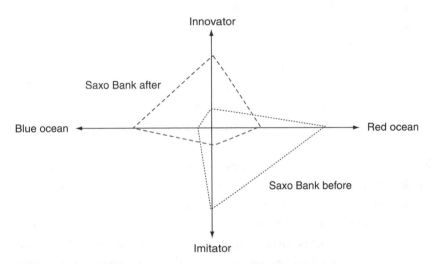

Figure 12.1 **The strategy system applied to Saxo Bank.**

In addition, plotting a company's strategy along all four dimensions of the strategy system allows for the strategist to explore the possibilities of bridging the four strategic perspectives and how such bridge building can lead to potentially new and unconventional strategies.

Just plotting a company's strategy along the four dimensions alone will not yield passage to the X-factor universe, which is exactly what the key success drivers may help realize. In Chapters 6–11, six key success drivers were identified as a non-exhaustive list of those that the companies analysed have used in unconventional ways in order to break free of the recipe universe and to enter into the X-factor universe.

The Strategic Engine: The Key Success Drivers at Work

As described in Chapter 4, the key success drivers are those that are significantly utilized by the companies analysed when the strategic engine has been started in order to achieve a high Return on Strategy. The companies have also deployed unconventional methods and out-of-the-box thinking in order to achieve their success and place in the X-factor universe in a variety of ways regarding the following six key success drivers:

- Customer attitudes
- Product portfolio
- Financial circuit
- Organizational design
- Technological chain
- Leadership genes.

Each of these six key success drivers may furthermore be broken down into what is termed "bearing points". These carry some resemblance to indicators in that a key success driver is easier to cover and explain, the more relevant the indicators and bearing points are. However, bearing points take the reader one step further than do indicators, because bearing points also suggest a desired action or direction. It is a matter of fact that companies belonging to the X-factor universe are actively pursuing many of the bearing points identified.

Bearing points cover, for example, the ability to involve the customer in the production of goods, the ability to short circuit existing pricing mechanisms or the ability to deploy proven technology to produce innovative products. As such, the bearing points act as directional signs on road maps.

In the following sections, the six key success drivers and the bearing points identified will be presented using a road map tool. This tool allows the strategist to map the bearing points of a company for each key success driver to either gain a picture of how they fare compared with their peers or to understand how the strategy has evolved or should evolve over time. As such the "Key Success Driver Road Map" allows for a static view of the company compared with its peers or a dynamic view of the company and the strategic journey it undertakes in order to increase the likelihood of reaching the X-factor universe destination and subsequently also the achievement of a high Return on Strategy.

As is the case with directional signs on road maps in the traffic, the onlooker may always look for more in order to be sufficiently guided. However, there is always a balance to strike, and the bearing points in the following sections do therefore not purport to be exhaustive.

CUSTOMER ATTITUDES

By analysing how companies have approached customer attitudes, these being the attitude towards customers as well as the attitude of customers, some bearing points were identified as unconventional and instrumental in the assessment of how companies reached and maintained their position within the X-factor universe.

Four bearing points were identified as important (although not purporting to be fully exhaustive):

- Customer involvement – pro-sumer
- Customer-centric marketing
- Customers as viral ambassadors – WOW & WOM
- Channel utilization – channel conflict.

Companies such as Google, Facebook, Ryanair, Saxo Bank and Dell all involve the customers in the production of their goods and services, and by doing so short circuit traditional thinking. Similarly, traditional theory on marketing is circumvented by the customer-centric marketing used by, for example, Procter & Gamble, whereas using the customers as viral ambassadors was essential to the achievements of, for example, Google, Face-book, Hotmail and Ryanair.

In terms of channel conflict, Saxo Bank has very successfully implemented a strategy which in a traditional sense is ill advised as they target both the retail and wholesale segments simultan-eously and therefore work on the basis of potential channel conflict.

Using Saxo Bank as an example, the Key Success Driver Road Map can be developed to encompass how it fares on the four bearing points and how these have changed over more than a decade when compared with the initial strategy of the company as shown in Figure 12.2. The figure illustrates the dynamic nature of both the road map and the Return on Strategy. First of all, companies are usually "underway", and the road map in Figure 12.2 precisely illustrates a dynamic development from "point A to point B", i.e. from the initial to the current strategy. Second, strategies may change over time, and the road map tool allows for alterations whereby the slope and the level of the curves may change. The tool also allows for the identification of additional or changed bearing points.

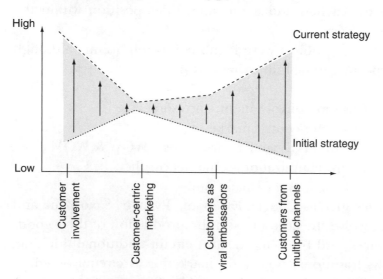

Figure 12.2 **The Key Success Driver Road Map for customer attitudes and Saxo Bank (illustrative).**

As seen from Figure 12.2, Saxo Bank has changed its focus to involve the customer to a high degree as the users of their online trading platform place their own investments – they act as producers of the product. This involvement of the customer also translates to a medium degree of customer-centric marketing as the users are very much at the centre of the products developed. Using customers as viral ambassadors has likewise been a growing feature of Saxo Bank given the increased information sharing among online investors. Finally, Saxo Bank's ability to exploit channel conflict by servicing the retail and wholesale segment simultaneously truly sets them apart.

Saxo Bank's ability to utilize customer attitudes as a key success driver in a unique way is what Figure 12.2 captures. It must, however, be noted that the bearing points and the key success driver as a whole should be used in a dynamic way to allow for the changes that continuously occur in the marketplace.

PRODUCT PORTFOLIO

Where the customer attitudes belong to the demand side of the company's ecosystem, the product line of the company is a key success driver which is more closely tied to the supply side. However, to some extent, companies in the X-factor universe are able to blur or manipulate this distinction, which is evident from some of the five most salient bearing points identified:

- Stickiness of the core product
- Products constitute a proprietary ecosystem
- Products as business modelling
- Creation of demand pull
- Product life-cycle management attention.

As an example, companies like Skype and Google have been diligently blurring or manipulating the demand by creating an unprecedented strong pull effect in the market zone towards their product offerings.

With Skype as an example, the bearing points and the road map is displayed in Figure 12.3 based on a paired comparison with traditional incumbents. This figure displays how Skype has been utilizing specific bearing points in order to outperform traditional incumbents within the communications industry. By way of a product with stickiness, Skype has been able to create a new ecosystem and blur the distinction between supply and demand relations as viewed in the traditional micro-economic theory. By excellent downloadable software that is free of charge and utilized on investments already made by the customers, Skype has been able to create a strong demand pull effect.

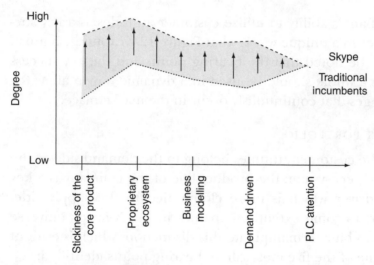

Figure 12.3 **Product portfolio: Skype compared with traditional incumbents (illustrative).**

Moreover, Skype has shown that its business model is viable, whereas the longer term calls for considerations with regard to life-cycle management of the products in order to sustain its place in the X-factor universe. A company like Novo Nordisk has shown the way forward in that they have high spending on research and development, making the insulin and related line of products tuned to stay competitive with products from other pharmaceutical companies that have a much broader and less focused product portfolio.

FINANCIAL CIRCUIT

In the recipe universe, the financial aspect is only (part of) the outcome. Not one of the recipes actually included financial aspects as a driver (independent variable), so financial aspects only came into the equation when measuring the outcome of companies following a recipe. More specifically, financial aspects are then often reduced to stock listing and profitability criteria.

Within the X-factor universe, financial aspects play a different and, from time to time, more prominent role. Rather than viewing financial aspects as an outcome, financial aspects become a significant independent variable, i.e. a key success driver which may be broken down into several bearing points. Some of the most important bearing points that were identified in relation to how X-factor universe companies took advantage of this key success driver covered the following:

- Price killers
- Cost innovators
- Reverse cash flows
- Co-opetition/Financial partnering.

The price killers mainly consist of companies using reverse pricing mechanisms in order to generate revenue from third-party resources, allowing them to offer their core product or service free of charge or at an unprecedented low price (see Appendix I and the notion of the so-called zero-SAC business cases). Google, Facebook and Skype are prime examples of such companies. Hot on the heels of these, one finds the discount companies, such as Ryanair, that are able to break traditional demand curves by offering a discounted product that leads to overall value destruction for the industry as a whole.

The recent rise of the Chinese dragons has put cost innovation on the agenda, but this approach stretches beyond solely Chinese companies to also encompass companies such as Samsung Electronics and Dell who have innovated production processes in order to offer high quality at low price. By innovating their production process, Dell also managed to reverse the traditional cash flow, leading to them being paid by their customers prior to them paying their suppliers.

Saxo Bank successfully utilized co-opetition by offering their proprietary trading platform to the competition in order to grow the market as a whole and is a prime example of financial partnering. Financial partnering allowed Wahaha to break into the market for carbonated drinks in rural China as distributors were approached with considerable effect.

Dell is utilized as an example in Figure 12.4. Rather than comparing the initial strategy of Dell to their current, the Key Success Driver Road Map is here used to map Dell against its peers in the industry. As shown in Figure 12.4, Dell makes considerable use of the price killer model, given their focus on offering low-priced PCs to the end customer, whereas traditional manufacturers, such as Hewlett-Packard, charge higher prices. Likewise, Dell has innovated the value chain, notably by reducing the costs of producing PCs by selling directly to the customer, who in turn configure the PCs themselves via the online portal of

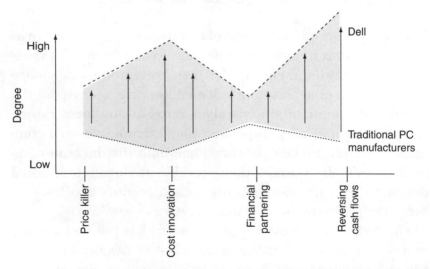

Figure 12.4 **Key Success Driver Road Map for financial circuit and Dell (illustrative).**

Dell. Financial partnering is an area with little difference between Dell and traditional PC manufacturers as all are seeking to partner with both suppliers, retailers and, to some extent, customers. Dell, however, has managed to refine its business model and its utilization of the financial circuit in such a way that it has effectively reversed the traditional flow of cash, which none of its peers has managed to do effectively so far.

By applying unconventional thinking to the financial circuit, Dell has developed its own unique road map to how the key success drivers can best be utilized in the pursuit of a high Return on their Strategy.

All the bearing points addressed in the context of the financial circuit as a key success driver fall within the market zone or competition in the traditional sense. Basically, the same applied to the previous key success drivers focusing on the demand and supply side, respectively. However, as touched upon in Chapter 7, some industries also bring significant resources in and out of the institutional zone. In some cases, financial bailout packages are established because an industry is already heavily regulated and considered vital, for example, the banking sector, leading forward to almost de facto nationalization as was the case in the UK. In other cases, some countries award bailout instruments to a sector like the automotive sector which seem somewhat better suited to work in the institutional zone than other sectors.

ORGANIZATIONAL DESIGN

Optimizing the organizational design is also a key success driver in the strategic engine, focusing on the internal zone within the company itself. Working with this key success driver could lead forward to many bearing points, however when narrowed down, the following seem to be the most important:

- Structural alignment
- Value driven
- Unique culture
- People oriented.

One prime example of a company which actively utilizes its structure as a central theme of its strategy is Naturhouse. Naturhouse has successfully utilized a franchise concept to grow its business. In this case, strategy followed structure, which is considered unconventional by many.

All the companies addressed hold a clear focus on their values. Values must be authentic and incorporate a long-term perspective, which translates to a value-driven organization that uses these to create a common purpose. Not surprisingly, the culture of these companies is centred on these values and furthermore aligned to the strategy of the company.

By focusing on their culture and values, X-factor universe companies are able to instil a passion among their employees that is aligned with the purpose of the company. In many of the companies, the passion is supported by people and performance incentives.

For Google the road map, and how this compares with a traditional ecosystem, can be illustrated as shown in Figure 12.5. The culture of Google is characterized as unique by many and this rests to a large degree on its authentic values and its people-

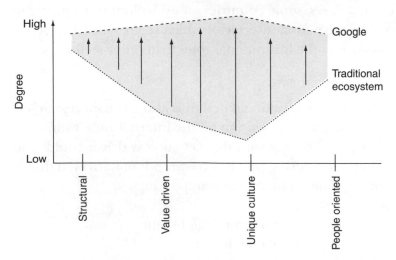

Figure 12.5 **Key Success Driver Road Map for organizational design and Google (illustrative).**

oriented approach. The innovative culture is furthermore supported by people and performance-based incentives.

Whereas authentic values may lie at the centre of traditional companies, these rarely drive the culture of the companies, which in many cases are driven by short-term financial targets. In addition, traditional companies are more oriented towards products rather than their people. Google has deliberately used the above bearing points to establish a unique competitive position that has assisted them to enter the X-factor universe and gain a high Return on their Strategy.

TECHNOLOGICAL CHAIN

To illustrate the bearing points that form some of the main pillars of how companies utilize the technological chain, the example of Saxo Bank is used. The Key Success Driver Road Map for the technological chain of Saxo Bank and how this compares with traditional brokerage companies is shown in Figure 12.6. It is worth noting that the profile of traditional brokerages, as shown in Figure 12.6, matches that of Saxo Bank prior to its strategic shift and its focus on becoming an IT-focused brokerage.

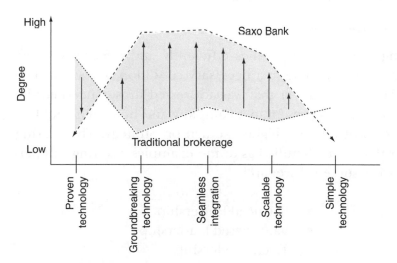

Figure 12.6 **Key Success Driver Road Map for the technological chain and Saxo Bank (illustrative).**

As can be seen from Figure 12.6, the five important bearing points that have been identified are:

- Proven technology
- Groundbreaking technology
- Seamless integration of technology
- Scalable technology
- Simple technology.

While Saxo Bank did not deploy proven technology to a high degree, this is indeed what characterizes companies such as Google, Ryanair and Skype. Having a high degree of proven technology does not exclude also having a high degree of groundbreaking technology as the examples of Google and Ryanair show.

Saxo Bank's ability to integrate its technology throughout its value chain has been instrumental in achieving straight-through-processing, leading to a high quality product and improved transparency. Additionally, the high degree of scalable technology and less focus on keeping it simple is what constitutes the unique Key Success Driver Road Map for Saxo Bank and how it utilizes the technological chain.

LEADERSHIP GENES

Driving the leadership genes efficiently and effectively is the closest one may come to a necessary condition of success. The final key success driver that was addressed thus concerned the leadership genes present in a company and how such could be used to navigate for a higher Return on Strategy. The bearing points that were identified as prime examples covering this particular key success driver are:

- Balanced leadership
- Value-based leadership
- Talent leadership
- Execution by leadership
- Aligned leadership.

Companies in the X-factor universe and the leaders of these are able to balance the vision and ideas of the top executive with those of the organization and as such manage to align these. This is true for companies such as Ryanair, Google, Huawei and Saxo Bank.

Developing talent or "talenting" is becoming an increasingly important bearing point given that human resources are the scarce capital of the future and, furthermore, that internally developed leaders will be better aligned to the organization and how to execute its strategy. Inspired by some of the leading talent factories such as General Electric, Procter & Gamble and Hindustan Unilever, Saxo Bank and Huawei have both formalized the development of internal talent. Such internal development will assist in executing the strategy. However, leaders must also show a talent for execution by continuously focusing on and evangelizing the need for execution. In addition to leading by example and thus instilling a sense of urgency and attention to execution, the entire organization must be aligned to execute, which is another feature of the X-factor universe companies. Ryanair is a prime example of a company that is aligned to execute from top to bottom.

The key success driver of leadership and the above identified bearing points all impact the other five drivers as a vision balanced to that of the organization will influence customer attitudes, product portfolio, financial circuit, organizational design and technology. This is also the case in terms of the values that are projected and used for leadership. Growing the talent base will invariably impact all the identified key success drivers as middle and executive managers are put in charge of the functional areas relating to these. Executing and being aligned for execution is a matter of mobilizing the key success drivers in the strategic engine.

The tasks and the challenges of leaders are to anticipate changes and proactively position their companies to be even more successful than they were under the status quo. A key leadership role is to, on a continuous basis, intervene, develop and transform the key success drivers of the company. This concerns the individual key success drivers and the combination of these. The leadership role is also to carefully position the company in the three zones as discussed earlier, and by this strive for durability in the X-factor universe.

The Return on Strategy Framework Revisited

The idea of issuing a framework in Chapter 4 for working with the notion of Return on Strategy was first and foremost to structure the highly complex groundwork for helping companies achieve a high Return on Strategy.

The framework has served as a framework, i.e. a map and a checklist rather than a recipe. The framework stands in contrast to recipes as it does not carry specific recommendations as to what exactly companies should do or abstain from doing. Rather, it provides a framework for launching and conducting the strategy process, and subsequently allowing for appropriate soft measuring on whether a company subsequently achieved Return on their Strategy.

However, some would naturally ask: Do we need to work equally thoroughly with all key success drivers? Likewise: Do we need to work with all the road maps and the bearing points in our strategy process going forward?

First of all, it is very clear that not all companies in the X-factor universe pay equal attention to all the six key success drivers. For example, a company like Hotmail paid considerable attention to viral marketing which they, in fact, invented. Less attention, if any, was paid to the financial circuit, the organizational design and the leadership genes, at least at the beginning of the venture. However, what is important in the strategy process of a company is that the attention given to a key driver is a deliberate choice.

Second, the key success drivers are interlinked to some extent, which is graphically expressed by the somewhat overlapping circles in Figure 12.7. The linkage is even more outspoken when it comes to the key success driver labelled leadership

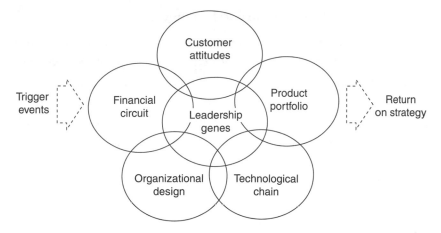

Figure 12.7 **The Return on Strategy framework.**

genes. The reason for this is that the entrepreneurial spirit behind the leadership genes and leadership in general is intertwined with all the five other key success drivers. In fact, the strategic leadership, including the execution of a strategy, is very much tied to the skills and the performance of the management. Consequently, leadership genes have a status as a necessary condition of achieving a high Return on Strategy.

Finally, one of the implications of this is that the bearing points identified are not fully mutually exclusive, far less exhaustive either. Rather, they are to be utilized as a checklist that may be added and subtracted during the strategy process.

However, with the Return on Strategy framework, the different types of trigger events and modes of strategy, the six key success drivers, the bearing points, the road map technique and the possibility of measuring Return on Strategy a toolkit has been presented to be used in the strategy process of a company.

Return to Strategy

Dynamism is increasingly interesting: "*The living company stands a better chance of living longer – of reducing the gap between the average and the maximum life expectancy of the corporate species*".[3]

As addressed earlier, crises are particularly important when it comes to the understanding of Return on Strategy. First of all, many companies begin the most important part of their journey during their own crisis and cross the chasm by out-of-the-box-thinking thereby reaching the X-factor universe destination. This was exactly the way that Skype, Hotmail, Ryanair, Saxo Bank and many others achieved a very high Return on their Strategy.

Many companies have been addressed in this book and not only the success stories in widely different geographies, but also unfortunate failures. Inevitably, most readers will now pose the following question: "The successful companies that you have depicted – will they remain in the X-factor universe during the next decade and continue achieving a high Return on Strategy?" The answer to this straightforward question is not a roaring "YES", it is rather a silent "yes" in a few cases, a "maybe" in other cases, and a "no" in some instances.

However, the book started off with Saxo Bank which is definitely depicted as a company with the potential to continue in the X-factor universe, based on its strong IT platform, the growing international brand recognition, its strengthening of the top level management and its ability and eagerness to exploit the financial crisis starting in 2008. Continuing on this road and constantly staying tuned will probably yield a high Return on Strategy going forward.

The company may put this in danger if it diversifies into activities where there is no strategic synergy with its present core competence, if it moves into shareholder or stakeholder conflicts, or even if it develops different lines of business activities successfully but without alignment, for example, if a strong global brand is built up expensively but without an appropriate match with current and future products and services. Invariably, all companies may expose themselves to such risks and thereby extinguish any reasonable momentum achieved.

By consistently focusing on the various key success drivers, subscribing to unconventional thinking and exercising leadership on how to achieve Return on Strategy many companies, including Saxo Bank, may mitigate risks considerably and continue achieving a disproportionately high Return on Strategy compared with their peers.

Some companies do not walk the last mile and undertake the accountability of assessing and ensuring the achievement of a satisfactory Return on Strategy. Other companies do not deal with strategy at all and far too many companies strategize at a symbolic or rhetorical level. Arguably, for most companies a prerequisite for achieving Return on Strategy is a return to strategy.

APPENDIX I
Zero-SAC

By implementing the zero-SAC profile, a financial gain can be achieved compared with a conventional, costly SAC profile. With zero-SAC there is room for more competitive prices. Due to the price elasticity effect this leads to an increase in turnover. Higher quantities of sales eventually results in a financial gain for the zero-SAC provider in a standard competitive environment. Finally, a zero-SAC strategy implies a much more attractive risk profile than is the case with a conventional, costly SAC profile.

Structure of this Strategic-Financial Report on Zero-SAC

This appendix starts with a definition of zero-SAC. Next, there is an explanation of the model and the mathematical approach behind the model. Subsequently there follows a four-step procedure explaining the benefits of the zero-SAC profile, backed up by the mathematical fundamentals of the model. After that, the Net Present Value (NPV) effect is taken into consideration. Lastly, we arrive at the conclusion, addressing both the attractiveness and the risk profile of the zero-SAC approach compared with the conventional approach. Moreover, some perspectives are outlined. Additionally, there is an explanatory mathematical appendix.

Zero-SAC – Definition

Sales and acquisition costs or subscriber acquisition costs (SAC) is the average cost of taking up a new customer. Taking the mobile communications sector as an example, mobile "cellular" operators and – to a lesser extent – virtual operators frequently pay incentives to retailers, who bring in customers to their networks. They also usually subsidize the costs of mobile phones (heavily so in the case of contract/subscription customers). The SAC of contract connections is usually far higher than that of prepaid connections because of the greater incentives and subsidies.

By zero-SAC we refer to a profile were the SAC by definition is zero (or close to zero). This means that there is room for lowering the prices of the services for the zero-SAC operator. With more competitive prices, the zero-SAC operator will attract more customers from higher priced competitors. All other things being equal, the favourable prices of the zero-SAC operator will lead to an increase of minutes of usage (MoU) for its customers. This increase in MoU will eventually lead to a financial gain for the zero-SAC operator.

Elaborating the Model

Next, we will compare two profiles.

- The premium profile (costly SAC)
- The discount profile (zero-SAC).

Assumptions for the Model

- The average subscriber life-time is given (all customers have the same profile)
- The costly SAC and zero-SAC profiles intersect at the "neutral point".

Mathematical Approach

X = neutral point of average life-time

π = Profit

α = Constant

β = Coefficient

$\pi = \alpha + \beta X$

where

α (premium profile) < 0
α (discount profile) = 0
β (premium profile) > β (discount profile)

In the model, the following numbers are assumed:
Costly SAC (premium profile)
Profit = −60 + 10X
Zero-SAC (discount profile) → without effect of MoU increase
Profit = 0 + 2.5X
Zero-SAC (discount profile) → with effect of MoU increase
Profit = 0 + 5X
We assume in this report that the customer's average lifetime,
X = 8.

Step 1. The "Normal" Costly SAC Profile

Profit = −60 + 10X
Profit = −60 + 10 × 8
Profit = 20

The premium profile attracts customers, i.e. by subsidizing the cost of mobile phones. Therefore, they have a high SAC (negative: −60) as illustrated in Figure A.1. Due to premium prices the cash flow profile has a relatively steep slope (in this case: 10X). Notice that the company's break even point is close to the end of the average customer life-time. At the neutral point, however, the premium profile generates a profit as illustrated in Figure A.1 (however, reaching the neutral point is not given if the customer churns or does not pay the assumed amount before the cash profile curve intersects the X-axis).

Step 2. The Reduced Tariff with Zero-SAC Profile

Profit = 0 + 2.5X
Profit = 0 + 2.5 × 8
Profit = 20

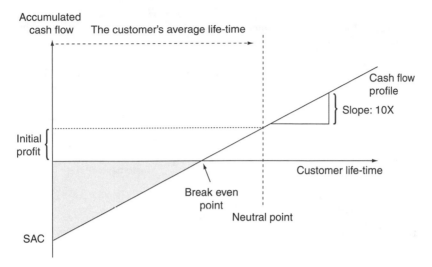

Figure A.1 **The conventional approach.**

If the company instead chooses a zero-SAC profile, the SAC is by nature never negative.

A part of this discount profile is, naturally, that they compete on prices, resulting in a lower profit margin. Therefore, the cash flow profile from the zero-SAC profile has a less steep slope than the more costly SAC profile (in this case: 2.5X versus 10X). So far, the discount profile and the premium profile are cqually profitable given the average life-time of a customer (see Figure A.2).

Step 3. The Increase of MoU (Minutes of Usage) with Zero-SAC Profile

Profit = 0 + 5X
Profit = 0 + 5 × 8
Profit = 40

Due to lower prices for the discount profile the price elasticity of the customers leads to an increase in MoU. This results in an upside potential for the zero-SAC profile resulting in a shift in the zero-SAC curve to the new MoU increase curve. Due to an increase in MoU (higher quantity), the cash flow curve in this case shifts to 5X (from 2.5X). This is illustrated in Figure A.3.

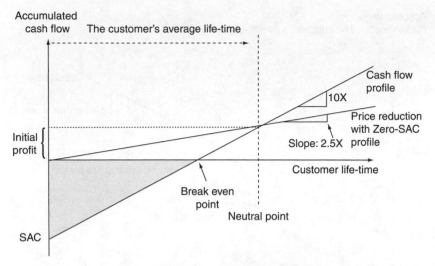

Figure A.2 **Reducing the tariffs.**

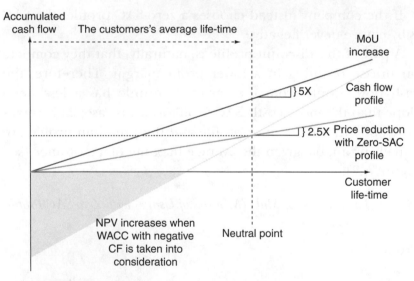

Figure A.3 **The increase in MoU.**

Step 4. Financial Gain

Below is a comparison of the new cash flow profile with the MoU increase and the ordinary cash flow profile with the costly SAC.

The increase of MoU with the zero-SAC profile:

The costly SAC profile.
Profit = 0 + 5X   Profit = −60 + 10X
Profit = 0 + 5 × 8   Profit = −60 + 10 × 8
Profit = 40   Profit = 20
Zero-SAC (with MoU increase effect)   > costly SAC
                                      40 > 20

The MoU increase results in a financial gain expressed as the difference between the current cash flow profile (costly SAC) and the MoU increase profile caused by the zero-SAC profile. With zero-SAC there is considerable room for more competitive prices. Due to the price elasticity effect, this leads to an increase in MoU. Higher quantities of sales eventually result in a financial gain for the zero-SAC operator. The shaded area in Figure A.4 shows this increase of cash flow over time by the MoU increase effect.

The costly SAC profile for the premium profile results in high negative cash flow in the beginning of the period for this

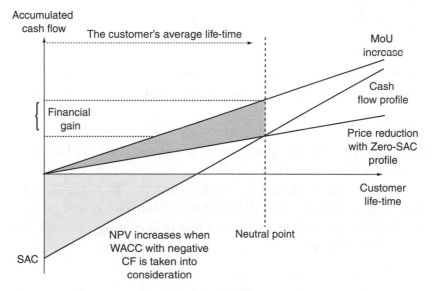

Figure A.4 **The two approaches and the financial gain.**

strategy. When we take into account the Weighted Average Cost of Capital (WACC) of the negative cash flow, the zero-SAC profile is even more beneficial.

Calculating and Comparing the NPV Effects

In addition to the upside potential of the MoU increase, the NPV effect of the costly SAC profile further promotes the zero-SAC profile. An example of this is given below.

Assumption: WACC of 10% per period. Figure A.5 illustrates the time value of money effect of the costly SAC versus the zero-SAC profile. Column 1 illustrates both the positive and negative effects of the costly SAC profile. Column 2 illustrates the NPV effect of the SAC profile. Column 3 illustrates the NPV effect of the zero-SAC profile.

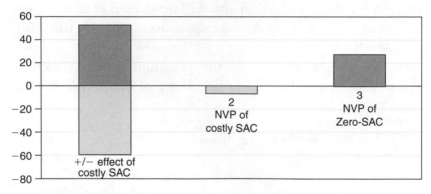

Figure A.5 **The time aspect in conjunction with NPV.**

In this extreme example, the costly SAC profile gives a negative NPV (–6.65) compared with a substantially higher NPV (26.67) of the zero-SAC profile.

Although this is just an illustrative example, it clearly demonstrates the benefits of a zero-SAC profile. With no initial outlays, the time value of money effect is less dominating than for the costly SAC profile.

Table A.1 **NPV with regard to the costly SAC approach**

Period	0	1	2	3	4	5	6	7	8	
Costly SAC	−60	10	10	10	10	10	10	10	10	NPV
	−60	9.09	8.26	7.51	6.83	6.21	5.64	5.13	4.67	(6.65)

Table A.2 **NPV with regard to the zero-SAC approach**

Period	0	1	2	3	4	5	6	7	8	
Zero-SAC	0	5.0	5.0	5.0	5.0	5.0	5.0	5.0	5.0	NPV
	0	4.55	4.13	3.76	3.42	3.10	2.82	2.57	2.33	26.67

Conclusions and Perspectives

Evidently, the zero-SAC approach implies a financial gain which does not exist with the conventional, costly SAC approach. Invariably, this prompts reflections on the risk profile of the two approaches addressed.

Generally, the zero-SAC philosophy has a more attractive risk profile than the conventional approach comprising a high SAC level; see Table A.3, where this is illustrated with examples including the case of terminal subsidies within the mobile communications industry.

The conclusion is, therefore, that the zero-SAC approach is not only the most profitable approach in churn-rich environments but also the approach with the most attractive risk profile. There are important wider repercussions of this finding for industries other than the mobile communications business, for example Google and Skype. Moreover, the zero-SAC concept also forms some of the theoretical background for what Ryanair did in practice. Essentially, Ryanair extinguished as much SAC as it possibly could – electronic ticketing, guerilla-based marketing in the press (better than getting advertisements for free), no agents or dealers ("Agents are a bloody waste of time"), plus the WOW and WOM effects. Thus, the zero-SAC is one of the tools companies can use in order to approach the

Table A.3 **Risk profiles**

Issue	The conventional SAC risk profile	The zero-SAC risk profile
Cash flow	High – due to high up-front costs	Low – due to low (zero) up-front costs
Customer retention, short-run	Low – due to lock-in of the customer with a high terminal subsidy	Low – as the customer has just signed up to a cheaper offering
Customer retention, long-run	High – many customers would like to have a new terminal subsidy or churn	High or low depending on whether a terminal is provisioned at an attractive price point (1)
Aggregate	*HIGH RISK*	*LOW RISK*

Note
1 As the zero-SAC strategy generates high volumes, terminals may be provisioned attractively without subsidies or it may become rational for the zero-SAC provider to use some of the excess proceeds (see the financial gain in Figure A.4) to partially subsidize terminals.

X-factor universe. As mobile companies (mobile operators and virtual providers alike), Google, Skype and Ryanair were able to exploit the zero-SAC tool, many other companies could potentially do the same in other industries.

APPENDIX II
Foremost Case Companies

Apple
Body Shop
British Airways
Canon
CBB Mobil
Charles Schwab
Chrysler
Cisco
Costco
Dell
Digital
Disney
easyJet
eBay
Facebook
General Electric
General Motors
Google
Hewlett-Packard
Hindustan Unilever
Honda
Hotmail
Huawei
IBM
IKEA

Lego
Microsoft
Motorola
Naturhouse
Nintendo
Novo Nordisk
PayPal
Porsche
Procter & Gamble
Quantas
Ryanair
Samsung
Saxo Bank
Scandinavian Airlines System
Skype
Southwest Airlines
Starbucks
Tata
Texas Instruments
Vestas
Virgin
Wahaha
Wal-Mart
Xerox
Yahoo!

NOTES

2 THE RECIPE GAME

1 Peters, T.J. & Waterman, R.H. (1982) *In Search of Excellence*. Harper & Row, p. 22
2 *Business Week*, (1985), November 5
3 http://en.wikipedia.org/wiki/Atari (seek additional resources)
4 Form 10-K for the fiscal year ended December 31, 2007
5 McGill, Michael. (1958), *The American Business and the Quick Fix*. Henry Holt & Company, Inc.
6 Yahoo finance, charting the period from August 1994 to August 2008
7 Rosenzweig, P. (2007), *The Halo Effect: ... and the Eight Other Business Delusions That Deceive Managers*, Free Press
8 "What is permitted to Jupiter is not permitted to the ox."

3 THE STRATEGY LANDSCAPE

1 Weick, K.E. (1995), *Sensemaking in Organizations*. Sage Publications, p. 54
2 Whittington, R. (1993), *What is Strategy – and Does it Matter?* Routledge, p. 14
3 Andrews, K. (1971), *The Concept of Corporate Strategy*. Dow Jones-Irwin Inc.
4 Whittington, R. (1993), *What is Strategy – and Does it Matter?* Routledge, p. 14
5 Ibid., p. 24
6 Pettigrew, A., Thomas, H. & Whittington, R. (2002), *Handbook of Strategy and Management*. Sage Publications
7 Prahalad, C.K. & Hamel, G. (1994), *Competing for the Future*. Harvard Business School Press
8 Mintzberg, H. (1994), "The Fall and Rise of Strategic Planning". *Harvard Business Review*
9 Eisenhardt, M.K. & Sull, N.D. (2001), "Strategy as Simple Rules". *Harvard Business Review*

10 Kim, W. Chan & Mauborgne, R. (2005), *Blue Ocean Strategy: How to Create Uncontested Market Space and Make the Competition Irrelevant*, Harvard Business School Press

11 Lele, Milind, M. (2005), *Monopoly Rules: How to Find, Capture, and Control the Most Lucrative Markets in Any Business*. Crown Business

12 D'Aveni, R. (1994), *Hypercompetition*. Free Press

13 Andersen, M.M. & Poulfelt, F. (2006), *Discount Business Strategy: How the New Market Leaders are Redefining Strategy*, John Wiley & Sons

14 Markides, C.C. (1999), *All the Right Moves: A Guide to Crafting Break-through Strategy*. Harvard Business School Press

15 Mintzberg, H, Ahlstrand, B. & Lampel, J. (1998), *Strategy Safari. The Complete Guide Through the Wilds of Strategic Management*. Prentice Hall, pp. 118–120

16 *The Academy of Management Executives*, Vol. 15, No. 3, August 2001

17 Kim, W. Chan & Mauborgne, R. (2005), *Blue Ocean Strategy: How to Create Uncontested Market Space and Make the Competition Irrelevant*, p. 18

18 Lele, Milind, M. (2005) *Monopoly Rules: How to Find, Capture, and Control the Most Lucrative Markets in Any Business*, p. 93

4 THE STRATEGY SYSTEM OR HOW TO COMBINE PERSPECTIVES

1 Markides, C.C. (2008) *Game-Changing Strategies: How to Create New Market Space in Established Industries by Breaking the Rules*. John Wiley & Sons, p. x

2 The PEST framework, Political, Economic, Social and Technological, or alterations of this, is often used when working with forces pertaining to the institutional zone

3 Andersen, M.M & Poulfelt, F. (2006), *Discount Business Strategy: How the New Market Leaders are Redefining Strategy*. John Wiley & Sons

5 WHAT TRIGGERS STRATEGY?

1 www.amazon.com/Founders-WorkStories-Startups-Problem-Solution/dp/1430210788/ref=pd_bbs_sr_1?ie=UTF8&s=books&qid=123835050&csr=8–1

2 Quote taken from the Saxo Bank A/S 2002 Annual Report p. 3

3 www.virgin.com/AboutVirgin/WhatWeAreAbout/WhatWeAreAbout.aspx

4 Gloria Miacias-Lizeso Miranda & Kiko Thief, *McKinsey Quarterly*, 2007, No 1

5 Interview with employee at Saxo Bank spring 2008

6 Andersen, M.M & Poulfelt, F. (2006), *Discount Business Strategy: How The New Market Leaders are Redefining Strategy*. John Wiley & Sons

7 www.ryanair.com/site/DA/about.php?page=About&culture=DA&pos=HEAD

8 Ryanair Annual Report 2008

9 Annual reports of Scandinavian Airlines and easyJet

10 www.amazon.com/Founders-Work-Stories-Startups-Problem-Solution/ dp/1430210788/ref=pd_bbs_sr_1?ie=UTF8&s=books&qid=123835050& sr=8–1

11 The Honda Motor Company 1994 Case, Mintzberg, H. *et al.* (2002), *The Strategy Process: Concepts, Contexts, Cases.* Prentice Hall

12 Quote from Felix Revuelta, *The Naturhouse Case* (2004), p. 2, IESE Business School

13 http://naturhouse.com/index.php?language=en-us

14 Facebook Case, (2006), Stanford Graduate School of Business, p. 3

15 www.facebook.com/press/product.php

16 https://www.paypal.com

17 Livingston J. (2007), *Founders at Work: Stories of Startups' Early Days*, Apress

18 www.aboutschwab.com/about/overview/history.html#early

19 Samsung Electronics Case, (2006), Harvard Business School

20 The Google Case, (2006), Harvard Business School

21 Kim, W. Chan & Mauborgne, R. (2005), *Blue Ocean Strategy: How to Create Uncontested Market Space and Make the Competition Irrelevant*, Harvard Business School Press

22 Andersen, M.M. & Poulfelt, F. (2006), *Discount Business Strategy: How the New Market Leaders are Redefining Strategy.* John Wiley & Sons

6 EXPLOITING CUSTOMER ATTITUDES

1 Disney Annual report 2007, p. 24

2 Ibid., pp. 25

3 Kotler, P. & Armstrong, G. (2006), *Principles of Marketing*, 11th edition. Prentice Hall, p. 35

4 Quote by Sue Boche, Director of Guest Relations in the Toys "R" Us corporate office, Disney case study: Toys "R" Us

5 Kotler, P. & Keller, K.L. (2006), *Marketing Management*, 12th edition. Prentice Hall, p. 211

6 Naturhouse web site: www.naturhouse.com/index.php?content=naturh ouse&language=en-us&label=Naturhouse&din_pass=&js=

7 Quote from Hartmut Jenner, CEO, Alfred Kärcher GmbH, IBM Global CEO Study, p. 27

8 The Google Case, (2006), Harvard Business School

9 Facebook Case, (2006), Stanford Graduate School of Business, p. 10

10 Saxo Bank Press Release, July 11, 2007

11 IBM Global CEO Study, *The Enterprise Of The Future*, 2008

12 Mossberg, L. (2003), *At skapa upplevelser – från OK til WOW*, Studentliteratur, Lund

13 Cook, S. (2008), "The Contribution Revolution. Letting Volunteers Build Your Business", *Harvard Business Review*, October 2008, p. 62

14 Ibid., p. 64
15 Putnam, R., (1993), *Making Democracy Work. Civic Traditions in Modern Italy*, Princeton University Press.

7 REVISING THE PRODUCT PORTFOLIO

1 Michael E. McGill, (1988), *American Business and the Quick Fix.* Henry Holt and Company, New York, p. 20
2 Ibid., p. 19f., has given inspiration to the following sections
3 Ibid.
4 See for instance *A compact plan for a full-sized problem*, Merrill Lynch, December 3, 2008, p. 1.
5 *Financial Times*, March 24, 2009
6 Michael E. McGill, (1988), *American Business and the Quick Fix*, p. 46
7 See Andersen and Poulfelt (2006), *Discount Business Strategy*, p. 181
8 See *Fortune Magazine*, February 16, 2004
9 See Andersen and Poulfelt (2006), *Discount Business Strategy*, p. 5
10 *Harvard Business Review*, January–February, 1976

8 LEVERAGING THE FINANCIAL CIRCUIT

1 Skype news archive, http://about.skype.com/2003/08/
2 http://about.skype.com/news.html
3 The Google Case, (2006), Harvard Business School
4 http://searchenginewatch.com/3632382
5 Google annual reports
6 www.researchandmarkets.com/reportinfo.asp?report_id=660478&t=d&cat_id=
7 www.facebook.com/press/info.php?statistics
8 Ibid.
9 Williamson, P.J. & Zeng M. (2007), *Dragons at Your Door.* Harvard Business School Press
10 www.huawei.com/corporate_information/milestones.do
11 http://en.wikipedia.org/wiki/Samsung_Electronics
12 Dell (2008) Annual Report
13 The Dell Case, (2007), University of Hong Kong
14 The Wahaha Case, (2003), Richard Ivey School of Business, University of Western Ontario
15 www.indiaresource.org/news/2006/1039.html
16 Brandenburger & Nalebuff (1996), *Co-Opetition: A Revolution Mindset that Combines Competition and Cooperation*
17 Davison, L., Brown, J.S. & Hagell III, J. (2008), "Shaping Strategy in a World of Constant Disruption", *Harvard Business Review*, October 2008, p. 89
18 In a sense, Google has become incumbent in its original ecosystem and

has to capitalize on that, thereby avoiding the risk of being subjected to competitive disruption, see the notion of "Failing to capitalize on the incumbent's advantage is to invite almost certain competitive disruption" in "The Incumbent's Advantage" by Ian C. Macmillan and Larry Selden in *Harvard Business Review*, October 2008, p. 120

9 OPTIMIZING THE ORGANIZATIONAL DESIGN

1 Tang, R. "Hungry Like the Wolf", *The Standard*, Hong Kong, September 24, 2004
2 *China Labour Bulletin*, "Is corporate wolf-culture devouring China's overworked employees?", www.clb.org.hk/en/node/100253
3 Huawei Annual Report 2007
4 Ibid., p. 29
5 Interview with employee at Saxo Bank
6 Saxo Bank Factsheet, http://saxobank.com/?id=424&Lan=EN&Au=1& Grp=5
7 Ayn, R. (1957), *Atlas Shrugged*. Random House
8 Bryan, L.L & Joyce, C.I, (2007), "Better strategy through organizational design", *McKinsey Quarterly*, no. 2, p. 23
9 Goold, M. & Cambell, A. (2002), *Designing Effective Organizations*. Jossey-Bass
10 www.naturhouse.com/index.php?language=en-us
11 From Saxo Bank press release, "Saxo Bank announces new top leadership team", August 4, 2008
12 The Procter & Gamble: Organization 2005 (A) Case, Harvard Business School, (2007), p. 8
13 Procter & Gamble Annual reports
14 Quote from Steve Jobs taken from the web site: www.1000ventures.com/ business_guide/crosscuttings/leadership_values-based.html
15 Henderson, M., Thompson D. & Henderson S. (2006), *Leading through Values: Linking Company Culture to Business Strategy*, HarperBusiness
16 Quote from Jack Welch taken from the web site: www.1000ventures. com/business_guide/crosscuttings/leadership_values-based.html
17 www.ge.com/annual00/values/index.html
18 www.valuewiki.com/w/AAPL
19 http://money.cnn.com/2007/01/05/magazines/fortune/Search_and_ enjoy.fortune/index.htm
20 www.valuebasedmanagement.net/methods_schein_three_levels_culture.html
21 www.southwest.com/careers/culture
22 Smith, G. (2004), "An evaluation of the corporate culture of Southwest Airlines", *Measuring Business Excellence*, Vol. 8, No. 4
23 www.southwest.com/about_swa/southwest_cares/our_people
24 Milliman, J., Ferguson, J., Trickett, D. & Condemni, B., (1999), "Spirit

and community at Southwest Airlines: An investigation of a spiritual values-based model", *Journal of Organizational Change Management*, Vol. 12, No. 3

25 http://en.wikipedia.org/wiki/Roy_Edward_Disney

26 Andersen, M.M & Poulfelt, F. (2006), *Discount Business Strategy: How the New Market Leaders are Redefining Strategy*. John Wiley & Sons, p. 191

27 Goo, S.K. (2006), "Building a 'Googley' Workforce", *Washington Post*, October 21.

28 Ibid.

29 http://news.cnet.com/Meet-Googles-culture-czar/2008-1023_3-6179897. html

30 Chambers, E.G., Foulon, M., Handfield-Jones, H., Hankin, S.M. & Michaels III, E.G. (1998), "The war for talent", *McKinsey Quarterly*, No. 3

31 Livingston, J. (2007), *Founders at Work*, APress, p. 127

32 www.universumawards.com/dk/files/pressemeddelelse_dc.pdf

33 Kjær, E. & Sørensen, D. (2008), *Talentfabrikken*, Børsens Forlag. Introduction by Lars Seier Christensen

34 Huawei presentation, "HR Building & Culture Building in Huawei", Huawei Technologies.

10 SPINNING THE TECHNOLOGICAL CHAIN

1 Arnold, S.E. (2005), *The Google Legacy*. Infonortics, p. 66

2 Ibid., p. 59

3 http://en.wikipedia.org/wiki/Skype

4 The Dell Case, (2007), University of Hong Kong, p. 5

5 www.amazon.ca/direct-dell-audio-michael/dp/product-description/0694520233

6 Samsung Electronics Case, (2006), Harvard Business School

7 Christensen, Clayton M. (2003), *The Innovator's Solution*. Harvard Business School Publishing, p. 33

11 DRIVING THE LEADERSHIP GENES

1 The Jan Carlzon: CEO at SAS Case, (1992), Harvard Business School

2 Article in *Business.dk*, "Carlzon indrømmer at have kostet SAS 2 mia. kr.", (January 26, 2007)

3 Michael Maccoby (2000), "Narcissistic leaders – The incredible pros – The inevitable cons", *Harvard Business Review*, January–February, p. 75

4 www.chiefexecutive.net/ME2/Audiences/Default.asp?AudID=257093C D337F495B86A6A07046702F8C

5 Freeman, R. Edward, Gilbert Jr, Daniel R. & Stoner, James A.F. (1995), *Management*, 6th edition. Prentice Hall, p. 470

6 Tsun-yah Hsiek & Yik, Sara (2005), "Leadership as the starting point of strategy", *McKinsey Quarterly*, No. 1

7 Levinson, M. (1993), "Can he make an elephant dance?", *Newsweek*, April 5
8 Slater, R. (1999), *Saving Big Blue*. McGraw Hill, p. 109
9 Levitt, Raymond E., Malek, W. & Morgan, M. (2007), *Executing your Strategy*, Harvard Business School Press
10 Kaplan, Robert S. & Norton, David P. (2008), *The Execution Premium: Linking Strategy to Operations for Competitive Advantage*, Harvard Business School Publishing
11 Ibid., p. 4
12 Axelrod, B., Handfield-Jones, H. & Welsh, T. (2001), "The War for Talent, Part Two", *McKinsey Quarterly*, No. 2
13 http://money.cnn.com/magazines/fortune/leadership/2007/global/index.html
14 Colvin, G. (2007), How top companies breed stars, CNN Money.com, October 1
15 Kjær, E. & Sørensen, D. (2008), *Talentfabrikken*. Børsens Forlag
16 www.youtube.com/watch?v=6-IvKE1stIo
17 Sharp, C. (2007), "Moments of truth: global executives talk about the challenges that shaped them as leaders", *Harvard Business Review*, January, pp. 15–25
18 www.easyjet.com/common/img/Andy_Times_ban_old_aircraft.pdf
19 Ruddock, A. (2007), *Michael O'Leary. A Life in Full Flight*. Penguin Books, pp. 215
20 Holst-Mikkelsen, Mark & Poulfelt, Flemming (2008), *Strategi med mening. Hvordan sikrer virksomheder strategisk effektivitet?* Børsens Forlag

12 INROADS TO THE ACHIEVEMENT OF A HIGHER RETURN ON STRATEGY

1 Gladwell, Malcolm (2008), *Outliers*. Allen Lane
2 Moore, Geoffrey A. (2007), *Crossing the Chasm. Marketing and Selling Technology Products to Mainstream Customers*. Capstone Publishing Limited
3 Geus, Arie de (1997), "The living company", *Harvard Business Review*, March–April

BIBLIOGRAPHY

Andersen, M.M. & Poulfelt, F. (2006) *Discount Business Strategy: How the New Market Leaders are Redefining Strategy.* John Wiley & Sons

Andersen, Henrik & Ritter, Thomas (2008) *Inside the Customer Universe. How to Build Unique Customer Insight for Profitable Growth and Market Leadership.* Wiley

Andrews, K. (1971) *The Concept of Corporate Strategy.* Dow Jones-Irwin Inc.

Ansoff, H.I. (1993) *Corporate Strategy.* Penguin Modern Management Readings

Arnold, S.E. (2005) *The Google Legacy.* Infonortics

Axelrod, B., Handfield-Jones, H. & Welsh, T. (2001) "The war for talent, part two". *McKinsey Quarterly.* No. 2, pp. 9–11

Ayn, R. (1957) *Atlas Shrugged.* Random House

Bardwick, Judith M. (1991) *Danger in the Comfort Zone: From Boardroom to Mailroom – How to Break the Entitlement Habit that's Killing American Business.* Amacom

Barney, J. (1997) *Gaining and Sustaining Competitive Advantage.* Prentice Hall

Bosshart, David (2006) *Cheap. The Real Cost of the Global Trend for Bargains, Discounts & Consumer Choice.* Kogan Page Limited

Bossidy, Larry & Ram Charan (2002) *Execution. The Discipline of Getting Things Done.* Random House Business Books

Brandenburger, A.M. & Nalebuff, B.J. (1997) *Co-Opetition: A Revolution Mindset that Combines Competition and Cooperation: The Game Theory Strategy that's Changing the Game of Business.* Doubleday Business

Bryan, L.L & Joyce, C.I. (2007) "Better strategy through organizational design". *McKinsey Quarterly.* No. 2, pp. 21–29

Chambers, E.G., Foulon, M., Handfield-Jones, H., Hankin, S.M. & Michaels III, E.G. (1998) "The war for talent". *McKinsey Quarterly.* No. 3

Chandler, A. (1962) *Strategy and Structure: Chapters in the History of the Industrial Enterprise.* Cambridge: The MIT Press

China Labour Bulletin (2008) "Is corporate wolf-culture devouring China's over-worked employees?"

Christensen, C.M. (1997) *The Innovator's Dilemma: When New Technologies Cause Great Firms to Fail.* Harvard Business School Press

Christensen, C.M. & Raynor, M.E. (2003) *The Innovator's Solution: Creating and Sustaining Successful Growth.* Harvard Business School Press

Clausewitz, Carl Von (1997) *On War.* Wordsworth Editions

Collins, J. (2001) *Good to Great. Why Some Companies Make the Leap ... and Others Don't.* BookHouse Publishing

Collins, J. & Porras, J.I. (1994) *Built to Last: Successful Habits of Visionary Companies.* Harper Collins

Colvin, G. (2007) "How top companies breed stars". *CNN Money.com.* October

Cook S. (2008) "The contribution revolution. Letting volunteers build your business". *Harvard Business Review.* October–November, pp. 60–70

D'Aveni R.D. (1994) *Hypercompetition: Managing the Dynamics of Strategic Manoeuvring.* Free Press

Davis, Stan & Mayer, Christopher (1998) *Blur. The Speed of Change in the Connected Economy.* Addison Wesley

Davison, L., Brown, J.S. & Hagell III, J. (2008) "Shaping strategy in a world of constant disruption". *Harvard Business Review.* October–November, p. 89

De Wit, B. & Meyer, R. (2005) *Strategy Synthesis.* Thompson

Eisenhardt, K.M. & Brown, S.L. (1998) *Competing on the Edge.* Harvard Business School Press

Eisenhardt, K.M. & Sull, D.N. (2001) "Strategy as simple rules". *Harvard Business Review,* January–February, pp. 107–116.

Finkelstein, Sydney, Harvey, Charles & Lawton, Thomas (2007) *Breakout Strategy. Meeting the Challenge of Double-Digit Growth.* McGraw Hill

Freeman, R. Edward, Gilbert Jr, Daniel R. & Stoner, James A.F. (1995) *Management* (6th edn). Prentice Hall

George, Bill (2003) *Authentic Leadership: Rediscovering the Secrets to Creating Lasting Value.* Jossey-Bass

Gladwell, M. (2008), *Outliers.* Allen Lane

Gleeson, R. (1987) *The X-Factor: Business Winners Reveal their Success Secrets.* Information Australia

Gloria Miacias-Lizeso M. & Thiel, Kiko (2007) "Improving organizational speed and agility". *McKinsey Quarterly.* No. 1, pp. 14–15

Goffee, R. & Jones, G. (2000) "Why should anyone be led by you?" *Harvard Business Review.* September–October

Goo, S.K. (2006) "Building a 'Googley' Workforce". *Washington Post,* October 21

Goold, M. & Campell, A. (2002) *Designing Effective Organizations.* Jossey-Bass

Gottfredson, M. & Schaubert, S. (2008) *The Breakthrough Imperative: How the Best Managers get Outstanding Results.* Bain & Company, Inc.

Grant, R.M. (1991) "The Resource-Based Theory of Competitive Advantage: Implications for Strategy Formulation". *California Management Review,* pp. 114–129

Hamel, G. & Prahalad, C.K. (1994) *Competing for the Future.* Harvard Business School Press

Henderson, M., Thompson, D. & Henderson, S. (2006) *Leading through*

Values: Linking Company Culture to Business Strategy. Harper Business

Herzberg, F. (1968) "One more time: how do you motivate employees". *Harvard Business Review.* January–February

Hofer, Charles W. & Schendel, D. (1980) *Strategy Formulation: Analytical Concepts.* South-Western, Division of Thompson Learning

Holst-Mikkelsen, Mark & Poulfelt, Flemming (2008) *Strategi med mening. Hvordan sikrer virksomheder strategisk effektivitet?* Børsens Forlag

Hougaard, Søren & Bjerre, Mogens (2002) *Strategic Relationship Marketing.* Samfundslitteratur

Hsiek, Tsun-yan & Yik, S. (2005) "Leadership as the starting point of strategy". *McKinsey Quarterly.* No. 1, pp. 66–73

Johnson, Lauren Keller (2004) "Execute your strategy – without killing it". *Harvard Management Update.* Vol. 9, Issue 12, pp. 3–5.

Joyce, W. & Nohria, N. (2003) *What Really Works: The 4+2 Formula for Sustained Business Success.* Harper Business

Kaplan, R.S. & Norton, D.P. (1996) *The Balanced Scorecard: Translating Strategy into Action.* Harvard Business School Press

Kaplan, R.S. & Norton, D.P. (2008) *The Execution Premium: Linking Strategy to Operations for Competitive Advantage.* Harvard Business School Publishing

Kjær, E. & Sørensen, D. (2008) *Talentfabrikken.* Børsens Forlag

Kim, W. Chan & Mauborgne, R. (2005) *Blue Ocean Strategy: How to Create Uncontested Market Space and Make the Competition Irrelevant.* Harvard Business School Press

Kotler P. (2003) *A Framework for Marketing Management* (2nd edn). Prentice Hall

Kotler P. & Armstrong G. (2007) *Principles of Marketing* (12th edn). Prentice Hall

Kotler, P. & Keller, K.I.. (2008) *Marketing Management* (13th edn). Prentice Hall

Lele, Milind, M. (2005) *Monopoly Rules. How to Find, Capture, and Control the Most Lucrative Markets in Any Business.* Crown Business

Levinson, M. (1993) "Can he make an elephant dance?" *Newsweek.* April 5

Levitt, Raymond E., Malek, W. & Morgan, M. (2007) *Executing your Strategy.* Harvard Business School Press

Liker, Jeffrey K. (2004) *The Toyota Way: 14 Management Principles from the World's Greatest Manufacturer.* McGraw-Hill

Livingston J. (2007) *Founders at Work; Stories of Startups' Early Days.* Apress

Lynch, Richard (2006) *Corporate Strategy* (4th edn). FT Prentice Hall

Markides, C.C. (1999) *All the Right Moves: A Guide to Crafting Breakthrough Strategy.* Harvard Business School Press

Markides, C.C. (2008) *Game-Changing Strategies: How to Create New Market Space in Established Industries by Breaking the Rules.* John Wiley & Sons

Markides, C.C. & Geroski, P.A. (2004) *Fast Second: How Smart Companies Bypass Radical Innovation to Enter and Dominate New Markets.* Jossey-Bass

Mayo, Anthony J. & Nohria, N. (2005) *In Their Time: The Greatest Business Leaders of the Twentieth Century.* Harvard Business School Press

McGill, M. (1988) *The American Business and the Quick Fix.* Henry Holt & Company Inc.

McKiernan, P. (ed.) (1996) *Historical Evolution of Strategic Management,* Vols I & II. Aldershot. Dartmouth

Michelli, Joseph A. (2007) *The Starbucks experience: 5 Principles for Turning Ordinary into Extraordinary.* McGraw-Hill

Milliman, J., Ferguson, J., Trickett, D. & Condemni, B. (1999) "Spirit and community at Southwest Airlines: An investigation of a spiritual values-based model". *Journal of Organizational Change Management.* Vol. 12, No. 3, pp. 221–233

Mintzberg, H. (1994) "The fall and rise of strategic planning". *Harvard Business Review.* January–February, pp. 107–114

Mintzberg, H., Ahlstrand, B. & Lampel, J. (1998) *Strategy Safari. The Complete Guide Through the Wilds of Strategic Management.* FT Prentice Hall

Moore, Geoffrey A. (2007) *Crossing the Chasm. Marketing and Selling Technology Products to Mainstream Customers.* Capstone Publishing Limited (a Wiley Company)

Morgan, M., Levitt, Raymond E. & Malek, William (2007) *Executing Your Strategy: How to Break it Down and Get it Done.* Harvard Business School Press

Mossberg, L. (2003) *At skapa uplevelser – från OK til WOW.* Studentliteratur, Lund

Nelson, Richard R. & Winter, Sidney G. (1982) *An Evolutionary Theory of Economic Change.* Belknap Press

Nonata, I. & Takeuchi, H. (1995) *The Knowledge-Creating Company: How Japanese Companies Create the Dynamics of Innovation.* Oxford University Press

Pascal, R. (1984) "Perspectives on strategy. The real reason behind Honda's success". *California Management Review.* Spring

Peters, T.J. & Waterman, R.H. (1982) *In Search of Excellence.* Harper & Row

Penrose, E. (1980) *The Theory of the Growth of the Firm.* M.E. Sharpe

Pettigrew, A., Thomas, H. & Whittington, R. (2002) *Handbook of Strategy and Management.* Sage Publications

Porter, Michael (1980) *Competitive Strategy.* Free Press

Porter, Michael (1985) *Competitive Advantage. Creating and Sustaining Superior Performance.* Free Press

Prahalad, C.K. & Hamel, G. (1994) *Competing for the Future.* Harvard Business School Press

Prahalad, C.K. & Krishnan, M.S. (2008) *The New Age of Innovation. Driving Co-created Value through Global Networks.* McGraw Hill

Putnam, R. (1993) *Making Democracy Work. Civic Traditions in Modern Italy.* Princeton University Press

Quinn, J.B, Mintzberg, H. & James, R. (1988) *The Strategy Process.* Prentice Hall

Rosenzweig, P. (2007) *The Halo Effect: ... and the Eight Other Business Delusions That Deceive Managers.* Free Press

Ruddock, A. (2007) *Michael O'Leary. A Life in Full Flight.* Penguin Books

Rumelt, Richard (1984) "Towards a strategic theory of the firm". In Robert Lamb (ed.) *Competitive Strategic Management.* Prentice-Hall, pp. 556–570

Sheth, J. & Sisodia, R. (2002) *The Rule of Three: Surviving and Thriving in Competitive Markets.* Kindle Edition, 2002.

Slater, R. (1999) *Saving Big Blue.* McGraw Hill

Smith, G. (2004) "An evaluation of the corporate culture of Southwest Airlines". *Measuring Business Excellence.* Vol. 8, No. 4, pp. 26–33

Spector, R. & McCarthy, P. (2005) *The Nordstrom Way to Customer Service Excellence: a Handbook for Implementing Great Service in Your Organization.* John Wiley & Sons

Stiglitz, Joseph E. (2006) *Making Globalization Work.* Norton

Tang, R. (2004) "Hungry like the wolf". *The Standard, Hong Kong.* September 24

Trott, Paul (2005) *Innovation Management and New Product Development.* (3rd edn). FT Prentice Hall

Vise, David A. (2005) *The Google Story.* Pan

Weick, K.E. (1995) *Sensemaking in Organizations.* Sage Publications

Wernerfelt, B. (1984) "A resource-based view of the firm". *Strategic Management Journal.* Vol. 5, pp. 171–180

Whittington, R. (1993) *What is Strategy – and Does it Matter?* Routledge

Williamson, O. (1993) *The Nature of the Firm: Origins, Evolution, and Development.* Oxford University Press

Williamson, P.J. & Zeng, M. (2007) *Dragons at Your Door.* Harvard Business School Press

Wit, de Bob & Meyer, Ron (2005) *Strategy Synthesis. Resolving Strategy Paradoxes to Create Competitive Advantage.* Thomson

CREDITS AND PERMISSIONS

Chapter 2

p. 15, Table 2.1: Peters, T.J. & Waterman, R.H. (1982) *In Search of Excellence.* Harper & Row.

p. 20, Table 2.2: Collins, J. & Porras, J.I. (1994) *Built to Last: Successful Habits of Visionary Companies.* HarperCollins.

p. 23, Table 2.4: Collins, J. (2001) *Good to Great. Why Some Companies make the Leap... and Others Don't.* BookHouse Publishing.

p. 26, Table 2.5: Joyce, W. & Nohria, N. (2003) *What Really Works: The 4 + 2 Formula for Sustained Business Success.* HarperBusiness.

p. 27, Table 2.6: Joyce, W. & Nohria, N. (2003) *What Really Works: The 4 + 2 Formula for Sustained Business Success.* HarperBusiness.

p. 31, Figure 2.2: Rosenzweig, P. (2007) *The Halo Effect: ... and the Eight Other Business Delusions That Deceive Managers.* The Free Press.

Chapter 3

p. 45, Figure 3.1: Reprinted with permission of The Free Press, a Division of Simon and Schuster, Inc. from *Competitive Strategy: Techniques for Analyzing Industries and Competitors by Michael E. Porter.* Copyright © 1980, 1998 by The Free Press. All rights reserved.

p. 47, Figure 3.2: Jay Barney, "Firm Resources and Sustained Competitive Advantage", *JOM*, 1991, Vol. 17, p. 112. Reprinted by permission of SAGE Publications.

p. 48, Table 3.3: Jay Barney (1997), *Gaining and Sustaining Competitive Advantage*, pp. 29, 69–72, 74, and 81. Reprinted by permission of Oxford University Press.

p. 49, Table 3.4: Kim, W. Chan & Mauborgne, R. (2005) *Blue Ocean Strategy: How to Create Uncontested Market Space and Make the Competition Irrelevant.* Harvard Business School Press, page 18.

p. 51, Figure 3.3: Kim, W. Chan & Mauborgne, R. (2005) *Blue Ocean Strategy: How to Create Uncontested Market Space and Make the Competition Irrelevant.* Harvard Business School Press, page 32.

p. 53, Figure 3.4: Andersen, M.M. & Poulfelt, F. (2006) *Discount Business Strategy: How the new market leaders are defining business strategy,* pp. 156, 256. Reprinted by permission of Wiley Blackwell Publishing.

Chapter 7

p. 116, Figure 7.1: The BCG Portfolio Matrix from the *Product Portfolio Matrix,* ©1970, The Boston Consulting Group.

p. 132, Table 7.1: Sheth, Jagdish N. *The Self-Destructive Habits of Good Companies and How to Break Them,* 1st edition, © 2007, p. 3. Reprinted by permission of Pearson Education, Inc., Upper Saddle River, NJ.

Chapter 9

p. 177, Figure 9.2: Henderson, M., Thompson, D. & Henderson, S. *"Leading through Values: Linking company culture to business strategy,"* (2006), Harper Collins Publishers, New Zealand, p. 43.

Chapter 10

p. 199, Figure 10.1: Arnold, S.E. (2005) *The Google Legacy,* page 58. Reprinted by Permission of Infonortics.

p. 212, Figure 10.4: Christensen, C.M. & Raynor, M.E. (2003) *The Innovator's Solution: Creating and Sustaining Successful Growth.* Harvard Business School Press, page 33.

Chapter 11

p. 242, Table 11.2: C. Sharp, *"Moments of Truth: Global Executives Talk About the Challenges That Shaped Them as Leaders,"* (2007), Harvard Business Review, January 2007, pp. 15–25.

INDEX